Comprehensive Architectural Services
—General Principles and Practice

Comprehensive Architectural Services — General Principles and Practice

EDITED BY WILLIAM DUDLEY HUNT JR, AIA

The American Institute of Architects

McGRAW-HILL BOOK COMPANY

New York   San Francisco   Toronto   London   Sydney

Comprehensive Architectural Services: General Principles and Practice

BY WILLIAM H. SCHEICK, AIA *

The present book, a first, broad look at the whole field of comprehensive services, is the result of many years of study and work by a large number of architects and others who have devoted themselves to the expanding role of architect today; in the future, this great work continues on

*Executive Director,
The American Institute of Architects

This book is a "first reader" in comprehensive architectural services. Most of its chapters were originally published in the AIA JOURNAL. The book and the articles, along with the many seminars on the subject held over the past few years, represent the first answers to the challenge and problems of preparing the architectural profession for the expanded role it will assume in the future.

Need for Comprehensive Services

The need for expanding architectural services was presented to the profession in 1960, in the first report of the AIA Committee on the Profession. In 1962, this committee further defined the concept, which came to be known as comprehensive architectural services, in its second report. In the second report, the then president of AIA, Philip Will Jr., put it this way, "The objectives of the dynamic new concept are to increase our competence in design for today's society and improve our competitive position in today's economy." The report went on to say that comprehensive services constituted, "a program of practical action to expand the role of the architect in the creation of buildings and their environment for a restless and dynamic society in the complex and changing world of today."

What this book is about

In general then, this book is about principles of this sort. In particular it is about the things architects must know, the ideas they must espouse, the competence they must possess, the professional qualifications they must bring to the task of performing or coordinating all—or most—of the diverse activities necessary for the design and creation of buildings and their environment. A few of the activities, sometimes performed by others in the past without benefit of the services of architects, are these: feasibility studies, operational programming and planning, site analysis, selection and acquisition, project financing, promotional design and planning. All of these activities are vital to the performance of the total design process. All, and many others, are covered in the present book; not in minute detail but with enough depth to enable architects to gain some grasp of them and to point the way for further study and accomplishment.

For large and small offices

There is meat in this book for every architect, for every architectural office. For the large office already involved in some of the services covered, there is an opportunity to examine additional services not yet offered, the opportunity to see how the other fellow does it. For the smaller office, the book contains a great deal of information about how to organize a "compact" or "core" firm that freely uses various consultants from the socio-economic disciplines to offer to clients complete architectural services.

Contributors to AIA program

Many architects and others have made invaluable contributions to this book, as authors, consultants and in other ways. In all, some 1000 people have been involved in one way or another; too many to name, of course, but without their interest and help there could not have been a book on this subject at this time. As it is, it might be said that the book represents the best current thinking on the subject.

Work of AIA Committee on the Profession

However, it must be pointed out that the work of the AIA Committee on the Profession is the foundation for this book, not only its work in comprehensive services but also in registration, education, design, practice and relationships with other professionals and the entire building industry. For this reason, the members who served on that committee deserve appreciation, not only here, but by the whole profession. The committee members were Robert E. Alexander, Herbert L. Beckwith, Clinton Gamble, Robert F. Hastings, Perry B. Johanson, Vincent Kling, Frank R. Slezak, Hugh A. Stubbins, Philip Will Jr., and, notably, the last chairman of the committee, James M. Hunter. Also for several years, I had the privilege of working with the committee as ex officio member, as did Dudley Hunt Jr., the editor of this book, as consultant.

Toward the future

Finally, it should be pointed out that the Institute will continue to find means for exploration of comprehensive services in greater depth and to furnish the profession with additional educational tools fashioned to assist architects to continue increasing their design and business capabilities over the coming years.

Comprehensive Architectural Services: Potential, Performance and Alerts

BY DUDLEY HUNT JR, AIA

The great potentials inherent in the expanding role of the architect can be attained if the profession prepares itself for comprehensive services and, with deliberation, proceeds toward the end goal of excellence in architecture

The thousands of architects and others who have expressed themselves in one way or another on the subject of the Comprehensive Architectural Services Program have at least a couple of things in common. No two of these people are in perfect agreement on any of the details of the program; and, without exception, each questions certain other parts of the program. This is as it should be. The lack of agreement, the questioning attitude —these are signs of health and of an aptitude for growth.

At this point, however, enough time has passed since the beginning of the present program in 1962 for an effort to be made to answer some of the questions, if only imperfectly, and resolve some of the doubts, if only partially. While it is surely impossible —if not foolhardy—to attempt simple answers to complex, interrelated questions, it now seems imperative to ignore the danger and attack the impossible.

What are comprehensive architectural services?

Before the present program was launched, the Committee on the Profession had come to an agreement that comprehensive architectural services include all of the activities required for the creation of buildings and other environmental designs. As set forth in the outline prepared by the Committee, these activities were divided into analysis, promotion, design and planning, construction, supporting and related services. It was never intended, or even intimated, that all of these services would be necessary for every project, or that every architect must perform every service for his clients. In fact, many of the services would not be performed by architects at all, but might be arranged for, in the name of the owner, and directed or coordinated by architects.

Comprehensive vs basic services?

There is no conflict at all between comprehensive and basic services. On the contrary, basic services are actually included within the comprehensive services concept. The basic services are, of course, those listed in the B131 Owner-Architect agreement and in other AIA standard agreements: schematic design; design development; construction documents; administration of construction contracts. These are the services ordinarily performed for every architectural project. Comprehensive services include these and also the services listed as "additional" in the standard agreements: surveys, measured drawings, etc. The comprehensive concept also includes many services not found in the standard agreements at all: site analysis, selection and assembly, feasibility studies, operational and building analysis, etc.

Basic services are the foundation of architecture, the skeleton, the central theme. The additional activities that make up the complete comprehensive services concept build on the foundation, fill out the body and clothe it, develop the central theme. Just as the automobile that the industry calls "basic transportation" can be fitted with a heater for cold climates, air conditioning for hot, the basic vehicle of architecture can be fitted with accessory services.

Why comprehensive services?

Let it be put on the record that architects did not first create the comprehensive services concept, then scurry around looking for clients who would pay for its application. Comprehensive services were created to fulfill a need—or rather many complex needs. Recognizing these needs, clients—the consumers of architecture— then began to demand that the needs be fulfilled. The basic services of architects were often inadequate for the task. Therefore, the comprehensive services concept was delineated by men who believed that architects should answer the demands. It is well known that architects do not have the field entirely unto themselves; others have also heard the demands and have hastened to answer them. Architects must be prepared to do the job better.

Is there a philosophy of comprehensive services?

The purpose of comprehensive services is better architecture and other environmental design. The services that are additional to the basic have one main purpose: to place the architect in a position central to the entire design and construction process, a position from which he can exercise better control and perform more effective services. Beyond this, there is little complete agreement among those who have studied the subject. There is no "party line" adhered to by any group within the profession; no attempt has been made to "brainwash" architects into acceptance of rigid doctrine. Instead, what exists is a philosophy of architectural services expanded to range across the multifarious activities now necessary for the proper handling of architectural and other environmental projects. There is an attempt to unify the many diverse activities into a rational, coordinated system.

What is the role of architect in comprehensive services?

The central role of the architectural profession, then, is in the performance of the basic services on a high level. Additionally, the profession must itself be prepared to perform many of the additional services in certain cases, coordinate the work of others in other instances, obtain and direct some services, and analyze or review still others. On some large or complex projects, the architect's role will often be some combination of these functions.

In all of the aspects of comprehensive services applicable to their practices, architects must have sufficient knowledge to enable them to relate all of the aspects to over-all goals or purposes of projects. Architects must be prepared to cooperate with specialists of many kinds and to cause these specialists to cooperate with each other for the good of the projects. A big role yes, but not one that expects the architect to become the whole show.

For each architect, for each office, the role will no doubt be that required by clients, that answering the needs or wishes of the individual architect or office.

How are comprehensive services performed?

Architects may provide their clients the services required in addition to the basic in a number of ways. Among these are services performed in the architect's own office by his own staff; services performed in association with other architects who are skilled in needed specialties; consultation between architects; services performed outside the architect's office by specialists engaged by the architect under extended terms of the Owner-Architect agreement; services by outside experts engaged by the architect acting as the agent of the owner and as director or coordinator; services obtained by the owner apart from the Owner-Architect agreement; services performed by the owner and his own staff. In the two last-named cases, the architect should have an advisory relationship with the owner and those who perform the services.

Fees for comprehensive services?

At the present time, because of the breadth and diversity of comprehensive architectural services, the formulation of a single method of fees for services other than the basic is impractical. According to the standard AIA Owner-Architect agreements, all services other than those enumerated as basic are extra and are subject to extra fees. These fees may be based on a multiple of personnel costs calculated to include overhead and profit; in other cases, additional services are performed for agreed-upon set dollar amounts. If services are performed outside the architectural office by consultants or other specialists, charges to the owner are often expressed in the form of the actual costs of the outside services plus some amount for the coordination or other extra work performed in the architectural office. These principles are applicable to all additional services, whether listed as such in the standard agreements or among the expanded services envisioned in the comprehensive services system.

One important point to remember is that only the charges for basic services—schematic design, design development, construction documents and construction contract administration—are included in the standard fee. All other services are subject to extra charges. However, some architectural offices have found that they can offer many of the additional services to their clients without extra charges. For example, some firms perform a degree of analysis and programming, site advisory services, etc, without charging extra, in order to extend their control over the project. In this way, they feel they can perform the basic services more effectively than otherwise might be possible. Often, they find the additional services can be performed without increasing their office costs.

How to use this book

The content of this book is only intended to be a primer of comprehensive architectural services, a broad sketch of the principles and practice. There is not sufficient information in the present book on any single service to prepare any architect to offer that service. The chapters should only be used as guides to the subjects, a foundation upon which a system of comprehensive services can be constructed, a direction-finder pointed toward the development of information based on experience that can lead to the practice of the services. As a matter of fact, no two of the authors are in perfect agreement. Because of this and the even more divergent opinions held throughout the profession, eight alerts to the profession are discussed below. Perhaps these alerts can illuminate some of the misconceptions that creep into such a sweeping concept.

Alert No 1   A common reaction to the comprehensive services concept, particularly among more firmly established architects in larger firms, goes something like this, "What's all the fuss about? We've been doing these things for years." This attitude is, at the same time, both a great strength and a liability. One of the assets of the architectural profession is that so many architects have been doing comprehensive services "for years." Thus, there exists a vast source, within the profession, of virtually untapped knowledge on many of the services. In fact, this series of articles has its basis in this reservoir of knowledge.

At the same time, it must be remembered that until the time of the Committee on the Profession, no real attempt had been made to formulate the many services into a logical, workable system. Also, it bears repeating that no single architectural firm now—or probably even in the future—will perform all of the services. Yet even the firm that has been performing some of the services for years would do well to re-examine, periodically, the services it offers and how they are performed. The needs of clients change, as do the types of clients. Types of work change, and the size and complexity of work. In such a climate, the services of each firm should reflect a growing, changing world.

Alert No 2   Another reaction expressed, in good faith, by some architects takes some such form as, "Why are we trying to get into all of these things when we should be trying to improve the quality of architecture?" These people, for whatever reasons, have somehow missed the most important point of all. The purpose of comprehensive services is just that—the improvement of architecture.

For example, a bad site selected before the architect is retained often results in compromises in the basic services that lead to unfortunate compromises in the solution. On the other hand, if the architect participates in the selection of the site, then the act of selection becomes an integral part of the complete design process. It follows that the solution can then be improved. Similarly, feasibility, the operations within buildings, the program, etc, are all factors closely related to design. The comprehensive services concept envisions a definite role for the architect in all of these decisions, thus strengthening basic services.

Alert No 3   Unfortunately, some architects, quick to grasp the potential of comprehensive services, but unprepared, have with almost equal speed offered such services to their clients and then have been unable to deliver a high level of performance. This is both a temptation and a great danger. The offer of services without first preparing to perform the services on an effective level can only lead to sorrow for the architect and his clients and lasting ill-effects on the architectural profession.

Alert No 4   Some architects seem to have become so enamoured of the scope of comprehensive services that they sound as if they expect clients (and everyone else) to quickly deliver themselves unto the architectural profession which, in short order, will create for them a perfect, ordered and beautiful world. A seductive dream, but one no one seriously expects to come true. It is extremely reckless to project the role of the architect as that of the all-knowing, all-powerful, all-wise and beneficent.

Needless to say, the other professionals and specialists concerned with environmental design and construction are not going to deliver themselves into the hands of the architect, then perform their work at his beck and call. The owner is never going to be satisfied with only the furnishing of the capital.

In actuality, nothing could have been farther from the minds of those who have worked closely with the comprehensive services program. Instead, what they envisioned is a system that can better unify the design and construction toward the end of better results. The intent is to improve coordination of all the diverse elements of the process, in order to do a better job. For the architectural profession, the goals are improved relationships with all of those concerned with the design and construction processes, and more understanding of their roles. Importantly, the goal is better performance among architects, based on broader knowledge, clearer vision. Certainly, these goals are possible of attainment for architects, trained as they are in the general areas of environmental design. Certainly, improvements in performance will be forthcoming as the architectural profession prepares itself better, trains its students better. Certainly, it is possible for architects to stand at the center of the whole design and construction process without the necessity of indulging in running duels with all of those with whom architects must work in real estate, in finance, in other specialties.

Alert No 5   Some architects have intimated that one of the functions of comprehensive services is to allow the profession to "take over" the others involved in the process. Nothing could be farther from the truth. Architects are not going to become real estate brokers, or bankers, or builders, but architects are going to know enough to work closely with these interests and to coordinate them for the over-all good of the projects. Many people think that one of the strengths of the existing system stems from the interplay of the varied points of view of the people representing the various interests. In any case, to be very realistic about it, architects cannot really supplant these interests, nor will most architects have any desire to do so. Instead, it will be enough if architects can influence and coordinate the over-all processes for the good of architecture and the people who use it.

Alert No 6   In some instances, architects have offered to perform under the comprehensive services concept for clients who obviously were well-prepared to perform the services for themselves. This can be embarrassing. Every architect should make sure of his ground before putting himself in such a position. This is not to say that such proposals should never be made, for numerous clients have indicated that they would be only too happy to eliminate portions of their large real estate, planning and similar departments if they found that architects could handle these functions effectively.

Alert No 7   It has been said many times that, "Comprehensive services are only for the large offices." This definitely does not seem to be the case. A number of smaller firms have, in the past few years, reorganized themselves along the lines of the "core" office described elsewhere in the present book or on the model described many times in speeches by Henry Wright as the "compact" office. These firms have surrounded their permanent cores of architects with groups of outside expert specialists who are on call when needed. To potential clients, the "core" or "compact" firm stresses the fact that the experts are available when required, but that clients do not have to pay a share of their overhead; charges only accrue when the necessary specialists are called in for a particular service. In addition, the firm can obtain exactly the right outside expert who can tailor his services perfectly to the client's own problems. Therefore, the client is not stuck with an in-house expert who might not be exactly right for the job at hand. All in all, this makes a good story, and in many smaller offices, it seems to be working effectively.

Of course, other opportunities are available for the smaller firm: specialization by building type or, more recently, by architectural function (a few firms perform only analysis, others only design, master planning, etc); limitation of practice to less complex projects or those of medium size. One type of smaller practice, often overlooked but engaged in by a number of respected and well-known architects, is the practice of architecture in combination with teaching, consulting work, magazine editing, etc. One enterprising and hardy soul even tends bar part-time! These architects find they can assure themselves of steady, moderate incomes through their related activities and are free to be quite choosy about the commissions they accept. Their offices tend to build up in size when they have work and dwindle almost to nothing when the work has been completed.

Alert No 8

Undoubtedly every architect now recognizes that unless he is prepared to offer some degree of comprehensive services he will lose commissions to others who may be less ethical, less prepared for effective services. Often overlooked, but perhaps of even greater moment, are the commissions that do come to architects after many of the great and important decisions on feasibility, the site, financing, goals, operations, etc, have been made without the participation of the architect. In such cases, the architect finds himself bound up in a web of often unthought-out, arbitrary, unrelated decisions that may prevent the effective performance of the basic services themselves.

Where does it all lead?

At the risk of extreme oversimplification, perhaps it can be said that the response of the architectural profession to the needs and demands of clients and society has been to meet the challenge squarely, and with dedication. That response is embodied in what is now called comprehensive architectural services. With the help of all others who are concerned with the environment, with their talents, energies and abilities, the architectural profession envisions a community of efforts toward the creation of an environment that will be beautiful, comfortable and satisfying. To paraphrase Vitruvius, in the language of our time, our every action must point toward the creation of beauty, utility and value in our buildings, and in our environment, in our time.

Contents

Part One:

The New Role of the Architect

Comprehensive Architectural Services: The New Role of the Architect

BY DUDLEY HUNT JR, AIA

Society needs better environment and expects the need to be fulfilled; clients need more effective architectural services and demand their fulfillment; such are the great roles architects are called upon to perform at the present time

Architects of today seem destined to practice their profession in a kind of world that has no parallel in history. It is a world composed of revolutionary advances in technology, of exploding population, of a degree of complexity never dreamed of before now. A world of speed, of great leaps ahead in knowledge and know-how. A world of expanding social problems and lagging social answers. A world that makes much of the specialist, while thumbing its nose at the generalist and calling him dilettante. A world in which the scientist is accepted and esteemed, but the artist has become estranged from his fellow man. A world in need of order, but seemingly doomed to fragmentation.

The challenge of society   In all the seeming confusion of the world of today, there are signs of hope and light. One of the brightest signs is the growing demand of society for someone who can bring order into human environment, who can fill it with beauty, who can cause it to function better, who can create an environment that will contribute to the well-being and advancement of the human race. The most eligible candidate for such a role is the architect. Imperfect though his preparation for the role may be, the architect is a member of the only profession concerned with total human environment. The architect is the only individual who, in any useful degree, possesses all of the elements of such a

The response of the architect

role—the education, the will, the orientation, the desire, and the knowledge. Of course, it would be less than truthful to say that the architect is completely prepared for such a role. But the rudiments are in him, as in no other, if he only cares enough to develop them.

Society presents the challenge. Someone is needed who will take the responsibility for the design of human environment. Clients are demanding broader and more complete services for buildings and their environment. The opportunity for service exists. The challenges are directed first to the architect and his group of skilled and creative specialists. The opportunities are his, if he will accept them with the attendant responsibilities. If not, society will look elsewhere for the answers, for it will be served. There is an alternative for the architect. If he chooses not to involve himself in the creation of total human environment, the architect can retreat to some position of security from which he performs limited services, while others assume control of the over-all problems. Such a course is possible, but unlikely. Too many architects are deeply concerned with the entire show; too many firms have already begun working with the biggest problems.

Just what is architecture? A definition is desperately needed for registration, legal and other reasons. It is equally important to any discussion of great and expanded roles for the architect in our time. Since everyone seems to be attempting it, perhaps one more try might do no harm.

"The architectural profession should assume responsibility for nothing less than the man-made environment, including the use of land, water, and air, an environment in harmony with the aspirations of man."
Philip Will Jr, FAIA

The practice of architecture consists of the professional activities of architects required for the creation and construction of buildings and their environment. These activities include the consultation, analysis, and design necessary for the creation of buildings and their environment, the preparation of graphic and written documents that clearly show the intent of the design, administration of the construction to ensure that the intent of the design is fulfilled. The architect is responsible for the selection of the materials, equipment, and systems for buildings and their environment. The architect's services include the direction or coordination of the other professions and disciplines necessary for the accomplishment of the intended result—buildings and their environment that fulfill the needs they are intended to fulfill and contribute to health, welfare, safety, order and beauty in the community of men.

"The architect is the shaper of the physical environment. He is the manipulator and moulder of space. The architect keeps the balance between the old and the new. The architect, finally, acts as the reconciler of technics and esthetics."
August Heckscher

Individual architects are now performing, in greater or lesser degree, all of the services outlined in the definition. What may not be immediately apparent in the definition is that the accomplishment of buildings and their environment is a much more complex problem today than it was a few years ago. It is not enough, today, to conceive of a design, produce working drawings and specifications for it, and see it through construction. No longer does the client walk through the architect's office door, with a piece of land, a building problem, and money to finance its solving. The more likely situation today is a client with a problem but with no land and little money. Or he is the owner of

If not the architect, then who?

"The package dealer is in business solely for profit. His conflict of interest precludes professional service to his client. To him, design is secondary. If what he builds contributes to the community, it is a lucky accident."
William H. Scheick, AIA

Comprehensive Architectural Services

"To meet the challenges of today's society, architects must expand their practices to include the preparatory planning that makes buildings possible and must carry the projects through all of their phases."
Robert F. Hastings, FAIA

land and would like to see it developed. Or he is an investor or speculator. The architect's current role in the case of the client with a problem is likely to be 1) investigation of the client's problem, and as indicated by the research, advice on whether he should build or not and 2) if the decision is to build, the architect's next role will probably be that of getting the client and his problem together with land and money. If this sounds as if the architect is going to have to become involved with the client's problems before they become architectural problems, that is exactly the case. If it appears that the architect is going to have to become concerned with real estate and money, that also is so. And the architect is going to have to get involved in the programming and planning of the operation that goes into the building.

If the architect refuses to accept the role as described here, there are lots of others waiting for the chance. Some of these are already in serious competition with the architect. The package dealer. The industrial designer. Even people on whom the architect is dependent, if he is to offer complete services, such as the engineers and other consultants. It would be folly for the architect to consider that the competition offers only poor substitutes for the architect's own services. A few package dealers are very good indeed in their way. However, the architect possesses some valuable and necessary characteristics that no other can equal. The architect, as a professional acting as his client's agent, receiving compensation only from his client, effectively removes himself from any conflict of interest and can act purely in his client's behalf. This is a claim none of his competitors can substantiate. And the architect's historic role has been to take hold of a problem, organize it, bring the parts together into a unified whole, and cause the resulting structures and their surroundings to fulfill their purpose. No other can claim more than a specialized portion of this total process.

If the architectural profession accepts the big role being offered to it, certain additional services will have to be added to the basic or standard services. The profession must then develop, within itself, with the help of related professions and others, methods of handling the entire process of creation and construction. To put it another way, the profession will have to prepare itself for comprehensive practice in the area of buildings and their environment. One of the important elements of such a practice would be architectural analysis of feasibility, land, location, finance, and the like. The architect's work would involve him with promotional activities since many projects today are speculative or entrepreneurial in nature and public relations is a necessary tool for success in many others. The architect would find himself concerned with the nature of the operations to be performed in buildings, and would interest himself in operations programming and planning. He would play an increasingly important role in the construction industry as a consultant to manufacturers of building products. He would have much to do with architectural graphics, fine arts, crafts and a long list of other pursuits.

Of course, there are many ways to practice architecture under the comprehensive services concept, just as in the past. Some architects might choose to offer a wide variety of services with their own staff. Others might offer similar services with a smaller staff and outside consultants. Still others might specialize in limited building types, or in one or more phases of architecture such as building design or programming, offering their services as consultants to other firms. For many clients, particularly those with smaller or less complex projects, the basic or standard services might suffice. The small architectural office will survive under the comprehensive services system. It will continue to perform services on many of the buildings it now handles. At the same time, the small office will find its vistas opening up toward more complex and bigger work, if it prepares for it and builds a consulting force outside the firm. Or it can grow larger if that is indicated.

Ethically, comprehensive services are possible for architects under the principle of agency, the principle which makes it possible for one person, the client in this case, to vest authority in another, the architect, to represent him in business transactions with a third party, e.g. a real estate broker or banker. Agency is based on a principle of the law of contracts. There are two legal maxims in this: "He who acts through another acts in person," and "A person who has the power in his own right to do a thing may do it through another."

Every facility available to the profession must be put to work toward the goal of educating practitioners now. And it will take many years and much work to evolve a type of architectural education leading to master planners and architectural specialists in the science, art, and administration of architecture. Similarly, there is much to be done in the fields of internship, continuing education, and cross-fertilization between architecture and the related fields.

Finally, if the architectural profession is to perform the great role sketched here, it must first determine what image it chooses to project for itself. Then, every effort must be expended to impress this image on the public. If architects are to fulfill the great role being offered to them as the creators of better human environment, the profession must make its choice now. Otherwise it inevitably will retreat to a lesser position. And if the larger role is chosen, it will be mandatory on the profession to prepare itself to perform the required comprehensive services with high skill, or at the very least, with competence.

It would be foolhardy to underestimate the task that lies before the profession if it is to assume a position of leadership in the area of design for human environment. The problems are complex and interwoven. They cut across every level of the profession, affect every activity of the members of the profession. Many of the problems are related to the work of other professions and businesses, and will require close coordination of effort with them. Every individual concerned with human environment is touched by the problems in some manner, in some degree. Each

---

Ethics and the principle of agency

"The agency concept seems to be the root of professionalism and the hallmark of the practice of medicine and law."
James M. Hunter, FAIA

Preparation for the new role

"We must be very careful about selling the expanded services concepts to clients until we have prepared ourselves to provide them."
Clinton Gamble, FAIA

The image of the architect

"The image of the architect could be that of the creative coordinator, the systems engineer of design, the environment shaper, the analyst and synthesizer, the profession of creative thought and imagery."
Robert E. Alexander, FAIA

The task ahead of the profession

architect, of course, must have a vital concern in the program because each will be affected closely by the developments. The related professions will be affected, as will the draftsmen, detailers, and other employees of the architect. Without the support of such people, the program will have trouble succeeding.

The American Institute of Architects has taken a number of positive steps to inform its membership, and others concerned, about the elements of Comprehensive Architectural Services. Following up on the work of the Committee on the Profession, further study is underway by other committees of the Institute. The membership will be kept informed of this work as it progresses.

Several specific projects are now underway. A number of the regions have participated in the Institute-sponsored seminars on the principles of comprehensive services. These seminars are still available, and it is expected that other regions will avail themselves of this opportunity in the years to come. Other, more advanced, seminars on specialized subjects within the comprehensive services concept will be made available as the need arises in the future. In the recent past, the Board of Directors of the Institute has allocated funds for providing national speakers for these seminars; such funds will, no doubt, be available in the future if the demand warrants it.

The present book represents another big effort to inform the membership. Based on re-edited and updated articles that originally appeared over a span of two years in *AIA Journal,* this book is intended to fill a need among architects for a sort of primer on comprehensive services. Accordingly, it covers in broad strokes the entire canvas of the subject. The authors of individual chapters are either architects who have specific knowledge about various aspects of the field or experts outside of the profession. The intent here is to bring to the architectural profession the best thinking possible, but not to attempt any deep analysis of any of the specialized areas. Preliminary studies have been made of some of the specialized areas of importance, and a series of books on many of these subjects is under consideration. It is expected that 30 or more books may be required over the next few years, if the profession is to be informed adequately on the major sub-areas of comprehensive services.

As time goes on, other methods for informing architects about comprehensive services will no doubt become necessary— and the time is fast approaching when considerable research on the subject will be required.

Many other things must take place, if a program far-reaching as the present one is to succeed. There are searching questions to be asked of architectural education and of education of the related professions. There are problems of registration and licensing. Grave problems are faced in the area of relationships of architects with society, with engineers, with contractors, with clients, with all who contribute to the creation and construction of buildings and human environment. It will take a lot of conversation and a lot of doing. It will involve us all. It can be done.

The AIA Program of Action

Quotation Sources: Robert E. Alexander, "The Architect and Society", *Architectural Record,* July 1959, August Heckscher "The New Measure of the Architect, *Architectural Record,* September 1959.

2

An Outline of Comprehensive Architectural Services

I Project Analysis Services

A number of these services are more properly business functions, rather than professional. Many of them would be negotiated for the owner by the architect as the owner's agent. In such cases, the owner's interests must be closely guarded. For the architect to properly assist and serve his client in such areas, special training will be required leading to a broad background in real estate, finance, business, and taxation to supplement the architect's skills as an investigator, researcher, organizer, and coordinator.

A Feasibility Studies
1 Need for Facility
2 Method of Accomplishment
3 Economic Requirements
4 Location Requirements
5 Personnel Requirements
6 Legal Considerations

B Financial Analysis
1 Operational Financing
2 Capitalization of Project
3 Land Values and Availability
4 Taxes and Insurance Rates
5 Interim Financing
6 Long-Range Financing

C Location and Site Analysis
1 Survey of Locations and Sites
2 Land Uses and Functions
3 Relationships to Surroundings
4 Relationships to Labor Force
5 Relationships to Raw Materials
6 Availability of Markets
7 Population Trends
8 Relationships to Transportation
9 Climatological Considerations
10 Legal Considerations

D Operational Programming
1 Functional Requirements
2 Space Requirements
3 Equipment and Furnishings
4 Personnel Requirements
5 Financing Requirements
6 Organizational Requirements
7 Maintenance Requirements

E Building Programming
1 Basic Philosophy
2 Site and Climatic Requirements
3 Space Requirements and Relationships
4 Occupancy Requirements
5 Budgeting
6 Financing
7 Design and Construction Scheduling

II Promotional Services

In many cases, there exists a need for services in the actual assembly of land for projects, acquiring of financing, and other promotional activities required for projects to go ahead. Architects, with their own staffs, can accomplish many of these activities including preparation of promotional designs, drawings, brochures, and the like. As the agent of the owner, architects can also procure and coordinate the additional activities necessary for a complete service. In all such activities, the architect must maintain his professional status as the agent of the owner.

A   **Real Estate and Land Assembly**
B   **Financing of Projects**
C   **Promotional Design and Planning**
D   **Public Relations**
E   **Communications**

III Design and Planning Services

The operations to be performed in a building, such as production in an industrial building or sales in a shopping center, determine to some extent the architecture of the building. In order to maintain his control over all of the aspects of the design, the architect must prepare himself to perform or direct the operational design and planning, as well as the building design and planning phases. Reliable cost estimating is a necessity in both operational and building design and planning.

A   **Operational Design and Planning**
1   Operational Procedures
2   Systems and Processes
3   Functional Requirements
4   Layout and Relationships
5   Equipment and Furnishings
  a   Specifications and Purchasing
  b   Installation and Hookup
  c   Testing and Checking
  d   Maintenance and Upkeep

B   **Building Design and Planning**
1   Schematic Design
2   Preliminary Estimates
3   Design Development
4   Outline Specifications
5   Cost Estimating
6   Working Drawings
7   Specifications

IV Construction Services

Architects may not—ethically—engage in building contracting. During the construction phases, the architect's position is that of agent of his client for bid or negotiated contracts, force account work, or other variations of the standard construction contracts.

A   **Bids and Construction Contracts**
B   **Supervision and Administration**
C   **Job Cost Accounting**
D   **Construction Management**
E   **Post-Construction Services**

V Supporting Services

In working with the supporting services, the architect's role is one of collaboration with them so as to coordinate their activities into a comprehensive service leading to a unified result. While the architect may employ many of these professionals as members of his staff, a more normal arrangement of comprehensive services might include them as consultants to the architect. In either case, they are entitled to their professional status, and to the benefits and public acknowledgement earned by their contributions to the total effort.

A Supporting Design Services
1 Engineering
2 Urban and Regional Planning
3 Landscape Architecture
4 Site Planning
5 Fine Arts and Crafts
6 Interior and Furnishings
7 Sanitary and Utility Planning
8 Roads and Traffic Design
9 Others—Acoustics, Lighting, etc

B Special Consulting Services
1 Specific Building Types
2 Economics
3 Market Analysis
4 Merchandising Analysis
5 Law

VI Related Services

A great need exists for services of architects in fields other than those directly concerned with individual building or environmental projects. The architect may actually perform such services or may direct or coordinate the activities.

A Architectural Education

B Industry Consultation

C Research and Testing

D Product Design

E Architectural Graphics

F Prefabrication

3

Comprehensive Architectural Services: For Small Offices or Large

BY DUDLEY HUNT JR, AIA

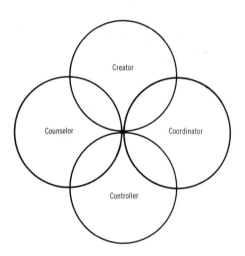

Role of the Architect

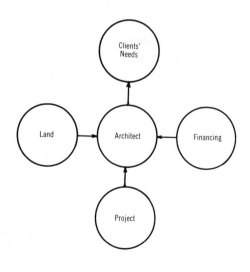

Architectural Practice Today

The concept of comprehensive services describes the role of the entire architectural profession and its collaborators in building and environmental design and construction. Within the concept, architectural firms of all sizes can practice effectively and creatively in any of a great number of ways

So vast is the scope of complete comprehensive architectural practice that only the architectural profession as a whole, with the help of talented and able consultants and collaborators, can hope to perform the entire range of services.

On the other hand, it is surely possible for individual architectural firms, large or small, to provide their clients with the comprehensive services required for particular projects.

Architectural firms of any size can practice effectively, creatively under the comprehensive practice concept if—to put it bluntly—they are competent and organized for it. The fact is that a number of firms presently are performing many services for their clients in addition to those of the standard design, production and construction supervision phases. Some offices now offer their clients professional services in such areas as building programming, master planning, feasibility and financial analysis, location analysis and site selection, space planning, or operational programming and design. Many larger offices are now prepared to perform these services and others according to the requirements of the particular types of work they handle. This fact is well-known. Not so common knowledge is the fact that a number of much smaller firms, having somehow acquired a degree of competence in such areas as finance and costs or real estate and land assembly, are regularly serving the interests of their clients in these or other areas not formerly thought of as architectural.

Whatever the size of a firm, the decision to go into areas in addition to those of the basic architectural services has usually come primarily as the result of recognition of the needs of the

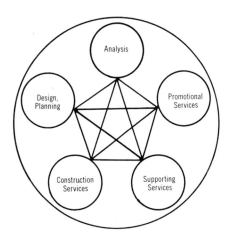

Comprehensive Practice

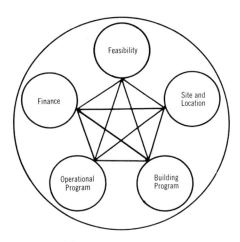

Architectural Analysis Services

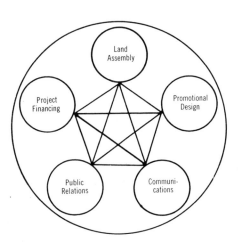

Promotional Services

firm's own clients. Perhaps equally important has been the realization that, in many cases, if it does not participate in the early real estate and financial operation, and similar decisions, the architectural firm will be prevented, by decisions over which it had no control or influence, from applying its best skills and talents to the solution of the more strictly architectural problems. Of course, the individual inclinations and desires of the firm's members also bear heavily on the question of whether or not a firm will offer some degree of comprehensive services. If a firm is to grow, it will inevitably face a long series of such questions during its life. If the decision at any point is for the firm to expand its present services, it then must follow that the firm will have to broaden its knowledge and attain an acceptable degree of competence in the newly added services.

The basic questions that must be answered by a firm considering the expansion of services toward some form of comprehensive practice would seem to be these: What are the major goals of the firm and the individuals that comprise it? What types of work does it wish to perform? What size of work? Work of what degree of complexity? What volume? What are the characteristics of the clients who commission this work? What requirements are peculiar to this work? What must be the scope and characteristics of services required for such work and for such clients? What kinds of people are needed to perform these services? How many? Where can they be obtained? How are they to be trained? How to organize them for efficient, effective, creative performance? Only with the help of realistic answers to questions such as these can the individual architectural firm plot its own course through the unruly waters faced by the profession. And the answer to the first question, and perhaps those to the succeeding three or four, provide the chart necessary if the firm is to avoid the dangers inherent in the other questions.

A given firm might decide, for example, that it will limit types of work it accepts, the size of its work, its complexity, its volume, or any combination of these because the major goal of the firm is selectivity of projects with a view toward excellence of performance within the limitations of the services it elects to perform on the projects it accepts. Another firm might gear its operation to growth and to the performance of expanding types of services on a growing number of projects of increasing size and complexity. A third firm might have a completely different view of itself. In any case, the individual firm will find it necessary to assess its position and its goals, if it expects to prosper and progress in today's world. Each firm must then prepare itself to perform the services required to reach the goals it sets for itself, with its own staff, with the help of outside consultants or collaborators, or by some combination of these methods. It goes without saying that the firm must somehow sell its potential for service to an adequate number of clients, and then perform the services commissioned by the clients, creatively and effectively.

All of this is undoubtedly easier to affirm than perform. Further clouding of the picture is caused by the existing need for vast improvement in the current average levels of performance of the basic services of design, production, and construction adminis-

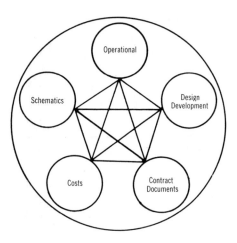

Design and Planning Services

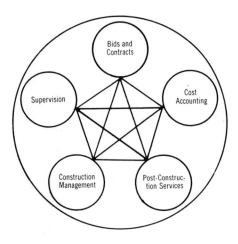

Construction Services

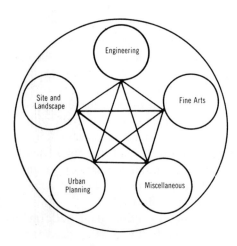

Supporting Services

tration. Greater competence in the areas of cost estimating and control of construction costs is sorely needed. And it is not easy to justify the current widespread practice of offering building programming only as an extra architectural service or performing it haphazardly, hurriedly and often for no fee primarily because the owner cannot or will not handle it himself. Without increasingly-improved levels of performance throughout the profession in these basic areas of practice, it is extremely doubtful that firms can perform effectively in such additional fields as land assembly or financial analysis. And it is even more doubtful that any large numbers of today's clients will allow such firms to advise them or act for them in these areas. The corporate client, the entrepreneur, the governmental client, the institutional board—the major clients of today—cannot reasonably be expected to entrust the analysis of the financing or feasibility of their important projects to architects other than those who have demonstrated their ability to perform efficiently the standard architectural services, including the preparation of realistic and reliable cost estimates and the exercise of cost controls to insure construction within budgets. None of these clients can be expected to commission an architect for services in programming or layout of production lines in an industrial building or in the market analysis of a shopping center, unless that architect is demonstrably competent in the performance of the standard architectural services, within reasonable and previously estimated limits of time. These are the sort of considerations that clients understand and have the right to expect.

Certainly a client is more likely to utilize services of an architect in such areas, if it is apparent that the architect's own functions are handled in an efficient and productive manner. And today's clients are looking for single authority over their complete building projects, something the knowledgeable and competent architect can deliver better than any other.

This is not to say that a firm or individual architect must provide all of the comprehensive services or even all of the standard services with his own staff. Growing trends toward consultation between individual architects and firms, associations, and joint ventures of various kinds are discernible. And the list of the architect's consultants and collaborators is growing.

It is within the realm of possibility, surely, that an architectural project might be handled in some way such as this: An architectural firm with a reputation for original and enlightened design might acquire a commission for which they intend to handle only schematics, preliminaries, and over-all coordination. The aid of knowledgeable real estate and financial consultants is enlisted for assembly of the necessary land for the site, analysis of financial requirements, and obtaining of financing.

A specialized consultant is asked to prepare an analysis of the operational and building requirements and eventually to prepare the program under the direction of the architects. An association is formed with an efficient and business-like firm of architects who are given the task of production of working drawings and specifications. Since the building is to be constructed in a location away from the home offices of either firm, still a third architectural firm of demonstrated ability in the area of construc-

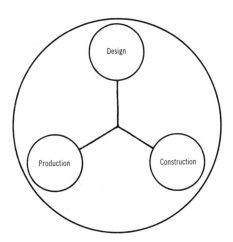

Former Organizational Pattern

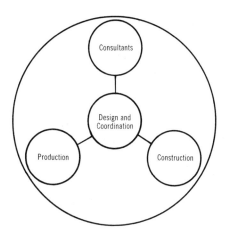

A New Organizational Pattern

tion is engaged to manage and administer the construction of the building. A hypothetical case this—but the fact remains that nearly every architectural firm in existence has, at one time or another, been involved in some project that was handled in a manner similar to that described.

The next step, perhaps, might be that the design-oriented firm might decide that the success of this project indicates they should handle more of their future work in this manner. Next might come a decision to concentrate the firm's efforts entirely in this one area of practice. How to get the working drawings done? Possibly with the aid of some other firm that has decided to concentrate in the production area. Possibly by a permanent association between the two firms. The combinations are virtually without limit.

Another architectural firm finds itself able to obtain commissions ever farther from home base. Inevitably, that firm must decide to limit itself geographically, refusing jobs that are too far away, or it may decide to create branch offices, or work out some other method of handling the work. Might not a more or less permanent association between a number of firms, removed from each other geographically but possessed of either similar or complementary interests, be an answer to this problem?

The hypothetical cases discussed only serve to point out, in a very limited way, that the architectural profession has available to it a great number of organizational patterns that might be utilized for meeting the complex requirements of comprehensive practice for the client of today. It is obviously impossible to describe definitively the types of architectural practice possible under the comprehensive practice concept. However, a brief discussion of a few of the major possibilities may be of some help.

In the recent past, and to a degree at present, the two most prevalent methods of organization for architectural practice have been general and specialized practice. For the most part, general practitioners have limited themselves to the offering of the basic services: design-production-construction administration. Such firms have usually offered their services for all, or almost all, building types. On the other hand, specialized firms have mostly confined themselves to services on a limited number of building types, offering the basic services, but increasingly finding they must perform additional services for their clients if they would maintain their positions of leadership in the specialized fields.

Today, general firms find it increasingly difficult to obtain commissions or to perform them well when they do obtain them, unless they equip themselves to do more than the basic services. For the most part, firms that specialize by building type learned this lesson earlier. At the same time, many of the specialized firms have begun seeking commissions in fields other than their specialties, and in so doing have had to prepare themselves for handling all aspects of the work necessary for success in the new fields.

In other words, general and specialized firms have inevitably found themselves expanding toward comprehensive services either from choice or as a result of the demands and needs of their clients. Of course, there have always been out-of-the-ordinary

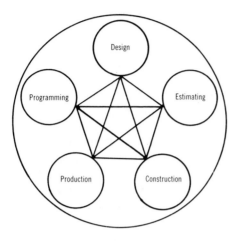

Limited Firm (Basic Services)

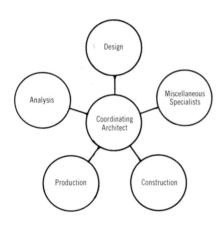

Specialization by Function

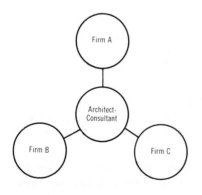

Architectural Consultant

methods of practice in addition to the two main types. Together with the general and specialized practices these have been evolving toward newer ways of organization for practice, all of them within the concept of comprehensive practices.

At the present time, it is possible to isolate and classify no fewer than five major types of firms now in existence, all operating within the comprehensive services concept: 1, Limited Firm; 2, Specialist Firm; 3, Architectural Consulting Firm; 4, Co-operative Firm; 5, Comprehensive Firm. Theoretically at least, it is possible to add to the list a sixth type, which might be called the Core Firm. While the activities of many—perhaps most—of today's firms cannot be said to fall strictly within the limits of any one of these groups, perhaps such classifications can be helpful in the establishment of guidelines for an examination of some of the growing organizational and functional tendencies in present-day architectural practice.

Many firms today limit themselves, by choice or because of particular circumstances, to a type of practice that is closely akin to the old concept of general practice. Such firms are currently finding that they must seek out special consultants to aid them in serving their client whenever their clients' problems escape from the accepted range of basic architectural services. It would seem inevitable that most such firms will eventually have to work out some sort of standing arrangements with special consultants or bring some of them into their staffs, if the firms are to continue to do large and complex work. In other words, this type of firm now seems to be approaching some degree of comprehensive practice.

Firms that specialize by building types do exist, but it would appear that such specialization is not so narrow as it once was. Other ways of specialization are now beginning to make their appearance, perhaps in answer to the growing complexities of present-day practice. For example, some firms today perform few or no services in the production and construction administration areas, relying almost entirely on associated firms to accomplish this work. Such firms tend more and more to become specialists in some combination of programming, design and architectural co-ordination. Other firms have split themselves into two parts, a production-construction division and an architectural division that does everything else. There are numerous organizations that specialize in analysis and programming. Though most of these do not call themselves architectural firms, architects are the owners of, and prime movers behind, many of them. There are, of course, a number of further possibilities.

In order to perform a degree of comprehensive services, architectural firms are finding they must provide themselves with increasing numbers of consultants in specialized, non-architectual phases of the work. Perhaps not so apparent is the growing tendency of architects to engage the services of other architects for consultation. For example, a top-flight, efficient firm might retain the services of a top-flight consulting designer-architect if it has no one of that caliber on its own staff. This sort of thing is being done rather often these days, and with satisfactory results. Many firms could benefit greatly from similar consultation with other

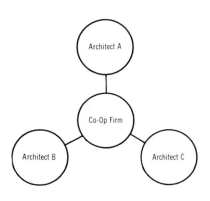

Cooperative Firm

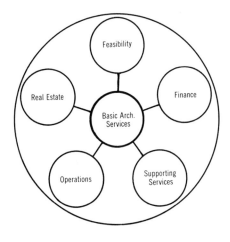

Comprehensive Firm

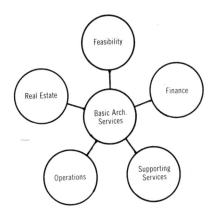

Core Firm

architects who have earned good reputations for such things as their organizational abilities, their talents in programming and analysis, their efficient procedures in the production of working drawings and specifications, or their ability to control construction costs.

One method of cooperative practice is that in which individual practitioners band together to share their overhead, certain facilities, and possibly the services of personnel. This method of organization is well established among doctors and lawyers. There would seem to be no insurmountable reason why architects cannot also benefit from the advantages of sharing such things as can be usefully shared while at the same time retaining the rights of each individual to practice in his own way. A further advantage is that greater opportunity exists in such organizations for constructive criticism among the co-op members.

It seems equally possible to set up cooperatives among firms rather than individuals, if there are important advantages to be gained through the actions of the larger groups, actions that might be ineffective if performed by single firms. As has been previously pointed out, such advantages might accrue to a group of firms, widely separated from each other geographically, if they made an agreement to cooperate with each other on certain types of work. Then too, there might be some advantages in a cooperative firm composed of divisions, each of which was devoted to a major sector of comprehensive services.

Firms deciding to organize for comprehensive services, in the fullest sense, must provide themselves with the capabilities necessary for performing all of the services needed by their clients. This can be accomplished either with people on the firm's own staff, or with outside consultants. In practice, the usual arrangement is a combination of the two. For the most part, specialized consultants whose services are required almost continuously by such firms are usually to be found on their staffs. Other experts, needed less frequently or those who are more extremely specialized, are usually brought in from outside when their services are needed.

What about small or medium-sized firms that wish to offer comprehensive services to its clients? Such firms may find themselves unable to perform more than the basic architectural services with their own staffs. Assuming that such firms are well-prepared to offer these services, it would seem entirely possible for them to make working agreements with outside specialist consultants who would remain on call until needed. As the number of projects handled by the firms together with their consultants increased, it should be possible to work out smoothly-operating and efficient procedures that would lead to quite satisfactory results. Such a firm would consist of a hard core of creative and productive people who would perform all or most of the purely architectural functions. This core would be surrounded by equally creative and productive consultants, selected by the members of the firm for their talent, ability, and compatibility. A firm organized along these lines might be hard to hold back in the years stretching ahead of the profession. Such a firm should be able to handle work of any size or complexity.

4

Office Organization for Successful Comprehensive Architectural Services:

BY RICHARD A. ENION *

For comprehensive services to lead to better buildings and environment, architects must so organize their offices that efficient business practices contribute to—rather than conflict with—the achievement of excellence

*The Author, who is president of Enion Associates, Inc. Management Consultants, of Philadelphia, designed and supervised the reorganization study of the Institute staff in 1960 and is now permanent consultant to the AIA on organizational and personnel matters

The practice of architecture in the complex society of today is in the throes of what appears to be a significant evolutionary change. Mass production, mass consumption, government directives, redevelopment, decentralization and urbanization affect not only the basic design concepts of the architect but his performance as an economic unit of society as well. The spirit of individual architects which created and built most architectural practices several decades ago is now slowly being replaced with the collective spirit of organizations of individual architects. Today, the *practice* of architecture is irrevocably complicated by the *business* of architecture. In addition to his essential design functions, the architect must now devote time to cost accounting, cash flow projections, image building and solicitation of new business.

Such trends and forces give many an architect pause for contemplation: What is his purpose? What is the philosophy of his practice? Which direction does he wish his office to take in terms of client assignments? In order to define his goals, the architect must find satisfactory answers to such questions.

Balancing design and business

It has been said that the role of the architect today is to design a hospitable environment for our scientific age. In such a role, the architect finds himself involved in conflict between his aspirations as an artist and his needs as an astute businessman. He must somehow strike a balance which will enable him to function as an artist, yet arrive at designs that will be compatible with his clients' needs within today's socio-economic environment. He must then maintain this delicate balance, yet handle himself in a businesslike manner.

Even the great cathedral builders of the Middle Ages could not escape the vexing problems of the market place, although this may often have interfered with their pursuit of design concepts. Master builders from William of Sens to Christopher Wren found it necessary to offer a version of comprehensive services. No doubt they often wished they could be free to create instead of becoming enmeshed in the details of hiring (or conscripting) masons, carpenters, ironmongers and tracers. They, too, wasted valuable time placating clients. However, time was less expensive in their time than in ours.

Time can be worst enemy

Time seems to be the worst enemy of the architect who hopes to realize reasonable profits on his commissions. Time lost in design alteration, time devoted to client consultation, time spent over the drawing board, time revising specifications, time supplying the incidental and supplementary services of a comprehensive practice. Time means man-hours—and additional technical man-hours expended beyond the time budgeted in estimates mean dollars deducted until, in the end, the predetermined profit on a project may be wiped out.

How many hours can an architect afford to spend in redesign, revision of working drawings or correction of specifications? How can a firm achieve excellence in design without too many revisions and without merciless reappraisal of design, drawings and specifications?

Establishment of design freeze point necessary

Architects constantly deplore the lack of a satisfactory design freeze point and feel that this is an insurmountable ob-

Management Case A: Budgeting Man-Hours

Firm A had evolved an empirical formula (based on experience) for breaking down a project fee, by dollars, for each step in the architectural process. Quite correctly, the partners first allocated a certain percentage of fee for anticipated profit. Dollars spent for manpower were posted (although not too regularly) against budgeted dollars. Over-rides mounted, budgets were exceeded and everyone talked dollars. After evaluating the situation, it was decided to take the dollar analysis one step further and convert dollars into technical man-hours. Then, through adherence to a better report schedule utilizing a specially created form, technical man-hours expended could be compared regularly with budgeted man-hours, resulting in closer control of production and a return to predetermined profits.

stacle to efficiency. Yet, when an informed observer follows a job through the shop, it often becomes apparent that failure to freeze design may be only a symptom of problems that are more basic.

Origin of design freeze point problems

Uncertainty about when to set a design freeze point may arise from several basic problems. Perhaps the creative team itself generates its own problem. Is the design freeze point actually an essential part of the architect's capacity to design? The desire to perfect design is a legitimate—and, in general, laudable—goal. Then why do many architects feel guilty about a series of revisions on the design board?

Is the problem one of lack of communications between the design room and the rest of the staff?

Is the inability to freeze a design characterized by constant revision of details in the design, while the initial concept remains static?

Or, is it possible that fluidity of design is the easiest thing for everyone to blame as a time and money waster, thus making it possible to gloss over the real and basic problems in the organization?

Other problems are basis of design freeze troubles

A firm suffering from chronic design freeze trauma should ask itself if its administrative organization and personnel are functioning properly. The principals should ask themselves:

1 Does our firm have a good grasp of job cost analyses? Is someone responsible for keeping man-hours within estimated limits? Technical man-hours, when properly planned and reported, can become one of the most effective budgetary tools available to the architect who expects to realize predetermined profits.

2 Have time estimates been followed closely in all phases of the project? Too much time expended in one phase can almost never be recovered in succeeding phases without adverse results.

3 What financial controls has the firm adopted? Is there responsible management of the office budget, as well as the budget of the job? Has the firm a reliable system of budgetary controls?

For each firm, for each architect, there exists a point of reconciliation of perfection in design and efficiency in execution;

Management Case B: Design Freeze

Firm B was growing rapidly and decided to departmentalize by technical skills in order to better handle the expanding volume of work. The contract documents department continually complained that they were receiving incomplete preliminary drawings. They added that the design department never stopped reworking design detail. Analysis of this situation revealed that there was little, if any, continuity of control over a project as it progressed between departments. The best solution appeared to be the introduction of the project manager concept, superimposed on the departmental concept. This, of course, meant added overhead, but when a predetermined volume of work was reached, this change in organization paid off handsomely in effecting design freeze and a return to healthy profits.

some achieve it automatically by an almost intuitive sense of balance; some will never achieve it; most find that they must struggle constantly with the shifting weights of the design board and the balance sheet. There is no single pat formula for efficiency in business organization any more than there is only one solution to a design problem. Each solution—whether of a design or a business organizational problem—depends upon the careful integration of the elements of the problem in terms of its affective environment.

Achieving efficiency and design excellence

It is possible, however, for architects to improve the efficiency of their organizations without sacrificing their goals of excellence. If a firm finds its percentage of profit slipping downward, if an office seems constantly at odds, then the principals of that firm might do well to check over the following areas of their own practice:

1 Is the atmosphere—or environment—of the office itself conducive to efficient work?

2 How clear are the communications between principals and associates, between associates and draftsmen? It has been truly stated that more men fail from a lack of understanding than from lack of ability.

3 What are the personnel policies and procedures of the firm? How are salary increases, bonuses and promotions decided upon? Do these incentives actually motivate personnel to optimum performances?

4 Do the principals spend the time necessary to develop and train assistants and to delegate authority? Do key associates feel that they have career growth opportunities, or is turnover a constant harassment?

5 Does only one principal meet clients? Have steps been taken to develop an associate who can support this vital activity?

Factors that affect the balance sheet

These are considerations which directly affect the firm's balance sheet. Every architectural practice has peaks and valleys of work. When the pressure is great, an atmosphere of ease speeds up the working efficiency and mutual cooperation of all members

Management Case C: Communications

An analysis of communications problems in Firm C revealed that some key members of the architectural team did not appear to be fully informed of what was happening in areas other than their specialties. Also each man needed to know his position in the total architectural process and what his degree of participation should be in areas other than his specialty. A vector diagram of the logical steps of the architectural process was drawn, showing the degree of participation of each key man in each step. A number of important facts were revealed by the diagram; for example, it became apparent that the firm's specialist in field supervision should not limit his activities to the construction phase but should participate to a certain degree in activities such as those occurring during the contract-drawing phase.

Profits tied to organization

of the firm; when there is discontent, the opposite will undoubtedly be the case. Probably more dollars are lost through personal conflicts within the firm then through the reworking of drawings necessitated by changes in design concepts. Yet, neither type of loss need occur. The working atmosphere of an office reflects the over-all timing and leadership of the senior members of the firm and the clarity and relevancy of reporting relationships in the structure of the organization. Members of a firm who feel that their practice should be more profitable might look carefully at the organizational structure of their office and ask themselves:

Is this the best organization plan for us? Do we have the right man in charge of design? Should the design function be directed by an administrator or a truly creative and inspirational type? Should we have a "new business" man?

To this list could be added a host of other self-searching questions. It is often difficult for members of a firm to appraise their own organization structure—and the people in it—objectively and accurately. Yet failure to do so can be extremely costly.

Many architectural firms have developed excellent plans for the logical steps which must take place in the architectural process, from programming through preliminary design, working drawings, specifications, engineering and construction, as well as the kindred areas involved in comprehensive practice. Yet many of these same firms have failed to evolve organizational structures, complete with defined areas of responsibility, authority, and accountability, to implement their architectural processes. And the failure to formulate carefully an organization that has logical and workable reporting relationships can smother the profit potentials of an architectural firm.

No one organization structure proper for all offices

There is no single optimum approach for properly organizing an architectural office. Each organization must be tailor-made to meet the needs of each practice. The departmentalized approach of one office may not meet the needs of another office. One office will utilize the "team" approach, while another uses project architects. Still another office makes better headway with

Management Case D: Compensation Plans

Firm D found itself paying recent architectural graduates as much as architectural graduates who had been with them one or two years. An analysis of the situation revealed that a wage and salary administration plan should be established which would set forth competitive compensation ranges for each position in the firm, complete with minimum and maximum salary points. In this way, "guesswork" was removed from the compensation process. The more formalized wage and salary plan made allowances for discrepancies between jobs, and among jobs based on seniority, by utilizing step-by-step increments of increase. Finally, the plan was tied into a performance review program so that each man could be compensated on the bases of the value of his position to the firm, assessment of his performance and his length of service.

project managers. Semantics also enters the picture here; for different offices—even those practicing in the same city—often interpret terms like "project architect" and "project manager" differently.

Importance of personal relationships within offices

Firms which have excellent personal relationships, within their organizations, may still lose money because of inadequate coordination of projects from inception to completion. Job functions may overlap too much or there may be too little supervisory push at critical points. It is in this area that a great many firms appear to have trouble.

In actual practice, it is always difficult for the principals of any firm to assess their own managerial performance effectively. An architect who will subject his design to merciless reappraisal may not always be as willing to evaluate his organization structure, personnel problems and budgeting functions in the same manner. Nevertheless, the architect must develop a working organization which is efficient and profitable so that he can be free to achieve excellence in design.

Often, the alternative to this is living with an ineffective, inefficient organization, one that lacks personnel alignment and whose troubles are compounded by hidden losses that stem from improper budget controls. Worries about inefficiency do not increase the effectiveness of design.

Purpose of organization is creation of architectural strength

If any of the foregoing seems to make the practice of architecture sound too businesslike, it will be well to remember that the strength of an architectural firm is not derived from over-conformity or from rigid adherence to set policies and procedures. Rather the strength of a firm comes from the creation of a vehicle of organization that will allow each man to perform, at his highest level, in his fullest capacity, within a total atmosphere that contributes to individual motivation. Accordingly, controls and procedures should be introduced into an architectural firm only to the extent that they can be expected to nurture an atmosphere of freedom and creativity, make it possible to capitalize upon it and thus provide an effective and profitable enterprise.

Management Case E: Job Performance

The partners in Firm E had a very successful practice and, furthermore, felt that they knew exactly how well each employee had performed for any given year. The truth is that the partners did know but, unfortunately, few of the employees knew how well they were making out. After a thorough review of the situation, it was decided to introduce a job performance appraisal plan. This plan not only sharpened the objectivity of the partners' review of each employee's over-all performance but also created a vehicle of communications by means of which each employee could learn just how well he was making out. Through the medium of confidential interviews conducted periodically, each employee is given counsel on what his strengths are, areas that need development and what he can do to improve his situation.

An indication of the sort of organizational problems frequently encountered by architects—and how they may be solved—can be gathered from the following examples selected from studies made for architectural offices by the author's firm.

1 Organization Structure: Modifications in firm's organizational structure complete with separate functional organization charts and manning organization charts for adopting quasi-departmental structure.

2 An Executive Committee: Creation of executive committee which reapportioned certain responsibilities among partners.

3 Incentive Bonus System: Adoption of incentive bonus system for selected employees.

4 Planned Annual Budgets: Incorporation of method of annual planned budgeting for specified expense items by departments on quarterly basis.

5 Project Plans, Control: Methods of planning and controlling progress of projects by determining variations between actual hours expended and hours budgeted at critical stages, with report forms.

6 Distribution of Profit: Method of recalculation of profit distribution to associates.

7 Partners' Compensation: Recommendations concerning partner compensation and techniques for tax-sheltered income.

8 Standards for Drafting: Establishment of drafting room standards.

9 Program for the Future: Introduction of specific programs for forward planning.

10 Specialized Functions: Creation of new departments encompassing specialized functions of service necessary if firm is to continue its rate of growth.

11 Functional Delegation: Recommendations concerning firm's personnel who should be able to assume more responsibilities, now and in long-range future.

12 Position Descriptions: Creation of position descriptions to define responsibilities.

13 Salary Review Methods: Creation of salary review procedures for both hourly and salaried personnel.

14 Performance Appraisal: Establishment of job performance appraisal program.

15 Fringe Benefit System: Establishment of system of broadened fringe benefits.

16 Drawing Account Plans: Establishment of partner drawing accounts (or changes in present drawing account procedures).

17 Public Relations Plan: Establishment of planned public relations program.

18 Diagrams of Work Flow: Introduction of work-flow diagram which specifies responsibility by job classification at each stage in progress of projects, with indications of amount of time needed at each stage.

19 Predetermined Profits: Establishment of a method, complete with control forms, for budgeting, planning and programming projects in order to arrive at predetermined percentages of profit.

20 Design Freeze Methods: Procedures for establishing methods of freezing design. (Vary according to particular needs of each firm.)

21 Improvement of Morale: Recommendations for improvement of morale in order to curtail turnover at essential middle-management level.

22 Better Communications: Recommendations for improving communications.

23 New Business Program: Planning and implementation of continuing new business program.

The Standards of Professional Practice

The following Provisions of the Bylaws of The Institute

form the basis for all disciplinary actions taken under the

Standards of Professional Practice:

CHAPTER 14, ARTICLE 1, SECTION 1 (c)

Any deviation by a corporate member from any of the Standards of Professional Practice of The Institute or from any of the rules of the Board supplemental thereto, or any action by him that is detrimental to the best interests of the profession and The Institute shall be deemed to be unprofessional conduct on his part, and ipso facto he shall be subject to discipline by The Institute.

Preface

0.1 The profession of architecture calls for men of integrity, culture, acumen, creative ability and skill. The services of an architect may include any services appropriate to the development of man's physical environment, provided that the architect maintains his professional integrity and that his services further the ultimate goal of creating an environment of orderliness and beauty. The architect's motives, abilities and conduct always must be such as to command respect and confidence.

An architect should seek opportunities to be of constructive service in civic affairs, and to advance the safety, health, beauty and well-being of his community in which he resides or practices. As an architect, he must recognize that he has moral obligations to society beyond the requirements of law or business practices. He is engaged in a profession which carries important responsibilities to the public and, therefore, in fulfilling the needs of his client, the architect must consider the public interest and the well-being of society.

0.2 An architect's honesty of purpose must be above suspicion; he renders professional services to his client and acts as his client's agent and adviser. His advice to his client must be sound and unprejudiced, as he is charged with the exercise of impartial judgment in interpreting contract documents.

0.3 Every architect should contribute generously of his time and talents to foster justice, courtesy, and sincerity within his profession. He administers and coordinates the efforts of his professional associates, subordinates, and consultants, and his acts must be prudent and knowledgeable.

0.4 Building contractors and their related crafts and skills are obligated to follow the architect's directions as expressed in the contract documents; these directions must be clear, concise, and fair.

THE AMERICAN INSTITUTE OF ARCHITECTS

AIA DOC. J330 REVISED JUNE 1964

Obligations

1. To the Public

1.1 An architect may offer his services to anyone on the generally accepted basis of commission, fee, salary, or royalty, as agent, consultant, adviser, or assistant, provided that he strictly maintains his professional integrity.

1.2 An architect shall perform his professional services with competence, and shall properly serve the interests of his client and the public.

1.3 An architect shall not engage in building contracting.

1.4 An architect shall not use paid advertising or indulge in self-laudatory, exaggerated, misleading or false publicity, nor shall he publicly endorse products or permit the use of his name to imply endorsement.

1.5 An architect shall not solicit, nor permit others to solicit in his name, advertisements or other support toward the cost of any publication presenting his work.

1.6 An architect shall conform to the registration laws governing the practice of architecture in any state in which he practices, and shall observe the customs and standards established by the local professional body of architects.

2. To the Client

2.1 An architect's relation to his client is based upon the concept of agency. Before undertaking any commission he shall determine with his client the scope of the project, the nature and extent of the services he will perform and his compensation for them, and shall provide confirmation thereof in writing. In performing his services he shall maintain an understanding with his client regarding the project, its developing solutions and its estimated probable costs. Where a fixed limit of cost is established in advance of design, the architect must determine the character of design construction so as to meet as nearly as feasible the cost limit established. He shall keep his client informed with competent estimates of probable costs. He shall not guarantee the final cost, which will be determined not only by the architect's solution of the owner's requirements, but by the fluctuating conditions of the competitive construction market.

2.2 An architect shall guard the interest of his client and the rights of those whose contracts the architect administers. An architect should give every reasonable aid toward a complete understanding of those contracts in order that mistakes may be avoided.

2.3 An architect's communications, whether oral, written, or graphic, should be definite and clear.

2.4 An architect shall not have financial or personal interests which might tend to compromise his obligation to his client.

2.5 An architect shall not accept any compensation for his professional services from anyone other than his client or employer.

2.6 An architect shall base his compensation on the value of the services he agrees to render. He shall neither offer nor agree to perform his services for a compensation that will tend to jeopardize the adequacy or professional quality of those services, or the judgment, care and diligence necessary properly to discharge his responsibilities to his client and the public.

3. To the Profession

3.1 An architect should promote the interests of his professional organization and share its work.

3.2 An architect shall not act in a manner detrimental to the best interests of the profession.

3.3 An architect shall not knowingly injure or attempt to injure falsely or maliciously the professional reputation, prospects, or practice of another architect.

3.4 An architect shall not attempt to supplant another architect after definite steps have been taken by a client toward the latter's employment. He shall not offer to undertake a commission for which he knows another architect has been employed, nor shall he undertake such a commission until he has notified such other architect of the fact in writing, and has been advised by the owner that employment of that architect has been terminated.

3.5 An architect shall not enter into competitive bidding against another architect on the basis of compensation. He shall not use donation or misleading information on cost as a device for obtaining a competitive advantage.

3.6 An architect shall not offer his services in a competition except as provided in the Competition Code of The American Institute of Architects.

3.7 An architect shall not engage a commission agent to solicit work in his behalf.

3.8 An architect shall not call upon a contractor to provide work to remedy omissions or errors in the contract documents without proper compensation to the contractor.

3.9 An architect shall not serve as an employee of unregistered individuals who offer architectural services to the public, nor as an employee of a firm whose architectural practice is not under the identified control of a registered architect.

3.10 An architect shall not be, nor continue to be, a member or employee of any firm which practices in a manner inconsistent with these Standards of Professional Practice.

3.11 Dissemination by an architect, or by any component of The Institute, of information concerning judiciary procedures and penalties, beyond the information published or authorized by The Board or its delegated authority, shall be considered to be detrimental to the best interests of the architectural professional.

4. To Related Professionals

4.1 An architect should provide his professional employees with a desirable working environment and compensate them fairly.

4.2 An architect should contribute to the interchange of technical information and experience between architects, the design profession, and the building industry.

4.3 An architect should respect the interests of consultants and associated professionals in a manner consistent with the applicable provisions of these Standards of Practice.

4.4 An architect should recognize the contribution and the professional stature of the related professionals and should collaborate with them in order to create an optimum physical environment.

4.5 An architect should promote interest in the design professions and facilitate the professional development of those in training. He should encourage a continuing education, for himself and others, in the functions, duties, and responsibilities of the design professions, as well as the technical advancement of the art and science of environmental design.

Promulgation

5.1 These Standards of Professional Practice are promulgated to promote the highest ethical standards for the profession of architecture. Thus the enumeration of particular duties in the Standards should not be construed as a denial of others, equally imperative, though not specifically mentioned. Furthermore, the placement of statements of obligation under any category above shall not be construed as limiting the applicability of such statement to the group named, since some obligations have broad application, and have been positioned as they are only as a matter of convenience and emphasis. The primary purpose of disciplinary action under these Standards of Professional Practice is to protect the public and the profession.

5.2 Since adherence to the principles herein enumerated is the obligation of every member of The American Institute of Architects, any deviation therefrom shall be subject to discipline in proportion to its seriousness.

5.3 The Board of Directors of The American Institute of Architects, or its delegated authority, shall have sole power of interpreting these Standards of Professional Practice and its decisions shall be final subject to the provisions of the Bylaws.

NOTE: This 1964 edition of the Standards of Professional Practice, AIA Doc. No. J330, is a complete revision of the previously existing document. It was unanimously adopted by the Convention in St. Louis, June 15-18, 1964.

6

Comprehensive Architectural Services: Practice and Professionalism

BY DUDLEY HUNT JR, AIA

The Standards of Professional Practice of the AIA have been revised to enable the profession to better meet the needs of clients and society, ethically and with competence, through comprehensive architectural services

Promulgation 5.1

Preface 0.1

At the most basic level, the Standards of Professional Practice of the AIA constitute a code of conduct for architects acting as professionals. In the words of the Standards themselves, the code's primary purpose is . . . *to promote the highest ethical standards for the profession of architecture.* And in addition, to ensure that an *architect's motives, abilities and conduct always must be such as to command respect and confidence.*

Clinton Gamble FAIA puts it this way: "Society expects professional groups to establish standards of conduct that are more restrictive than are the general laws of the land. These special restrictions tend to instill in society special confidence in the actions of the professionals. The restrictions are particularly valuable because of the personal nature of the services of professionals. Society expects professional groups to impose high standards of conduct upon themselves and to police the standards within the groups; at the same time, such self-restriction has the effect of granting higher status in society to professionals."

In the seventeenth century, in his "Preface to Maxims of the Law," Francis Bacon said much the same thing, "I hold every man a debtor to his profession; from the which as men of course do seek to receive countenance and profit, so ought they of duty to endeavor themselves by way of amends to be a help and ornament thereunto."

Such are the reasons for the existence of the AIA Standards of Professional Practice. What is the reasoning behind the revisions, adopted at the 1964 convention and based on recommendations made by the Committee on the Profession with the assistance of a large number of other AIA members?

Standards for comprehensive services

First of all, the purpose of the revisions is to clear the way definitely and unequivocally for all of the phases of comprehensive architectural services. While the old Standards did not preclude architects from expanding their services toward the goal of comprehensive services, some doubt existed—in the minds of numerous members—as to the exact interpretation of a number of the individual clauses. The revised Standards are intended to remove all such doubts.

Standards for professional competence

The second—and perhaps most important—reason for the revision of the Standards is the widely help opinion, among AIA members, that a reasonable degree of professional competence should be required by the Standards of those who subscribe to them.

Other reasons might be cited for the new changes—the need for simplification and clarification of the language of the Standards, the need for their modernization, the need for elimination of the great number of explanatory interpretations appended by Institute Judiciary Committees over the years. The original Standards were written by AIA members; they have been rewritten by AIA members in the past; they have been revised and interpreted innumerable times. If anything is sacred about the Standards, it is the intent of AIA members to provide themselves—in the Standards—with an ethical code of practice. The wording and content of the Standards, being only temporal, must also be contemporary if they are to serve the needs of the profession, its clients and the public.

Professional activities of architects

Generally, both old and new Standards define and limit the professional activities of Institute members in such areas as these:

1) Architects' relationships with society (the public);

2) Architects' relationships with their clients;

3) Architects' relationships with their profession and with individuals within the profession;

4) Architects' relationships with those with whose help complete architectural services are performed (employees, consultants, collaborators, the building industry).

New standards more explicit

Both old and new Standards deal with the actions of architects in all of these areas; the main difference is that the new version is more explicit in its exposition of what is expected of architects in each of these areas. Architects are specifically directed to guard against all commitments that might tend to compromise their professional judgment. In all of their actions, architects are expected to conduct themselves in a professional manner. And with competency and adequacy. These are some of the general tenets of the new Standards. But what of the specific points now made in the document that were only implied in the past? Or were taken for granted? Or simply ignored?

"Should" changed to "shall"

The new Standards specifically require Institute members to adhere to all tenets included. No longer do most of the individual clauses contain principles that "should" be followed. On the contrary, instead of the "should" clauses of the old document, the new Standards almost invariably say—simply—"shall." This is a great change indeed, for now the Standards, particularly in the areas of obligations to the public, the client and the profession, state that Institute members are expected, without exception, to adhere to the letter of the obligations. This is not to imply that the old Sandards were not enforceable. Actually, they were enforced quite effectively, in spite of the seeming weakness of the word "should." However, it would seem much better to state the case as it actually exists; and the case is stated accurately by the word "shall."

Preface 0.1

In the area of professional competence, the new Standards are also quite explicit. For example, in the words of the new document: *his services* [must] *further the ultimate goal of creating an environment of orderliness and beauty.* Clearly the intent of these provisions of the new Standards is to insure that architects never allow themselves to be placed in any position where conflicts of interest could arise between professional duties and non-professional considerations.

Obligation 1.2

This means exactly what it says—that Institute members are expected by their fellow professionals to perform their services with reasonable competence. If not, their fellow professionals expect to hold them responsible for the good of clients, society, and the profession as a whole. Other clauses of the new Standards also treat of such matters. For example, an architect is expect *to perform his professional services with competence, and shall properly serve the interests of his clients and the public.*

Obligation 2.1

Perhaps the most striking example, from among the new requirements of competence, is in the area of cost controls. The wording is that an architect *shall keep his client informed with competent estimates of probable costs.* Not "should" but "shall." Thus for the first time, the AIA has unequivocally gone on record —in its own code of conduct—to the effect that its members can be expected not only to provide their clients with reliable and reasonable cost estimates, but that these estimates will be based on knowledge of realities, and will contain the whole story without glossing over or hiding any unpleasant facts. This step can be interpreted as a move on the part of the architectural profession toward completely responsible control of costs, efficient cost estimating, and full disclosure of the facts to clients.

Mastery of construction costs

In the opinion of a number of Institute members who have been close to the revision of the Standards, the new clause requiring attention to construction costs may be the most important change of all. For the first time, the architect is saying, through the Standards of his professional organization, that he expects to be the master of the costs of construction and that he expects to keep construction costs within a reasonable range. Thus he has tackled what is probably the single most troublesome aspect of contemporary architectural practice, certainly the one for which architects are criticized most often by clients. And adequate performance in the area of costs may well be the one most powerful weapon architects can wield in the battle against those outside the profession who would usurp its prerogatives for themselves.

Obligation 1.3

The revised as well as the old Standards say: *An architect shall not engage in building contracting.* This clause does not preclude architects from administering construction projects through subcontracts, force account work or similar means. However, architects may not accept compensation from anyone other than their clients, and then only for the rendering of professional services. To put it another way, architects may not accept profits or compensation from activities that are related to—but not part of—their professional services. For example, architects may not receive compensation from contracting firms engaged in the construction of the work for their clients or from manufacturers whose products are used in the work. As stated in the revised Standards, an archi-

Obligation 2.4 and Preface 0.2

tect is expressly prohibited from having *financial or personal interests which might tend to compromise his obligation to his client. Also, his advice to his client must be sound and unprejudiced.*

Obligation 3.9

A new clause, related to those just discussed says: *An architect shall not serve as an employee of unregistered individuals who offer architectural services to the public, nor as an employee of a firm whose architectural practice is not under the identified control of a registered architect.*

In other words, an architect is expressly prohibited from engaging in building contracting and he is expressly prohibited from working for any unregistered individual or firm that offers to perform architectural services. On the other hand, there is nothing to prevent an architect from working for, or becoming a principal in, a consulting engineering firm or architectural-engineering firm provided that the architectural services of the firm are under the responsible control of a registered architect. Also, no architect is prohibited from becoming an employee of governmental or other organizations that does not offer to perform architectural services for the public. And in no case may an architect engage in building construction or contracting.

Agency of architects

Another important provision of the new Standards is the agency relationship to clients assumed by architects, at certain times, when they represent the interests of their clients with third parties. This new provision recognizes the agency position of architects who coordinate or direct—for the benefit of their clients—the services of the consultants and collaborators needed in certain of the newer areas of comprehensive architectural services. However, it is not only in the more unusual areas of comprehensive services that the concept of agency is required. Many of the more usual relationships of the past are based on the agency principle; for example, an agency relationship can exist when a client employs the services of a building type specialist, such as a hospital or educational consultant, for assistance in programming or analysis of a project. Of course, architects also furnish services directly to their clients, services that do not involve the agency position of architects when they act for their clients with third parties. Also, during the construction phase, architects sometimes perform as arbiters.

Obligation 2.1

A provision of the new Standards states: *Before undertaking any commission* [the architect] *shall determine with his client the*

Obligation 2.6

scope of the project, the nature and extent of the services he will perform and his compensation for them, and shall provide confirmation therof in writing. Another provision says: *An architect shall base his compensation on the value of the services he agrees to render.* Neither of these clauses is intended to mean that an architect cannot, if he so chooses, enter into an agreement with an entrepreneurial client to perform a certain amount of professional services, with payment of the fees for the services conditional on whether or not the job goes ahead. For example, an architect might agree to study a speculative building problem and prepare schematics or preliminaries at no cost to the entrepreneurial client, but the architect must have made an agreement with his client as to both his services and compensation should the work be built.

The important points bearing on such an arrangement, as brought out in the new Standards, are that there must be an agreement between the architect and his client before the professional services begin, and as stated in another portion of the revised Standards: *An architect shall not enter into competitive bidding against another architect on the basis of compensation.* Of course, it follows directly that architects are prohibited from making agreements with clients on a conditional fee basis, if other architects are still being considered for the work. The only time the conditional fee is allowable is when one architectural firm definitely has been given a specific job, and the owner has ceased consideration of all other architectural firms for the job.

Obligation 3.5

Speculative Ventures

It goes without saying, perhaps, that one of the prime considerations in a speculative venture of any kind—architectural or otherwise—is the possibility of greater than usual gain if the speculation is successful. This can be weighed against the loss if unsuccessful. Surely architects who make agreements of the sort described can be expected to enter such ventures with full cognizance of the facts of the individual situations. It would not seem unreasonable, in such cases, for architects to expect higher fees or compensation than are ordinarily attached to similar services of a non-speculative nature. Possibly the nature of a particular speculative project and the opportunity for a creative contribution in its design and construction may have an allure that is impossible for an architect to resist. Or the architect wants the work and cannot get it any other way. Whatever the reason for accepting such work, ventures into speculative architectural services, which are accompanied by agreements to waive compensation should the projects fall through, should of necessity be entered into with caution by architects if they are to abide by the provisions dealing with competition among architects as to compensation, definite agreements with clients, and compensation based on the value of services rendered.

Obligation 3.7

A very straightforward clause of the new Standards says: *An architect shall not engage a commission agent to solicit work in his behalf.* This is perhaps the best example of the clarification achieved in the new document, avoiding as it does the circumlocutions of the former wording. This clause now states the exact case —an architect may reward with bonuses or by other means for aid in obtaining work, only regular members of his own staff—no others.

7

The Legal Status of the Architect

BY JUDGE BERNARD TOMSON AND NORMAN COPLAN

As the architect enters the more unusual and newer aspects of comprehensive architectural practice, his legal status may be that of an agent, an arbiter, or of an individual who performs services directly for his clients

Comprehensive architectural services, of course, will initiate many contracts and relationships between the architect and third parties in addition to those ordinarily found in traditional practice. The architect, in furnishing the basic services of design, production and supervision, is generally concerned only with the contracts between architect and owner, owner and contractor, and architect and consulting engineer, and his responsibilities relate primarily to these parties. The architect's status, even in this relatively limited area, is not always understood and may be subject to question and uncertainty. In his expanded role the architect may well become involved in real estate, finance, business and tax problems, as well as operational programming and planning. He may be in contact with bankers, real estate dealers, public relations personnel, attorneys, and other experts and consultants in various fields. The definition and understanding of the architect's status in each of these areas is a matter of critical importance.

Architect's status must be understood

The architect's legal status, when furnishing architectural services, will certainly determine the respective rights and liabilities of the architect *vis-a-vis* his client and third parties. Further, this status —in many situations—will determine the respective rights and liabilities of the client in relation to third persons. Consequently, as the architect expands his role, both client and architect must be particularly concerned with the definition of that status in the architect's contract of employment and consequent documents.

Clients and third parties

The Committee on the Profession of The American Institute of Architects, in its interim or progress report on its work in the field of expanding services of architects, has emphasized the basic concept of "agency" as describing one status of the architect. This concept is reflected in the draft of the revised Standards of Professional Practice, now adopted, which were included in the Committee's report and which were prepared specifically to satisfy the ethical requirements of comprehensive practice. One question for analysis,

Agency of architects

therefore, is whether a description of the architect's status in terms of "agency" is adequate and accurate for the purposes of legal definition and ethical standard.

The former Standards of Professional Practice contain no express reference to the "agency" of the architect. The status of the architect is described, to some degree, in the existing contract documents of The American Institute of Architects. Legal relationships between architect and client, and architect and third parties, have been spelled out in particular situations by court decisions. However, the new Standards of Professional Practice state, in describing the obligations of practice, that *an architect's relation to his client is based upon the concept of agency.*

Does the express reference to the agency concept in the new Standards of Professional Practice require further clarification?— The concept of principal and agent is primarily of legal significance as it relates to third parties. For example, when an architect contracts with his client to furnish architectural services, he is not then acting as an agent, but as an independent provider of professional services. On the other hand, in his dealing with third persons the architect may or may not be acting as agent for his client. The architect-owner contract will ordinarily determine whether, in retaining consulting engineers, the architect acts in an independent capacity and is responsible to the owner for the engineer's performance (the usual situation), or whether in his dealings with such consultants, the architect acts as agent for the owner, without responsibility for the consultants' acts.

In dealing with the contractor, the architect may or may not be acting as agent for the owner, depending upon the circumstances. Article 38 of The American Institute of Architects' General Conditions of the Contract expressly provides that the architect *shall have authority to act on behalf of the owner only to the extent expressly provided in the contract documents or otherwise in writing, which shall be shown to the contractor.* The article defining the architect's status provides that he is, *in the first instance, the interpreter of the conditions of the contract and the judge of its performance. He shall side neither with the owner nor with the contractor, but shall use his powers under the contract to enforce its faithful performance by both.* Since an agent owes a duty only to his principal, the legal and ethical requirement that an architect, when interpreting the contract or judging its performance, shall favor neither side but shall act in a judicious and impartial manner, would appear to describe a status which is the antithesis of agency.

Commenting on Article 38 of the General Conditions, the Handbook of Architectural Practice published by The American Institute of Architects states that "the architect's status as agent of the owner is limited to certain special acts according to the terms of the contract."

Some of the confusion concerning the architect's status as "agent" arises from the fact that in a number of legal decisions the courts, in determining the propriety of certain acts of the architect which were not and should not have been performed as agent of the

Obligation 2.1

Agency significant as related to third parties

Agency or other status?

Agency limited to special acts?

Determination of agency by courts

owner, have at the same time defined the architect's relationship to the owner as that of agent. For example, in Hines v Farr, 112 SE 2nd 33 (So Carolina), the issue before the court was the validity of the architect's determination of a dispute between owner and contractor concerning the number of cubic yards of rock which had been removed from the site. The construction contract in this case provided that it was the responsibility of the architect to make written decisions in regard to all claims of the owner or contractor and to interpret the contract documents on all questions arising upon the execution of the work. Pursuant to this authority the architect had certified a payment in connection with the disputed yardage of rock. The court held that this was binding on both.

"It may be stated generally that any stipulation whereby the parties constitute an architect or engineer the final arbiter between themselves, as to any matter connected with the contract, makes the decision of the architect or engineer conclusive as to such matter. For example, where the contract provides that the work shall be done to the satisfaction, approval, or acceptance of an architect or engineer, such architect or engineer is thereby constituted sole arbitrator between the parties, and the parties are bound by his decision. The same rule seems to apply where it is provided that payments shall be made only upon the certificate of the architect . . ."

In the same decision, however, the Appellate Court, in reviewing the contention of the owner that it was erroneous for the trial court to charge the jury that the architect is the agent of the owner, stated that this charge was correct in that "an architect, in the performance of his supervisory functions with respect to a building under construction, ordinarily acts as the agent and representative of the person for whom the work is being done." The court did not reconcile, however, this general statement in the context of the appropriate status of the architect when acting as an arbiter of disputes between owner and contractor.

Agent or arbiter?

In a Wisconsin case (Foeller v Heintz, 137 Wisc 169) the court apparently sensed the inconsistency between a statement that the architect acts as agent for the owner when performing his architectural services and the principle that the architect must act impartially and without favor in determining disputes between owner and contractor. In this case the issue was whether the architect could approve a material departure from the plans for the building under the authority of a provision in the construction contract which authorized him to arbitrate any dispute between owner and contractor. The court stated that although an arbitrator is supreme within his jurisdiction, the act of the architect in question was void as an act of usurpation. However, in describing the status of the architect in his function of determining disputes between owner and contractor, the court ruled that he was an agent of *both* parties. Again, however, this resolution does violence to the true meaning of the concept of agency.

The issue of whether an architect acts as agent for his client or as an independent provider of professional services often arises in legal actions involving claims of damage or personal injury sustained by third parties arising out of the alleged negligence of the architect.

If the architect's status is defined or deemed as that of agent for the owner in furnishing plans and supervising construction, his negligence may be imputed to the owner and the owner held responsible for injury to third parties.

On the other hand, if the architect, in performing basic or comprehensive services, performs his role in such a manner as to be deemed an independent provider of services, he may be held liable for injury or damage arising from circumstances which are ordinarily foreign to his responsibility.

Problems of negligence

In dealing with problems of negligence involving plans and construction, the courts have treated the concept of agency in a somewhat different manner than in other contexts. For example, in Burke v Ireland, 166 NY 305, a party who was injured at a construction site charged that the architect's plans were defective and sought to recover against the owner for the injury sustained. The court, in dismissing this action, ruled that the architect who was employed to draw plans and specifications and to supervise construction, is *not* the agent of the owner and the owner cannot be charged with his negligence. The court stated:

"If the architect, who had general supervision, had insisted upon a careful inspection of every detail of the work and had been present when the concrete was about to be laid upon the disturbed ground outside the old cistern wall, he might have discovered the departure from the terms of the contract in that respect and prevented it. But the architect was not the agent or servant of the owner. He was in the exercise of an independent calling and held the same legal relations to the defendant that the builder did, and for the omissions of either in the execution of the plans, personal negligence cannot be imputed to the defendant."

Agents represent their principals

Dealing with the other side of the coin, the court in Manton v H. L. Stevens & Co, 170 Iowa 495, was called upon to determine a suit against an architect instituted by an injured employee of one contractor based upon the premise that a safe place to work had not been furnished to the employee of another contractor, which resulted in the injury in question. The plaintiff contended that the architect was responsible because he was acting as an independent contractor on the particular project in that he had entered into sub-contracts for material and labor, that the architect's recommendations were followed in every case throughout the construction of the building, and that, in fact, the architect actually controlled the method of construction. The court, in dismissing this action against the architect, stated that the relationship between architect and owner *was* that of principal and agent and that although the architect entered into contracts and exercised control of the project, he did so with the consent of the owner and subject to the right of the owner to overrule or change the recommendations of the architect. The court said:

"We reach the conclusion that the evidence is abundant to warrant the finding that Stevens & Co were not independent contractors in their relation to this structure, but that they sustained the relation of agents to the Mantons and that their power and duties were those of the architect and the engineer, coupled perhaps with a supervisory power under which they superintended the enterprise in its entirety."

Limitations of agency

In describing the relationship of architect and owner as one of agency, a further problem is engendered in respect to the limitation, if any, of that agency. This issue generally arises when the architect has taken an action which the owner contends is outside of his authority and the other party involved in the litigation contends that the architect is the general agent of the owner. Illustrative is Millard v Parry, 271 P 2nd 852. In this case a contractor reduced his bid for the construction of a particular building in reliance upon the promise of the architect that additional construction would be awarded to him. The court, in finding that this promise was outside the scope of the architect's agency, asserted:

"It must be noted that in the matters referred to, plaintiff relies chiefly upon alleged promises and representations of the architect, and upon the contention that the architect was agent for the defendants. An architect is not ordinarily a general agent of his employer . . . and in this instance it was expressly so provided in the contract documents. Clearly he did not have authority to bind Parry on a promise of construction of another structure."

Agency concept subject to interpretation

From the foregoing, it would seem that the concept of agency and its extent is subject to differing interpretation and measurement depending upon the context in which the issue is raised. If this be the fact, then does the statement in the recently adopted Standards of Professional Practice that the architect in furnishing services to his client does so as "agent," introduce an ambiguity into the description of his status for the purpose of ethical standard? Undoubtedly the goal of the Committee on the Profession was to articulate the ethical principle that an architect, in expanding his services under the comprehensive practice program, must act with undivided loyalty and good faith toward his client and without special advantage to himself. This is the traditional professional obligation of the architect which has been characterized by the courts as one of trust and confidence. "Good faith and loyalty to his employer constitute a primary duty of the architect. He is in duty bound to make full disclosure of all matters, of which he has knowledge, which it is desirable or important that his principal should learn." Zannoth v Booth Radio Stations, 333 Mich 233. These tenets describe, as well, the exact obligation an agent owes to his principal. As stated by Mr Justice Benjamin Cardozo in a famous case (Meinhard v Salmon, 249 NY 458) involving the respective duties of joint venturers who act in relation to each other as principal and agent:

Architect as a professional

"Many forms of conduct permissible in a workaday world for those acting at arm's length, are forbidden to those bound by fiduciary ties. A trustee is held to something stricter than the morals of the market place. Not honesty alone, but the punctilio of an honor the most sensitive, is then the standard of behavior."

Since the concept of agency incorporates the ethical standards which are sought to be articulated in respect to the architect's relationship to his client, this appears to be the motivating factor for the description of the architect's status in the draft of the Standards of Professional Practice as agent of his client.

However, if the architect must act within the ethical connotations of the agency concept, but is not legally deemed the agent of his client in various situations, it might be more accurate and meaningful to provide that in relation to the services which he undertakes to provide in behalf of his client, the architect shall act only in his "professional" capacity, with the express and implied standards that this concept includes. The "agency" concept may introduce other factors or problems which have no pertinency to the ethical standards sought to be defined in the Standards of Professional Practice. In this connection, the recently adopted Standards of Professional Practice expressly and specifically state that the architect may not have financial interests which might tend to compromise his obligation to his client, that he may accept compensation for his services only from his client, and that he shall not engage in building contracting, and so on. Consequently, it would seem, therefore, the statement in the newly adopted Standards that the architect shall furnish his services as "agent" of his client is accurate only with respect to certain aspects of the architect's professional practice.

This is not to say that the "agency" concept is not of primary importance in respect to a large part of architectural practice and of particular significance in the context of comprehensive practice. If the architect deals with the real estate operator in respect to land acquisition for his client, if he deals with the banker in respect to financing the project, and if he deals with the myriad of experts and consultants whose services may be required in connection with project analysis, promotion, design, construction, and supporting and related services, it must be clear to him, to the owner and to the parties with whom he is dealing that he is acting as agent for the owner. If this is not made explicit, the architect runs the serious risk of responsibility and financial liability for the contracts which he makes on behalf of his client. It is an old and fundamental principle of law that an agent of an undisclosed principal is responsible for the obligations of a contract which he makes on behalf of his principal. Thus, the architect's agency must be disclosed, not only to satisfy the requirement of good faith, but in self-protection.

The concept of agency cannot be over-emphasized in defining the role the architect should play in his relationship to third persons in performing comprehensive services. While the ethical connotations of "agency" may coincide with the professional standards to be met by an architect, the importance of that concept lies in the legal relationships which may be created as the architect expands his role under the comprehensive service program. The recommendation of the Committee on the Profession that "each architect contemplating the expanding of his services seek advice from his own counsel concerning the matter of agency, to determine the legal problems involved and the methods of clearly defining an agency position" is, indeed, well taken. It is also of vital importance that the architect's compensation reflect his exposure and responsibility as he expands the area of his services.

Principles of professionalism

Agency important in architectural practice

Legal counsel necessary

8

Comprehensive Architectural Services: Education for the New Role

BY ROBERT W. MC LAUGHLIN, FAIA *

In order properly to prepare the architects of the future for architecture of the total environment, many great changes in education will be necessary

*The author is Director of the School of Architecture, Princeton University

Architecture as practiced and as taught is in a constant state of interplay. The profession makes demands on education; education nudges and stimulates the profession. Right now our problem is not just a matter of one of these simple interactions. What we are faced with is a determination of the kind of education that might be contrived for a profession as we hope it will exist.

The profession to which we look forward (or fear as inevitable) has been described in rounded, high-sounding phrases about the architect as the creator of man's total environment. Statements have ranged all the way from the macrocosm of man's total environment to the microcosms of technical specializations, with everything between included in the architect's area of influence.

The future of architecture

In our cynical moments, we are plagued by a picture of our profession evaporating in an aura of flaming nothingness, as demands on the architect break the limits of his human capabilities. In our imaginative and constructive moments, we foresee the architect as a species to be developed with capacities well beyond those required for his present attainments: one able to deal with problems of a magnitude and variety that as yet we have not met. In our realistic moments we have to say that the exact nature of these problems cannot presently be defined.

There is nothing new about preparation for the unknown. That is what liberal education professes to do in both the arts and sciences, as contrasted with technological education which trains for more specific objectives. And let's not make the new role of the architect too mysterious by over-emphasizing the unknown. We know perfectly well, for example, that architects are going to continue to design buildings, that these buildings will have to meet human needs and aspirations and that in meeting these we will have to know a lot of specific techniques.

Breadth and depth needed

Architectural education will have to be broader and more encompassing than it is now, but it will also have to aim for greater depth and more precise understanding in specific areas. It will not be an either-or proposition. Why breadth? Because man's physical environment is wide, varied and changing. It stands between man and the universe. Why depth? Because this environment is changed through the application of precise knowledge working with forces, materials and techniques.

College, then graduate study

If architects are to be masters of the grand concept they will need the best that the universities can offer. Specifically this means going to college first and then on to intensive study at the graduate level. Law and medicine have long since come to this—a broad program first, leading to a BA or BS degree, followed by a professional degree. In architecture we do have one problem, not faced by law or medicine—our need to develop as early as possible the awareness and ability to use visual means of study and communication. While the development of verbal aptitudes is taken for granted from elementary school on, visual aptitudes are cultivated only to a minor degree. Words are the instruments with which lawyers largely work, and words are the instruments of thought and communication in most liberal arts courses. The study of history and political science leads naturally into professional study for the law. Future doctors find much in the undergraduate laboratories that prepares them specifically as well as broadly for medical school. On the other hand, there is little now in the liberal arts and sciences that involves visual communication. It is important for architects not to wait until graduate years to develop awareness and facility in visual representation through means such as drawing. For an architect to do so would be like a lawyer's waiting until after undergraduate years to develop a knowledge of sentence structure.

Architecture as a liberal art and science

The answer to this problem lies, to a large degree I believe, in the teaching of architecture during the early years of our liberal arts colleges as a liberal art and science; this means the study of what architecture is, as well as how architecture is done. We immediately enter dangerous ground that has been plowed over into maze-like patterns by some humanists and scientists who are terribly fearful of *doing* as opposed to *analyzing* and *discussing*. But a synthesis of thought and action in architecture is entirely possible —indeed necessary—and to the benefit of both understanding and doing. Architecture as a creative process has much to contribute to the synthesis, and so has the analytical study of architecture as an accomplished, historical fact. There is just as much reason for the combination of creativity with analysis in architecture as there is for combining writing with the reading of literature.

Humanism and usefulness not necessarily incompatible

We need to realize that broadening the curriculum for architects is going to raise some problems. Before getting up to our ears in academic culture, we shall want to take a good hard look at current offerings of the universities in the broadly based humanities and social sciences. How many of these offerings, presented under the noble guise of search for values, are really vestigial remains of once directly useful courses? Usefulness was once an accepted characteristic of the humanistic departments in the days before some of them became so precious in a pontifical custodianship of values. Studies of Greek, Latin or Italian can still be instruments for coming to know about Greece, Rome or Italy. Yet nowadays, in some academic circles, usefulness can be a naughty word and "instruments" categorized as courses for drudges.

There is no need for architects to waste time on the superficialities of outdated departments which have perpetuated themselves by staking claims to "values" in our society. And may we be delivered from sole dependence on Humanities I and II, those omnibus creations that try to cram the wisdom of all ages into a couple of weekly hours. By breadth we still mean breadth of knowledge, not warmed-up opinion. There is plenty of solid stuff for us in the liberal arts and sciences, provided we look for it, and don't tumble for wordy substitutes.

Architectural schools will do well to look with skeptical eyes on invitations to combine their activities with the catchall of a "Creative Arts Program." Of course architecture is an art; and what art isn't creative? But architecture becomes an art only as we practice it: as a profession, as a science, and yes, as a business. That last, essential word scares the daylights out of most of the boys who are engaged in teaching about the creative arts *per se*. Schools of architecture will want to stand on their own feet as professional schools of first rank. Creative arts centers on campuses, like some cultural centers in cities, are too often gimmicks for make believe. The arts and culture (whatever may be intended by that term) don't thrive by being *centered;* they flourish by *pervading.*

If the broadening of the training of architects is not without potential pitfalls, we can take comfort in the great richness within the study of architecture itself. In relating the liberal arts and sciences to our own bailiwick, we can find areas of study that reach into just about every channel of human development, and avoid those academic closed circuits that begin with words—and end with words.

Early architectural training

Basically, the early years in the education of the future architect will need a solid and continuing axis of architecture taught as a liberal art, involving both doing and understanding. This axis will be expressed academically in a series of courses that will take a gradually increasing amount of the student's time through the four years. The student will elect work in those areas of the humanities, natural sciences and social sciences that relate to the central theme of architecture. Actually just about every area in the undergraduate curriculum relates to architecture, certainly to the new role of the architect. A wide degree of election will be necessary, not just because no individual can cover everything, but primarily because individuals vary and will naturally emphasize different aspects of architecture and the forces that produce it.

As the four years of the undergraduate program develop, greater emphasis can be given, during upper-class years, to architecture as the subject of major concentration. There is much evidence that most architects decide on architecture as a career by the freshman or sophomore year. Late starters seem to be comparatively rare in our profession. Where they do occur, more than the usual four undergraduate years will have to be allowed, in order to bring the student to a stage where he has been well exposed to the understanding and doing of architecture, as well as to the seasoning of a broad, liberal, undergraduate education. These are the objectives to be attained with the awarding of the baccalaureate, which will of course not be a professional degree, but will be evidence of breadth of study.

Schools of architecture as such will, I am confident, become graduate schools, and the five-year curriculum leading directly to a Bachelor of Architecture degree is destined to become obsolete.

Later professional training

Before discussing the nature of the graduate professional schools, it is important to mention a secondary but important effect of the broad undergraduate program. By establishing architecture as one of the liberal arts and sciences in the university, it will be possible for non-architects to elect subjects in architecture. So far as I know, this is not presently true in any university. It is unfortunate that graduates of undergraduate colleges arrive in the world without having had an opportunity to study architecture as one of the important aspects of the lives they lead. They will be our clients, but will be much better clients if they have been exposed as students to some awareness of what we try to practice. We will meet them on zoning and planning boards and as corporate and governmental officials responsible for what we will advise them to do.

If the architect's undergraduate years are to be essentially characterized by breadth, graduate years will aim for depth. Throughout both periods will run the solid core of architecture viewed as a creative process.

Wide diversity in architecture

The areas with which the architect has to be familiar are so diverse that he never can be fully cognizant of all of them. Each contains a world of knowledge that is constantly expanding. Structures, environmental controls (that we used to call mechanical equipment), materials beyond counting, climate, methods of statistical analysis, the psychology of perception, lighting, the urgencies of social change the varied insistences of our more positive creative personalities, the economic facts of life, industrialization and automation—these are suggestive titles picked at random. If the future architect cannot master each of them, he will certainly have to be aware of all of them. He will have to respect every one of them and the people who do understand them. His education will have to expose him to all of them, but if his awareness is to be more than superficial, he will explore more of the areas thoroughly.

The graduate curriculum

The graduate, professional curriculum will continue in the foreseeable future to have a continuing core of design or composition, treated as the centripetal force in the synthesis that is architecture. I see nothing better ahead in this area than the present case method of specific projects, leavened occasionally with prototypes.

Courses will continue to be given in structures, the technology of environmental controls, urban theory and design, the economics of the building industry, professional administration. There is little use in dreaming up new names for them, but their content will be richer, deeper and more challenging. They will largely be taught by specialists from other disciplines who have an understanding of architecture, rather than by captive engineers, planners or economists within schools of architecture. To find such specialists with the ability to relate their specialties to architecture is extremely difficult now, because they rarely exist. Perhaps such teachers will come into being when architecture establishes itself as an important liberal art and science within the university. Perhaps engineers and sociologists will elect to study architecture as they now elect literature or history.

The success of these professional courses, now too often treated as necessary bits of pedestrianism in contrast with the glamor of design, can come from treating them not as adjuncts but as essential, if particularized, aspects of the central design process. In addition, our professional schools might well establish elective seminars where specific subjects can be thoroughly explored with research and scholarship. The nature of these subjects will depend largely on who the faculty are and what they know, as well as on the directions taken by the desires of students to learn. All schools can hardly be expected to offer all subjects; nor is this necessary.

Emphasis today on development of knowledge rather than education

Universities today have two stated purposes: the education of young people and the development of knowledge. The growing emphasis on the latter is indicated by the budget of my own university, for example, which now spends more than twice as much for research and scholarship as for teaching. Most of this shift in emphasis has happened within the past ten years. Schools and departments of architecture act generally as if they were unaware of what is happening in the universities of which they are a part. If we are to have a vital place in our universities, we shall have to wake up to our responsibilities for the development of knowledge, meaning research and scholarship, in our area.

Bridging the chasm between practice and education

We can best serve our profession in its greater role by searchings for knowledge that will enable us to solve the problems that underlie its practice. That is the job of the university and of its constituent parts. There is now a chasm between our practicing profession and the schools of architecture bridged only by tenuous bits of sentimental attachment. There is comparatively little flow of knowledge about architecture from schools to the practicing profession. A leading medical school in one state university tells its entering students that they have come for a forty-year course of which the first four will be full-time, and I am told that if you have to be sick in a country town, choose one in that state.

We need to take a hard look at our current insistence on teaching architecture as a series of contrived solutions, rather than emphasizing the knowledge and understanding that make valid solutions possible. In other words we need to emphasize the knowledge underlying the design process, making it available through carefully prepared courses which will then feed into the design process.

Graduate curricula leading to the first professional degree will ultimately require three years in addition to a broad undergraduate program with a core or major in architecture, once adequate content is available. Where there has not been study of architecture as an undergraduate, the time for graduate study will have to be longer. The necessary extensions of time had best come about gradually, since there is not now enough substance in most of our schools to extend over periods such as will ultimately be necessary. Efforts should be applied to creating content which will then demand proper time, not to creating longer time schedules that have to be filled out. There will be a danger of making too big a thing out of the academic phase of the architect's education. Plenty of time, largely in architects' offices, will be required for education beyond the university.

Postgraduate courses to develop varied skills

In addition to the program for the first professional degree we will need post-graduate programs of a specialized nature. We need variety in the skills of architects. There is now almost sole emphasis on visual design, and a student without particular aptitude for this, but with other capacities, may have a hard time. We need architects with special bents for structures, urban planning, environmental controls, building organization. There should be opportunities to develop these without undue insistence on proficiency in visual matters.

Importance of urban design

Urban design should run through our curricula. Our schools have made considerable progress here. An urban planner should be an architect with a specialized knowledge encompassing the wide economic, political and social factors involved. Postgraduate years are probably necessary for this. Urban planning ultimately becomes urban design. It is a fearsome sight to see statisticians taking over planning without knowing how to compose data into three-dimensional concepts. It is equally futile for architects to try to compose such concepts without understanding the underlying social, economic and political forces.

The architect of record must become the architect of fact

We have developed here some fairly sweeping statements, but they are meant to reflect the attitudes that I believe will be necessary unless we are willing to let architects, as we know them now, become limited specialists in the major enterprise of designing man's environment. Generically speaking, an architect is anyone who determines the quality of that environment. Entrepreneurs, engineers, statisticians, politicians, industrial managers and just plain people are now making the decisions of architecture to an increasing degree, without much influence from architects as a profession. The architects *of record* are too seldom the architects *in fact*. We have fought successfully to limit, legally and technically, the use of the term "architect" to members of our profession. Now we need to expand the capacities of the profession to serve widely as architects in fact.

Implementation will be difficult. A new race of architects will have to be developed. This is not for my generation, nor probably for yours if you are crowding or have passed forty. But the opportunity of our generation is to loosen some of the bonds that limit us, for the benefit of the generations that are to come from our schools. What are those bonds—or more positively—what are the visions of the future of architecture that will destroy them?

Primarily, we had better make up our minds that we are essentially a profession serving our era, a profession that is difficult and challenging because its activities include the development and application of knowledge in the natural, economic and human sciences, as well as the creative activities that lead to composing these forces into satisfying and effective projects. Discussions as to whether architecture is essentially a business, an applied science or an art have become debilitating to our effectiveness as architects and confusing to the public—when the public bothers to listen.

Goal of architecture, and of architectural education, is service

Much of our current discussion of architecture is just as fragmented as our published performances because our individual attitudes as architects are often diverse, arbitrary and intolerant. Exhibitionism on one side and pedestrianism on the other are names called across the fence. Undue emphasis on esthetic judgments and too little regard for making things work are offset by financial opportunism and just "getting the job built." The architect will resolve all these carpings if he is honestly aiming to practice his profession for the service of his community, nation and world. We have got to advance as a real profession that aims to serve, if we are to have professional schools that will train for the new role of the architect that we hope for.

Part Two:

Principles of
Comprehensive Architectural Services

9

Comprehensive Architectural Services: Principles

BY DUDLEY HUNT JR, AIA

Within the concept of comprehensive services, the architectural profession can serve the needs of its clients and society in the complete design and construction of buildings and environment. The new challenge is outlined here

"The conception which the new kind of architect has of his calling (is) that of coordinating organizer, whose business it is to resolve all formal, sociological and commercial problems and combine them into a comprehensive unit. . . ." (Walter Gropius, FAIA, "Scope of Total Architecture," Harper & Brothers, New York, 1955)

Comprehensive services

Creator of environmental design, counselor to his clients and to society, coordinator of the work of his design and construction collaborators, controller of the entire environmental design and construction process. These have been the traditional roles of the architect. They remain so today, but the scope of the environmental problems and the degree of their complexity have been magnified. The degree of change and the rate of change have speeded up. The needs of clients and society remain in evolution as they always have, but today the needs are swept up in a sweeping evolution of acceleration.

If it is to stay abreast of the wave of change, the architectural profession must expand its traditional services to meet the needs of the times. Such an expansion of architectural services has as its final result what might be called comprehensive architectural practice. Within this comprehensive practice concept, the architectural profession would be prepared to perform, or arrange for and coordinate, all of the many services needed to insure the success of today's complicated building and other environmental design projects. Individual architects would have to be knowledgeable in a number of fields in addition to those that are concerned directly with building design. Such fields might include, for example, real estate, finance, and operations programming and planning. It would not be expected that architects would actually perform services in such fields as these, but rather that they would act as the agents of their clients in procuring the necessary services and coordinating them. In this way, architects, acting for their clients, can retain the degree of control and coordination of their projects necessary to assure the clients of correct and unified results.

The new needs

There is scarcely any doubt today that the architect pictures himself as the central figure, the leader, in the process of bringing order into the design of human environment. Few architects would deny that their primary role is the creation of buildings and their surrounding environment in such a fashion as to cause them to contribute in positive ways to the well-being and progress of man. It is not in the definition of the architect's role, but in the limits of its scope and in the manner in which the role is to be played that some confusion and differences of opinion exist within the architectural profession. Most architects neither fail to recognize the importance of the role, nor do they doubt their own basic ability to play it. Only the details are not now clear. However, the time for clarification of the issues is here. For the profession must—at the present time—consolidate itself into a vigorous and united front against those who covet the great role of the architect for themselves. And the profession must meet the needs of its clients and the evolving society. While it is difficult to catch hold of a subject that is changing so rapidly, a few facts central to the whole subject of comprehensive architecture should help to clarify the picture.

The new methods

In order to make a positive contribution to the physical, social, intellectual and emotional needs of his clients and society, the architect must maintain his position at the center of the environmental design and construction processes. If the architect is not able to participate constructively in all of the basic decisions that go into a project, it becomes almost impossible for him to direct the unification of all of the variables into a satisfactory solution of the client's problems. And it will be very difficult for him to lead the group effort toward effective results.

The basic reasoning behind the comprehensive services concept is that the changing times have brought with them a situation in which the assembly of land, the financing of construction, the operations to be housed, and other similar considerations often determine whether a project will be undertaken; and if the project is undertaken, such considerations often determine in large degree the nature of the design and construction of the project. If the architect is not deeply involved in these considerations, he runs the risk of being forced to make unreasonable design and construction decisions based on dogma developed previously by others.

Architect's basic services

The standard services of the architect in preliminary design, development of working drawings and specifications, and construction supervision make up the nucleus of present-day architectural practice. Comprehensive services do not supplant the standard services but are an expansion of them, enabling the architect to retain his leadership of the entire environmental design process in the light of the realistic requirements of today.

Performance of services

An important aspect of the comprehensive-services concept is the need for constant improvement of design and the other basic services. For example, building programming and analysis and reliable cost estimating might be made phases of the basic services. Such improvements are an integral part of the solution of the overall problems of expanded practice.

Basically, preparation for comprehensive services is a job for the entire architectural profession. No one architect could hope to perform all of the services needed. Nor could any one firm perform all of them. The individual architect needs to be conversant with certain broad principles of all of the services. The individual firm should be prepared to offer certain portions of the services, in combinations required by the type and extent of its practice and its own objectives.

Supporting services

Many of the services included in the comprehensive architecture concept would not be performed by architects at all. The concept is not intended to make of the architect a grand master of all things. The architect would not become a real estate broker or appraiser. Rather he would have an understanding of their work and its relationships with the other elements of the total project. He would coordinate such work, as the agent of his client, to insure the success of the project. The architect would not become an expert on finance but would be prepared to consult with such experts in the interest of his client when a particular project required it.

The traditional and unique contributions of such professionals as the engineers, landscape architects, and urban planners are necessary to the success of the comprehensive architecture concept. If anything, their contributions would become even more valuable than heretofore since these professionals would become more integrally involved in the complete process than might otherwise be the case. To round out a comprehensive practice, other technical and specialist services such as those of the interior designers, sanitary and utility engineers, highway planners, and analysts of various kinds would be added as required for specific projects.

Types of firms

The result of all this would be that the architect could surround himself with the specialists needed to offer a complete environmental design service to his clients, and would coordinate and direct their efforts toward a unified end.

Under the comprehensive services concept, many different kinds and sizes of architectural firms can operate. Some firms may choose to include on their own staffs some of the specialists needed to perform services for their clients. For example, a firm doing a considerable amount of commercial work might employ on its staff, market or merchandizing analysts. One doing industrial buildings might employ on its staff one or more industrial engineers. Firms might very well make arrangements for outside consultation with specialists in various fields when required in operations planning, real estate, or finance, just as they now arrange for the services of outside engineers. The whole comprehensive-practice concept is extremely flexible. Within the concept, the possible methods of organization for practice would appear to be even more flexible.

The new practice

Actually, there is very little in the comprehensive-services concept that is new. For many years, architects have been studying means of offering more complete services to their clients, as a direct answer to their client's needs. For years, architects have been attempting to develop means by which they could maintain their traditional position as the leaders of the design and construction processes. At the present time, a great number of architects offer their clients some portions of comprehensive services. This in direct answer to their individual assessment of their client's needs and the threat of competition from outside of the profession.

What is new about the comprehensive-services concept then, lies not in its elements, most of which architects have been doing right along. The new part is that for the first time, an attempt is being made to organize all of the elements into a complete system. It is not feasible for one architect or one firm to participate in all of the activities of the entire comprehensive services system. What is important is that the profession as a whole be prepared to offer the complete services, each individual architect or firm performing that portion that seems needed or desirable.

Specialization

Under the comprehensive-services concept, it is possible for individual architects to specialize, if they so choose, in a variety of ways. Currently, certain individuals within firms specialize in various phases of the work such as design, production, or specifications. Firms specialize in one or more building types. Many individuals and firms specialize without losing the generalist approach of the whole architect or of the complete firm. A trend is discernible now toward other types of specialization; also a growing trend toward more consultation between architects. For example, Pietro Belluschi often acts as a design specialist and consultant for buildings under development by other architects. Carl Koch specializes in design for industrial production of buildings and components. Eliot Noyes specializes in consultation with large corporations on their architecture and complete design programs. None of the three allows his specialized work to interfere with the general practice of architecture. Many other architects have found methods of bringing their special talents to bear on problems greater than those of the design and construction of single buildings.

Needless to say, a great number of architectural projects will never require anything like the whole extent of comprehensive services. Many will only need the standard services performed by architects, perhaps with more emphasis on analysis, programming, and cost controls. For these projects, architectural firms of all sizes will be able to perform their services much as in the past. This will also be true when firms perform services for less complex buildings.

The smaller office

It is by no means out of the ordinary for smaller offices to offer some degree of comprehensive services. Many already do. Some accomplish this through specialization in limited building types and by providing, within their own staffs, the specialists needed. Others carry on more diversified services by staffing themselves with talented generalists, and sometimes a few specialists, supplementing their abilities with those of outside consultants or collaborators. A smaller office with the right kind of staff talent theoretically could make arrangements to utilize exactly the best combination of consultants for each project that comes along. To put it another way, the smaller firm with exactly the right combination of its own and outside talents for a particular project might be preferred by a potential client over the larger firm forced to use its own specialists just because they are on staff, not because they are necessarily the best choices for the particular project.

10

Comprehensive Architectural Services:
Techniques

BY DONALD H. LUTES, AIA

How a relatively small firm, organized only six years, in a small community practices comprehensive architectural services with the aid of consultants

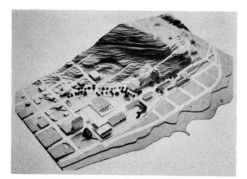

Site model, urban renewal,
Coos Bay

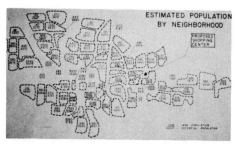

Neighborhood population map,
Eugene-Springfield

When asked to prepare this article, my partner said, "Are *we* practicing comprehensively?" I am sure this invitation would have been received in a similar manner in most offices, for many architects practice comprehensively now, but do not consider it anything special.

There are many architects who *wish* to practice traditionally, and each practitioner must decide if, and to what degree, he wishes to expand his services. It is, however, the obligation and opportunity of all professionals to learn about comprehensive service and the problems and rewards thereof.

Our office is both young and small. We have been organized for six years in a community of 20,000, and a metropolitan area of 100,000. There exist three other offices of our size, and ten of smaller size. We have a staff of eleven consisting of two partners (one of whom is a planner), three project managers (one of whom is a planner) and six draftsmen, including one planner. We also employ a secretary and a field coordinator.

Comprehensive services came as a natural extension of our philosophy of practice, inasmuch as we believe the future of architecture is concerned with total environment. Our practice was based on social concern and understanding of forces which shape environment, combining the two with knowledge of related fields. Comprehensive service began with public service based on this philosophy and then was used to expand client vision.

Our office was engaged to design a low rent housing development for the elderly and, in addition, was commissioned to work with the citizens' committee, developing information on population types, services available and needs for elderly housing. Besides the feasibility study, a survey of sites available throughout the metropolitan area was conducted by our office, presenting these to the owner and committee for evaluation and selection. The value of these studies was proven when the project became em-

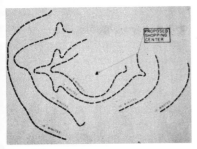

Travel-time map,
Eugene-Springfield

Westmoreland Village,
Eugene

Space diagram, Public Library,
Springfield

Model, Public Library,
Springfield

broiled in political controversy. The general knowledge and acceptance gained by the public through the feasibility studies assured the completion of the project, fulfilling a real social need.

Financial analysis can be the most important ingredient in any owner's development plan. Normally, outside consultants are employed by us to do this work. Such was the case in a small urban renewal project. Here, during development of the project plan and at all stages of its study, economic consultants were brought into the design process. These people determined potential salability of parcels of land, as well as providing advice on economics.

Ordinarily, location and site analysis for the small entrepreneur are done on a "seat of the pants" basis. As a result of conflicts with land-uses around this existing development, as well as access, egress and parking problems, a location and site analysis commission came to us from the developer of a new community shopping center. Analysis was made of locations within the region for community centers, examining the relationship of centers to existing and future neighborhood population, as well as to travel time from key population areas. Included in the study was a schematic analysis of the site, proposing sizes and locations of tenants, alternate uses of portions of the site, and recommendations on additional land to acquire for access. This study was followed by the commission to do the major building, which we hope will upgrade the developer's standards of architectural design as well as aid in obtaining satisfactory leases. It should be noted that this study was for a community center only, and we would seek consulting market analysts for a commercial operation on a larger scale.

Many projects, whether they be residential, industrial or commercial, have land-use problems. With no attempt to get into the field of the realtor, our firm is often involved in the early stages of a project with land assembly. In a development for 400 units of married student housing, land which was dedicated for street right-of-way was traded to the owner for alternate rights-of-way, part of the site design. Then, various odd-shaped parcels were traded for street closures and sewer easements. The result was lower street cost to the owner, as well as saving the city $75,000 in bridge construction costs. This land assembly permitted the owner to better utilize the land through higher density and obtain a more satisfactory grouping of buildings.

On all projects, after investigation, programming and design, the architect knows more about the project than any other person involved with it. For this reason, we must be aware of the public relations uses of this knowledge. A small library is an example. The programming steps and site studies were carefully documented for the Library Board. These, in turn, were used in the explanation of the needs for a new library. Frequent news releases on the progress of the planning were made, reminding the public of the pending bond issue. The final presentation was made in model form and photographed for use at public meetings, assuring the passage of the bond issue and the ultimate construction of the building. Such service as this is not considered to be an extra service, only a reorientation of regular services to the particular public relations needs of the client.

Guy L. Lee Elementary School,
Springfield

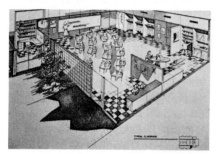

Classroom study, Lee School,
Springfield

Traffic volume diagram,
Albany, Ore

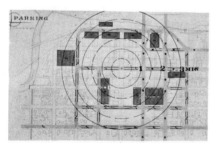

Central business district study,
Albany

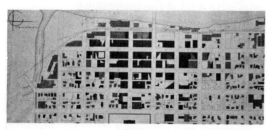

Central business district study,
Albany

In design, planning and construction services, our practice follows traditional lines—with emphasis and expansion of some aspects. In the case of the design of an elementary school, the school district had realized its first bond issue defeat in a decade. Few changes had been made in the pattern of teaching over the years, but many were pending. There existed the need for updating the school district staff in their educational thinking and presenting to voters of the district an economical building.

Programming began by a thorough investigation of the good and bad aspects of the existing elementary buildings in the district. A teachers' and citizens' committee was formed to analyze educational methods. The operational problems brought about by new teaching devices and equipment were analyzed, cataloged and coordinated. As the program evolved into studies, these were presented in a form the teachers and the citizens could understand. Rough models were made to demonstrate the unique educational characteristics of the building and illustrate its economy. Cost estimates were made, breaking down component part costs to determine relative savings for the scheme being considered over buildings which the district had previously built. Finally, the findings of the committee and the designs of the architect were presented as preliminary plans in brochure form. This brochure became widely circulated as a public information tool prior to the successful vote on the bond issue.

The construction process was closely scrutinized by the architect's full-time field representative. Professional liability and responsibility to our clients require expanded supervision practices. Thus, an example of traditional planning and construction services with added emphasis on programming, operational design, cost estimating and supervision, the architect's follow-up service included a pamphlet explaining the new school.

The provision of community planning services in our office, however, is perhaps the most unique aspect of our practice. Even though the architect may normally not be a city planner, he must be sufficiently conversant with the problems of the planner to at least keep his clients out of trouble. At best he can solve some of the problems of the city, too. Working on projects which include downtown redevelopment, land-use, parking and arterial studies for small communities, the architect's unique background for design, organization and presentation can go far in taking the statistical concerns of the planner and making them acceptable and understandable to the people.

Also, the architect must be sufficiently conversant with the mechanics of planning to properly represent his clients when zoning issues are involved. The architect cannot merely represent his client as an attorney would, but must show the worth of the proposal to the total physical community. Thus, we made a presentation for rezoning a parcel of land for a clinic, such rezoning being a logical terminus for an existing commercial area as well as providing an ideal site for the medical group.

Landscape and site-planning services are handled both in our office and by consultants. The total range of the landscape architect's capabilities are used, not just his services as a bush planter.

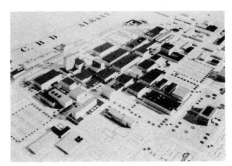

Business district study,
Albany

Model, Westmoreland Village,
Eugene

Aerial view, Westmoreland Village,
Eugene

Mark Sponenburgh sculpture,
Springfield Public Library

The grading, drainage and topographic problems inherent in large-scale development require the knowledge of the landscape architect, as does the organization of plant materials. Such service is provided as. a standard part of our contracts.

A standing list is maintained in our office of artists and sculptors who are capable of collaborating on architectural projects. We have found an initial reluctance to, then an astonishing acceptance of, the work of artists by commercial and public clients. No matter how lacking in artistic talent the owner may be, he logically turns to the architect for guidance in these matters, and the architect must be prepared. The artists' enthusiasm for incorporation of their work into architecture is boundless.

On commissions which require utility and traffic analysis, understanding is required of the effect of these elements upon site planning and architectural solutions, and to work within the limitations of these problems. On a 150-unit housing development, the state highway department, the country road department, the soil conservation service, a county, a city, three power companies and two water service districts were all involved in the traffic and utilities. The resolution of this hodgepodge into a pleasing solution integrated with the community required far more patience than consultants. Here again, the architect's awareness of the problems, his ability to find sources of solutions, and patience in resolving issues can provide a comprehensive service without the necessity of leaving the office. In this case, the consulting services of civil engineers were widely used to solve the technical problems once the design and political ones were resolved.

More and more, public and private clients are turning to the architect who is prepared and has broad scope as well as technical knowledge to conduct research studies on environmental design, which may or may not lead to actual architectural commissions. We recently completed such a pure research study, analyzing university dormitory policies as well as construction methods and cost alternates. Once, we had the opportunity of carrying a research project from beginning to end such as the downtown redevelopment proposal illustrated. Here, not only were we able to guide the committees drumming up interest in the study, but prepared the news releases and designed the theme, as well as planning the layout, utilizing artists, landscape architects and planners, and coordinating the activities of the city and the state highway department. The evaluation of this study, also prepared by us, for better or worse, has resulted in a lot of pedestrian-automobile separation experiments since 1957.

Our basic charging method is to raise fees based on the additional services provided. If at all possible, we determine the scope of extra services and incorporate them in the initial contract. Our standard services include programming, urban planning relationships, landscape design, engineering, acoustic analysis, cost estimates at each stage, arts and crafts coordination and promotional services, depending on form. Extra services include feasibility studies, research, financial analysis, site analysis and master planning. An alternate method which is frequently used is a per diem charge, with a maximum, for extra services.

Aerial photo, low rent housing,
Springfield

Shopping experiment,
Springfield, 1957

Shopping experiment,
Springfield, 1957

Shopping experiment,
Springfield, 1957

We must face some facts, however, in any discussion of fees. Clients frequently do not know the nature of the architect's basic service, and explaining comprehensive services is difficult. Our firm attempts to do this in a brochure which describes services available, both basic and comprehensive. By describing this type of service in detail, competition on the basis of fee is eliminated. We can, and do, compete with even the architectural "giants".

I would not be candid if I did not admit that comprehensive service presents some problems. This type of service takes preparation and research time on the part of both principals and employees to acquire additional knowledge. Not everyone is prepared to offer this type of service and we learn rapidly the limitations of our formal training. Also, a particular type of temperament is required—lots of patience and the ability to work with people over an extended period. Still I believe the architect is better prepared to provide this service than any of the other design professions.

We must be careful not to practice other professions such as law, land sales and building contracting.

The responsibility (and probable liability) of this type of practice is appalling.

Good consultants are difficult to find and cost money.

We must be careful not to lose our professional status as advisors, particularly when we come in contact with the other environmental influencers—politicians, real estate operators and the public.

Extra service may detract from our basic service, but I do not agree that basic service must reach perfection before embarking on at least some aspects of comprehensive service. As important as knowledge in this area are enthusiasm and determination.

The rewards of comprehensive service are many. This type of practice broadens your scope, which in turn obtains commissions and insures repeat clients. In this type of service the control of the job by the architect is more complete and assures payment for such services as programming and operational design for which we are now indirectly responsible.

Comprehensive service insures client respect. No job is based on mere sketches, as each commission is on a solid basis: programming, basic to a good solution; economics, basic to getting it built; and public relations, basic to understanding of others.

Some package dealers cannot compete with comprehensive services as they do not know local planning problems and lack knowledge of local costs. On two occasions in our experience, we have built buildings in competition with package dealers, and in both provided a more complete building, better located, for the same cost as the package dealer.

To conclude, almost all projects can use some facet of comprehensive service. In some, only an awareness of the total picture through the architect's fully developed knowledge is needed. On other projects, all facets of service are employed utilizing a full range of consultants. In our brief experience, we have received commissions on the basis of comprehensive service and been able to do a better job through expanded knowledge.

11

Comprehensive Architectural Services:
Industrial Buildings

BY ROBERT F. HASTINGS, FAIA

How comprehensive architectural services may be performed in the industrial building field by architects and their collaborators in related areas

Industrial clients' needs

If the architect is to serve efficiently the needs of many of today's industrial clients he must be prepared to perform more than the minimum basic services often offered in the past. Industrial projects today tend to be complex and large. In many instances, such factors as feasibility, operations programming and design, or financing must be thoroughly researched and analyzed before the building design can begin. If the architect cannot perform or arrange for and coordinate these services, he may lose control of portions of the design and construction process that may well be vital to the success of the project.

All of this simply means that the architect must be adequately trained in the areas of analysis, managerial, promotional, operational and supporting design services in addition to his training in the building arts and sciences in which he has traditionally served his clients. This means that the architect must have a broad enough vocabulary to enable him to call upon appropriate advisers to help him develop solutions to problems in areas in which the architect is not himself specifically qualified. In the industrial building field, such problems might well include those concerned with finance, real estate, marketing, manufacturing, and processing.

The architect's position in this would be that of agent for his client. His compensation would be based on the value of the specific services he renders his client. Trained in the broad requirements of all the related fields, the architect would have the vital role of coordinator of the total process, as well as that of adviser to his client. The services of the architect would not, of course, supplant the knowledge and skills of his client, but would supplement and complement them.

Expanded services

Types of services

Analysis, Promotional,

Managerial Services

Establishment of needs

Project economics

Feasibility studies

The following description of the types of services that an architect might provide for his industrial clients will give some indication of the dimensions of the role of the architect. In specific instances, services in addition to those discussed might be required for certain types of projects. On the other hand, only rarely would it be necessary for any single architectural firm to provide itself with all of the skills described. Those skills needed by individual firms will be determined by the scope of their work, the types of clients they serve, and other variables. The present description is only intended to show the scope of the problems of practice today, and to serve as an illustration of the type of comprehensive or diversified services needed by many of today's clients, particularly today's industrial clients.

For many industrial projects, there is a need for professional services in such fields as feasibility, financing, operations, and site selection. Architects who are experienced in industrial building design should be prepared to serve their clients in these and often in other related fields.

Before a client makes a capital investment in a plant, it is essential that the need be established. This can be determined by analysis of the potential markets and studies of existing sources of supply. From such studies, it will be possible to relate, geographically, the sources of supply to the markets. This and similar considerations have a decided bearing on the need for creating a new manufacturing facility.

In addition to determination of needs, it is essential to study possible methods of meeting the needs. Studies of this sort would include surveys of appropriate manufacturing methods, distribution methods, and methods for obtaining the necessary raw materials and partially processed components. To these should be added studies of such factors as location of the plant in relation to the sources of raw materials, markets, and labor sources.

Finally, the economics of the proposed project must be completely studied and developed. These studies should give attention to such things as capital investment in real estate, plant facilities, and manufacturing facilities, the investment needed to develop the required organization and staff, and the costs of raw and partially processed materials, manufacturing, and financing. It should also include data on costs of sales, distribution, and taxes. All such cost factors, and any others that have a direct or indirect bearing on the final return on investments, should be analyzed. On the basis of such analyses, it is possible to advise the client on the risks involved in launching a new manufacturing facility and the prospect of a reasonable return on the investment.

In order to serve his industrial clients' requirements in the area of feasibility studies, the architect must have an adequate general grasp of the subject. In addition, he will have to make available to his clients the knowledge and abilities of experts in these areas. This can be accomplished with the architect's own staff people or with consultants from outside the firm.

By means of feasibility studies, it is possible to establish needs and to determine whether or not the development of a new facility is economically justified. When it has been established that a need exists and methods of meeting the need are feasible, it is then

Financial services

necessary to thoroughly explore possible sources of financing for the project. Usually such an exploration would include interim financing as well as long-range financing. Often interim financing is furnished by local banks or by initial investment in stocks or other securities by a limited number of people. Long-range financing, on the other hand, is most often supplied by large trust funds, insurance companies, and other financial institutions interested in investments that promise reasonable rates of return over longer periods of time.

Financing projects

Long-range financing can be provided for in a number of ways, such as direct loans, issuance of additional common stock, or issuance or debt securities such as bonds. The sale and leaseback method should not be overlooked. By entering into such a sale-leaseback agreement with an investor, the manufacturer can often gain a number of financial advantages under certain circumstances.

Interest rates vary from time to time. Investment regulations change. Accordingly, the financing of a project must be thoroughly explored in relation to current realities of interest requirements and legal regulations that tend to limit or encourage capital investment.

The architect can be of inestimable aid to his industrial clients in the financing of their buildings. The architect's own understanding of the over-all requirements of industrial projects can be combined with the specialized financial knowledge of his staff specialists, consultants from outside the firm, and experts from financial sources themselves.

Comprehensive Architectural Services

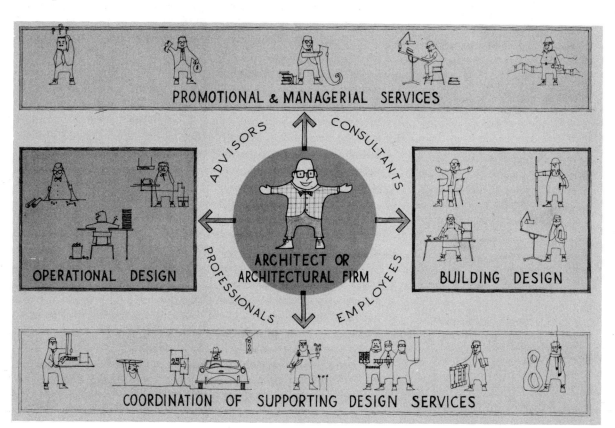

Operations programming

For industrial projects, programming of the operations to take place within the buildings is almost always necessary before the programming of the buildings themselves can be accomplished. Operations programming involves detailed study of the total manufacturing process. At this point the broad objectives of an industrial project must be clearly defined. Here the information developed through studies of feasibility and financing is brought to bear on the over-all problem of the industrial project. Working from the principles developed in the previous studies, the general requirements for manufacturing, sales, organization, production facilities and so on are outlined. From such requirements, the detailed processes to take place in the plant may be determined and the basic decisions concerning manufacturing equipment and furnishings can be made.

During the operations programming phase, it is necessary to determine the types and numbers of personnel required to operate the facility. Detailed organization requirements must be developed. Job descriptions must be drafted and key personnel should be selected. Financing arrangements will have to be worked out in detail to assure that adequate amounts of money will be available when needed for various phases of the project.

Operations decisions

It is in the operations programming phase, and the operational design and planning phase that follows, that many of the major decisions that affect the outcome of the building design are made. If the architect is deeply involved in the decisions made at this time, he can relate them to the complete design and construction phases. In this way, he can more nearly assure his client of a successful solution of his problems than would be possible if the operational decisions were made independently of the architect or if the decisions had been made before the architect was engaged.

Building programming

Having established the operational needs of the manufacturing facility in the operations programming phase, it is then necessary to determine the type of environmental facility that will best satisfy those needs. This is where building programming of an industrial building begins. The basic philosophy of the building design must be established. Site and climatic requirements for the building must be determined. Space relationships must be defined. Building occupancy requirements must be spelled out in great detail. The design and construction phases must be scheduled, as must construction financing.

When the feasibility, financial and operational requirements of the project have been established, appropriate sites may be surveyed to determine which one best meets the established needs of the project.

Building Design and Planning

The next step in the development of an industrial facility is the beginning of the actual design and planning based on the analysis studies and the operations and building programs. Before design of the building itself can proceed, it is necessary to work out the design of the processes to be housed.

In an industrial building, the design and layout of the industrial processes are usually important keys to the design of the building. Operational procedures must be designed and laid out. The systems and processes to be used must be finally determined. It is

Analysis, Promotion, Management

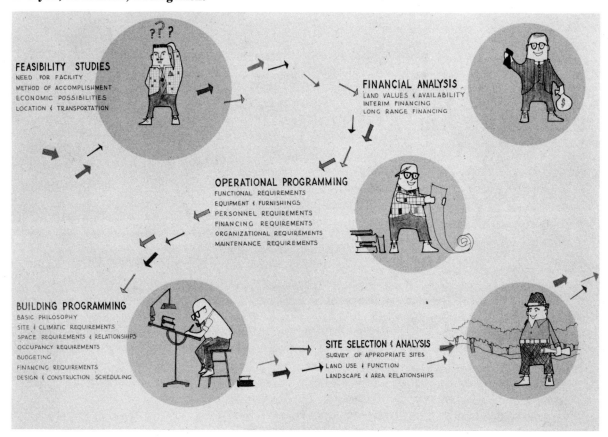

Operational Design and Planning

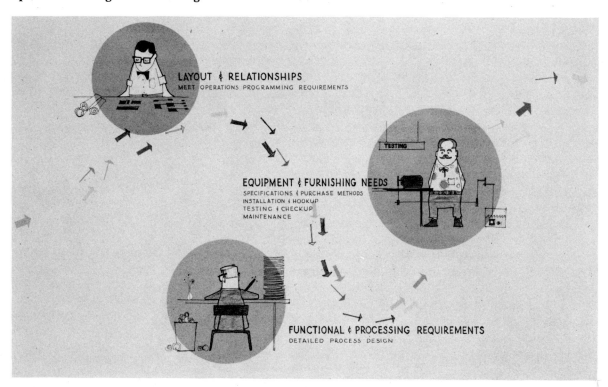

Building Design and Planning

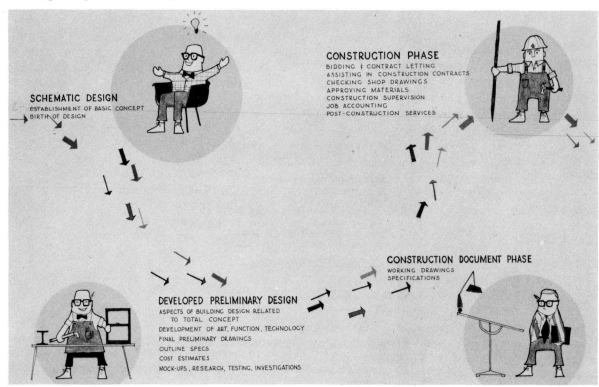

Supporting Services

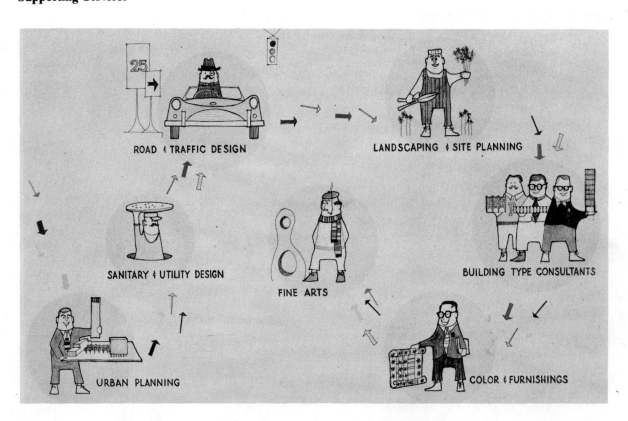

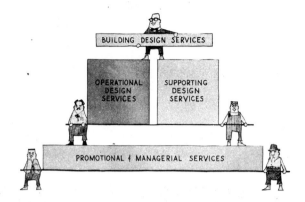

necessary to develop a complete and detailed process design. From these designs, a plant layout can be made that will meet all of the operations programming requirements in the most efficient manner. At this stage, equipment and furnishings requirements to carry out the manufacturing operations can be clearly defined. These can then be specified and placed on order or purchased. Installation and hookup drawings can now be developed. At a later time, these drawings will be used in the supervision of the installation and hookup of equipment.

The scope of the services of the architect during the building design and planning phase is well established. For industrial buildings, these services will closely parallel those performed for other building types. However, it may be worthwhile to stress again the importance of close coordination of the work of all of the many professionals and others who participate in this phase. Accurate cost estimating is of utmost importance, as are proper scheduling and adherence to schedules, since budgets are often extremely limited and time almost always limited in the industrial field.

Construction Services

The architect's services during construction traditionally include, among other things, the taking of bids, recommendations for construction contract awards, approval of materials and equipment, checking of shop drawings, and supervision of the construction. In industrial building work, when the architect has been involved in the programming and planning of the operations, he will also have the responsibility for final approval of operational equipment installations. When the building has been completed and the equipment is in place and the hookup made, the entire assembly should be thoroughly checked and tested. In this way, it is possible to make sure that the process lines and all equipment meet the needs of the manufacturing processes with regard to accuracy, quality, quantity, and unit costs.

Supporting Services

In the development of a complete industrial project, the architect will be working closely with engineers and a number of other supporting design and consulting services. The architect should always keep in mind the importance of such supporting services as urban or community planning, landscaping, sculpture and the other related arts. These supporting services are necessary to the architect if he is to complete an industrial facility that is not only feasible and functional, but one that will also satisfy the environmental needs of persons who operate the manufacturing facility and of the people who live in the community.

12

Comprehensive Architectural Services: Shopping Centers

BY CLINTON GAMBLE, FAIA

Comprehensive architectural services as related to analysis, promotion, programming, design, and construction of shopping center developments

Need for expanded services

The shopping center is a prime example of one of the many building types that require from the architect more than the basic services of design, production, and supervision. In order to practice successfully in this field, the architect must expand his services to some degree of comprehensive practice. This is not meant to imply that the architect must take over all of the functions needed for shopping center development. On a typical project, a long list of other professionals and specialists will often be involved. Such a list might reasonably include market analysts, real-estate agents, mortgage brokers, land planners, traffic consultants, all kinds of engineering consultants from soil analyst to airconditioning, bankers, chain store real-estate and building departments, government officials, landscape architects, accountants, appraisers, investment syndicate representatives, interior designers, lending institutions, insurance brokers, attorneys, general contractors, and sub-contractors.

Enlightened coordinators

In the kind of comprehensive practice needed in the shopping-center field, the architect's role is truly that of the enlightened and knowledgeable coordinator. The nature of this role and the fact that the architect can be counted on to act as a professional in his relations with the owner and others connected with the work may very well be the key reasons why the architect is necessary.

While it is obviously impossible to describe adequately all of the aspects of comprehensive services for shopping centers, the following will give some indication of the more important considerations.

Analysis, Promotional, Managerial Services

Feasibility must be established

Market analysis for department stores

Landowner vs entrepreneur

Method of accomplishment

In the establishment of the need for the facility, no building project is more susceptible to market analysis than a shopping center. Since the chain store nucleus is the key to its development, it is almost axiomatic that if the market for the largest store—the department store, or recently the large discount store —can be demonstrated, the total need for the center is almost completely established. Since the shopping center is completely dependent on the major tenants for its initiation and existence, the feasibility study is primarily a matter of enticing these tenants to lease in the center. It is not an over-simplification to say the lease for the major store spells the success for the promotion. Consequently knowing the expansion plans for the major stores in an area is the best practical adjunct to feasibility.

The architect who maintains a constant study of major store locations can be helpful to the owner or rental agent—many times in a negative way—by objectively relating new locations to his continuing study of present locations and advising whether a real opportunity exists or not for successful lease negotiations. It seems to be traditional that architects are more conservative in their approach to these matters than real-estate agents.

The technique of market analysis for the major department store is well established. There are two or three well-known national consultants who specialize in this field. The department-store chains themselves have well-developed analysis departments as part of their real estate operations and most other major chains also have similar departments. The architect must be knowledgeable enough to interpret the analysis quickly so that in preliminary conversations he may play a key role as part of the development team.

It is important to maintain a balanced position between the chains and the land owner or entrepreneur if such is the case, in interpreting the analysis in terms of land, building size, and costs against well recognized "rules of thumb." In this way, all of the factors that tend to produce a successful center, or vital factors that may be lacking, may be quickly recognized. In some cases in smaller centers, the architect may well have to act as the market analyst.

The technique of analysis has been well explored in publications of the Urban Land Institute and the International Council of Shopping Centers and the two organizations are continuously publishing new material. Any architect who intends to practice in the field of shopping centers might well belong to these organizations and take an active part in them.

The major decisions in the method of accomplishment of a shopping center are mainly dependent on who the final owner turns out to be. A center may be held by the original land owner, a private syndicate, the major store, a sale lease-back, or others. In one center designed by our firm, there have been three changes of ownership over a seven-year period. First this was a small center planned to expand; next, fringe expansions took place; recently a major expansion has been accomplished and there is still more expansion to come. We found ourselves in the position of minor-league city planners in effect, since we have been the only member of the team retained through all the changes. Time and again we found ourselves being called upon to evaluate the center and its potential, while new groups negotiated for ownership. Improvements, land leases, long term sale contracts on the land, refinancing of mortgages, lease of specific land with option to buy—all these methods have been used in this one center. Recently we have been employed by the present owner as the key figure in negotiations with an investment group considering the purchase of the entire center. We were instrumental in bringing this group into contact with a management group who will contract for management if the investment group actually buys the center. Obviously, the services in this center have gone far beyond the role that the architect's basic contract envisages. The total building program in this center will probably amount to $8 million when completed, yet fully half of the time of our principal-in-charge has been spent on matters entirely outside the specific design of these buildings.

Economic possibilities

In shopping centers, the knowledgeable architect will often find himself acting as a true coordinator. Standing in a position between the merchant with his needs and desires and the translation of these needs into buildings, the architectural firm will find itself, time and again, preparing the initial tables showing the relationship of building cost, size, rents, maintenance, and so on, even before tentative schematics are considered.

Building costs and rents

Since all figures of this sort must be related to one another, the first step is to agree what type of square-foot figures are to be used. Our firm prefers using the "rented area." In other words all comparisons of the total area of the store or the center are based only on the rented area, regardless of whether the area is sales or service. Common areas such as sidewalks, canopies, covered truckways, malls, and vaults are excluded from the figures. Related to rented area, a store might cost $15.00 per square foot. A breakdown of this cost might show that airconditioning will cost $1.25 of the $15.00, light fixtures seventy-five cents per sq ft, exterior paving and site work $1.15 and so on. When negotiating the leases these figures give the rental agent exact information as to the probable cost differentials he is working against when he agrees that the landlord will furnish certain items or argues that the tenant should furnish them.

Rents are commonly discussed on this same rented square-foot basis. The $15.00 per-sq-ft-store in this example might rent for $2.50 per square foot. Of this rent the owner might pay $1.50 per sq ft amortization and interest on the mortgage, thirty cents for taxes and insurance, and fifteen cents for the landlord's share of operation and maintenance. Consequently, fifty-five cents would remain to give the landlord a return on his equity. By keeping all these costs on a pro-rated square foot basis, it is easy to make direct comparisons, between tenants, of returns against investment and to answer many other questions. The most important thing is that everyone working on the project will be talking in the same cost terms. In this way, all the wild speculations regarding costs that often result when unlike comparisons are used may be avoided.

The figures used in this example are based on reasonable assumptions, conservative or optimistic depending on the results of market analysis, existing market costs, probable interest of merchandise and so on. It should be remembered, however, that the success of a shopping center is entirely determined by economics.

The old adage in real estate about the three important factors being location, location, and location, is most certainly applicable to shopping centers. Driving-time or transportation time of potential customers to the site is a part of market analysis, and the actual location of a center cannot be determined until the need, methods of accomplishment, and economic possibilities have been determined. Sometimes, strangely enough, the architect may find himself in the position of having a project well along in terms of these three studies before he actually knows who "the owner" will be.

Location and transportation requirements

If a shopping center project has developed to the point discussed here, various locations must then be evaluated in terms of cost. Economical appraisal of the land value is of paramount importance since the "intrinsic value" or "comparison value" may be entirely out of proportion. Since shopping centers require large land areas, and these areas are subject to tremendous variations in cost, the services performed by the architect up to this point are of great importance here. Probably the greatest change in "before" and "after" values of land occur with the development of a shopping center. Most projects will stand or fall on the "before" land value determination.

Land values and availability

In shopping centers, site selection and land assembly go hand-in-hand with feasibility. The problem is quite clear-cut. When it is known that a major store is interested in establishing a new location, the proper approach is to find the land for the tenant, and not to find the tenant for the land. A great deal of time is spent by land owners who happen to own a large tract and are dazzled by the profits that might come from a shopping center on their site. Such owners often disregard the fact that no real reason exists for the development of a center at their location, nor any reason for a major store to consider the location. As the shopping center field has become better defined it is quite clear that chains of centers, just as there are chains of stores, are coming. These chains of centers are being established by finding the land for the tenant. Probably the most important factor for the architect in this case is to be of assistance in the chain's location problems in an effective way. The proper service in some cases where his client is a land owner might be for the architect to show that while the land may not constitute a good shopping center location, that it will be good for something else.

Land assembly and feasibility

Shopping center chains

More and more we are dealing with corporate clients in shopping center work. These are often clients with a continuing series of projects. If the architect can take a place at the Board table when the company policies are being discussed and can help shape the general direction of the company effort, he can provide truly expanded service. Being an effective mem-

Working with corporate clients

Average Life of a Hypothetical Shopping Center Building			
	COST ($)	LIFE YEARS	LIFE X COST
Foundations	10,000.00	40	400,000
Walls, Floor, Roof, Structure	20,000.00	40	800,000
Doors, Windows, Millwork	6,000.00	20	120,000
Roofing	2,000.00	15	30,000
Acoustical Ceiling	1,500.00	15	22,500
Tile & Terrazzo	2,500.00	20	50,000
Electrical—Wiring	3,500.00	20	70,000
—Fixtures	2,500.00	10	25,000
Plumbing—Piping	5,000.00	20	100,000
—Fixtures	4,000.00	15	60,000
Airconditioning—Ducts	5,000.00	15	75,000
—Machinery	10,000.00	10	100,000
—Grilles	1,000.00	10	10,000
Movable Partitions, Cabinets	11,000.00	10	110,000
	84,000.00		1,972,500

1,972,500 ÷ 84,000.00=approx. 22.5 years average life for this building. For depreciation purposes, an average life of 25 years might be used.

ber in such a discussion is an entirely different matter from the direct job of design or planning. The emphasis must be on the general over-all background, on the total problem.

Long-range financing

Almost all shopping centers are premised on large institutional first mortgages. With institutional mortgages, a preliminary commitment is necessary so that the equity requirements can be determined. The guaranteed rents must support the institutional loan and should come from the triple-A rated stores. By estimating the triple-A rents and deducting fixed charges (taxes, insurance) the remainder can be capitalized into the probable commitment. The architect may well be the best equipped person at this stage for developing a realistic estimate.

Determination of the life of buildings

Due to the income tax structure, "depreciation" of buildings has a very special meaning. By using rapid depreciation schedules, the Federal government has opened up a method for substantially reducing the apparent income and its resultant tax. Depreciation involves two steps. The first is the determination of the "life" of the building. Traditionally the government has allowed forty years as the normal life. However, by breaking the building into its component parts it is clear that some parts wear out faster than others. A simple table for determination of the average life is shown above.

Depreciation

If the various "life" figures such as those given in the table are agreed upon by the Federal tax examiners, then a life of twenty-five years calculated by the "sum of the digits" or by the "descending balance" method (which starts off at roughly double the constant rate) means that the depreciation allowed for tax purposes the first year would be eight per cent of $84,000 or $6720 in the example. Twenty-five years equals four per cent a year; this rate doubled equals eight per cent. This is not to say that it would be good judgment to use all these calculations in a particular case. This must be decided at a Board meeting such as that mentioned before. The architect can make a knowledgeable breakdown of costs based on principles such as those discussed, analyze them with regard to the real useful "life," and advise the owner on the use of the figures.

Interim financing

Since most shopping centers will require interim financing for construction purposes only and this financing exactly parallels the mortgage commitments discussed above, the interim financing can be quickly determined. It should be emphasized that owners are concerned with total costs and financing. The architect, while maintaining a high degree of professional responsibility, can discuss these matters from a completely objective point of view. In most cases, the architect's compensation for such services can be determined on a direct hourly basis, not dependent on "speculation" or contingency. The architect can—indeed must—avoid letting himself be placed in a bargaining position. He must always remain in a status from which he can constantly advise on the total picture.

Operational Programming

Functional requirements

In order to determine the functional requirements of a shopping center, the store rental pattern must be programmed and then designed, since each center, having a known market (average of incomes, probable drawing power against competition) will have a different emphasis on types of tenancy. The relationships between building costs, sizes, rents and so on developed earlier can now be revised and studied to meet this market. Peculiar individual requirements, particularly of chains, can be equated into this analysis.

Equipment and furnishings

At this point, the type of center and its rental pattern will indicate the equipment and furnishings required for general use. Arrangements for tenant equipment are a major part of the lease agreement. The architect must establish ground-rules with the rental agent so that he may be of real service before signed leases are executed. These items may be the crux of the lease negotiations.

Personnel and maintenance

Personnel requirements and maintenance requirements are closely connected. Realistic estimates of these requirements must be made for inclusion in the total picture mentioned before. The net return against equity can only be determined after all costs are nailed down; some of the most illusive of these are operational costs.

Financing and organizational requirements

The total picture requires conservative and adequate provision for the financing of operation. The proportion of chain to local stores is the exact measure of the business risk.

Planning to get the best operation possible is involved not only with the direct management of the center but also with such things as public relations. Preliminary decisions on how management is to work may be made in this stage.

Building Program

Basic philosophy

Up to this stage of development of a shopping center, only rough schematic layouts required to make early determinations will have been prepared. A determination to negotiate a building general contract would mean that a broad outline of preliminary specifications and memos agreeing to areas, unit-costs, etc, would now be required. In such a case, the architect would work closely with the selected general contractor. An entirely different concept is required if the general contract is to be bid. The method of ownership of the center must also now be firmed up.

A review of the site and climate requirements follows the actual site selection. Even before this, the climate and site requirements of the general geographical location will have been considered.

Space relationships

Definite and meaningful schematics must be done now to spell out the space requirements. The types of stores to be adjacent to one another is most important. The architect will wish to give his full attention to maintaining a realistic *parti*.

Scheduling

The exact date of opening for a shopping center must be determined. Merchants have very critical requirements as to the time of year they begin business. Their entire stocks change every few months; in fact even a week's difference may change a merchant's whole approach toward initial inventory. Exact schedules must be planned and maintained.

Operational

Design Services

The operational design of common areas, the method of airconditioning whether individual or central, the lighting of the site, whether there will be a meeting-hall for civic functions— all of these must now be considered and policy determined. These reflect in the building costs to be sure, and might properly be considered as covered in building programming. General layout and relationships, and common equipment and furnishings, must now be given design considerations.

Design development

During the leasing period, which occurs during the time of preliminary sketch development or in what might be called the operational design development stage, the architect will need to be in close contact with the rental agent, furnishing him comparative costs for the variety of building decisions that occur. A guarantee-plus-percentage lease is a delicate formula with many

Guarantee plus percentage leases

variables that can be adjusted in relation to each other. The more the owner provides, the more rent he gets; but there are many shades of meaning in this statement. Approval of the lease itself, and particularly those sections dealing with the building requirements is a very important part of an architect's expanded service. The architect in some ways will be working with two owners. Extensive contact with the tenant (who is the real owner in the sense of using the building) is often necessary. How well the architect handles this relationship, as a direct personal service, will reflect on the effectiveness of his comprehensive services.

Preliminaries must follow other phases

Up to this point, outside of the direct schematics mentioned, no preliminary sketches in the usual sense have been prepared. Indeed it is important to restrain everyone else involved in the planning from asking for sketches, renderings, models, etc—the usual tools of architectural practice. It is entirely possible that a year or more will have been taken up with the other considerations. During this period, large files of memos, tables, letters of intent, all sorts of communications, and not one drawing of consequence will have been prepared. The point is, of course, that without the exhaustive determinations that have been described, dozens of perspectives could have been made, and none of them would reflect the exact scheme that now must be developed. An architect could well have earned a good many dollars up to now and not have furnished any of his traditional services. In these studies, compensation based on a percentage of building costs would be unrealistic. Instead, a simple hourly charge arrangement, scaled according to the kinds of personnel involved in the work, is often used by architects.

Building Design and Construction Services

Most of the building design and construction functions are so normal and usual in shopping center work it is probably unnecessary to discuss them in detail. Two points are worthy of attention, however—the negotiated construction contract and the need for close and continuous attention to project costs.

Negotiated construction contracts

In most cases, shopping centers can best be built by negotiating a contract with the general contractor. This requires complete and mutual confidence and respect between the general contractor and the architect. It requires complete disclosure and constant coordination. Interestingly enough, it also demands many of the same ethical requirements from the general contractor that are subscribed to by architects.

The negotiated construction contract is useful for a shopping center because, unlike other building projects, the center is almost always actually under construction long before a final set of working drawings are completed. For example, on one project a 220,000 sq ft department store was under way and the steel frame erected before the drawings were finished. A major part of the electrical work could be finalized and priced only after the interior fixtures were designed and bids let four months after the building construction started. Similarly, another 125,000 sq ft in the same project had the steel frame in place when only sixty-five per cent had actually been rented. By negotiating a guaranteed maximum with a fixed fee, many months had been saved. It is doubtful that a large center could possibly wait for the entire contract to be defined in working drawings before beginning construction.

Negotiated contract problems

The potential disadvantage in the negotiated contract is that a great deal of mutual confidence is required among owner, architect, and contractor. The moment that any one of these three tries to take advantage of the situation, it falls apart. The architect must produce a set of plans that the contractor agrees are within the scope of the work he contemplated. The contractor must agree to sufficient flexibility in his calculations to fit the final job conditions the architect finds as he completes his plans. The owner must be entirely fair in relating the tenants and their actual requirements to what has been previously determined as probable requirements. Probably no other building operation requires more reliance on a proper professional attitude, more experience and application of good judgment. When it does work on this basis, however, this is really a team effort that produces buildings that are better integrated, better designed and more quickly built than by any other method.

Need for cost analyses

Continuous cost analyses must be made during the construction of shopping centers; and most centers are never really finished. Most have a continuing building program, of alterations and changes in operations or maintenance. Consequently, for post-construction services, it may be best to revert to the hourly compensation arrangement, after the contract work has been accepted.

13

Comprehensive Architectural Services: Multifamily Housing

BY NEIL A. CONNOR, AIA *

The practice of comprehensive architectural services for multifamily housing is closely related to the practice of such services for other building types

* Director, Architectural Standards Division, FHA

Financial and market analysis needed

The days of the patron of architecture are past. Today's multifamily residential buildings are invariably financed with borrowed funds, and the primary incentive prompting the entrepreneur is usually profit, regardless of any secondary motives. This means that sound financial analysis is necessary to ascertain whether this objective can be attained. If not, there will be no building. Preparatory to such analysis, market analysis is necessary to ascertain the extent of the market in the various income brackets, what types of accommodations and services are needed and what the anticipated tenants or purchasers will pay. It is also necessary to ascertain the amounts of housing of various types that are available and the price or rentals being obtained. The architect and sponsor are comparable to a manufacturer who is proposing a new product; they must also, like the manufacturer, ascertain the market, market preferences and taboos, and make a complete and detailed financial analysis.

It can be argued that such investigations are not architecture, and that this phase is properly the work of market analysts, appraisal and real estate specialists, or even the owner or sponsor who, many times, is largely guided by optimistic opinions rather than data and impartial analysis. However, when it is realized that miscalculation in the initial determination of the market, rentals or types of accommodations and services, or in the financial analysis, can result in major deficiencies and, possibly, the failure of the project, and inasmuch as these are directly related to all aspects of the project design, the architect ought to be vitally concerned. No architect relishes the thought, or the effect on his reputation, of being the designer of an unsuccessful project, even though his fee was earned and no legal responsibility rests on him.

The analysis of the market, the needs of tenants, and the

motives or purposes and needs of the sponsor closely parallel the architect's traditional consideration of "use and function" in design.

Similarly, financial analysis brings home the limitations on cost and the effect of costs, as well as the effects of operating and maintenance expense. Financial analysis can also be adapted to save architects useless hours of work and expense in providing an upper limit of cost for physical improvements as a guide in design. This would minimize much of the trial and error approach to design.

Market analysis of multifamily housing

The purpose of market analysis is to ascertain the need for the project, whether there is sufficient demand to provide a continuing supply of tenants, sizes of families, types of housing and services preferred, and the rentals that can be obtained; also, the housing presently available or proposed and at what cost or rentals. All such housing is—in effect—competitive.

Market analysis provides the basis for determining need and the type of housing that must be provided to attract the desired clientele; in other words, it is the basis of planning. In planning multifamily projects, it is of utmost importance that accommodations and services be designed to meet the desires and preferences of the market segment which is to be accommodated. This selection is not entirely arbitrary but evolves from a number of factors, such as that project location must be attractive to the market segment. The cost of land must be in appropriate relation to the budget cost resulting from income expectancy. Size of market segment: a broad market is desirable, that is to say, there must be a sufficient amount of unsatisfied, financially able and willing, demand to justify and fill the project. The types of living units, number of rooms, arrangement, room sizes, finish, equipment and services must be commensurate with anticipated rentals; likewise, the total environment and appearance must be similarly appropriate. Competitive property and existing housing inventory: the project in its essentials must compare favorably with—or be superior to—competitive housing. Feasibility: the architect and proponent must discover that they can provide accommodations and services that will have continued appeal to the market segment at the obtainable rentals, and that such rentals will provide adequate income to meet all expenses and provide a reasonable profit.

Form for market analysis

Federal Housing Administration Form 2401, *Appraisal Data and Project Information,* is a type of data sheet which may be used for market analysis. This form deals with city, neighborhood, site, comparable site prices, comparison grid, competitive rentals, operating costs, taxes and other data, and is indicative of the number of families in various income groups and rental brackets and their general living habits and preferences. All are pertinent to design and operation of successful projects. Actual market investigations would probably be done by market analysts and appraisers in the employ of the sponsors of the project or by their bankers.

Financial analysis of multifamily housing

The purpose of financial analysis is to ascertain the financial feasibility of a project. This is done on the basis of approximations in the initial stage but must be refined, using careful estimates and known costs, as soon as the project sketches are sufficiently crystallized.

FHA uses a *Project Income Analysis and Appraisal Form* which is designed to record analysis data pertinent to the full valuation of a multifamily housing project. This form, when combined with the *Appraisal Data and Project Information* form and an estimate of reserves for replacement to be required, makes up a complete and comprehensive appraisal report. These data are recorded as estimates of gross rental income at full occupancy, vacancies, operating expenses, taxes, net income and the value found by its capitalization, replacement cost of property (which includes physical improvements, architects' and builders' fees, land and costs inherent in creating a project such as interest and taxes during construction, title costs, legal and organizational fees, etc) for the purpose of arriving at a conclusion as to the fair market value of the property. The value conclusion reached may be the total cost, the amount justified by earnings, or the known market price of an equivalent property, whichever is lowest.

Full and intelligent use of this appraisal form, or some other appraisal device, requires study of appraisal practice and valuation procedures. Most architects might find it better to employ or retain a qualified appraiser, rather than attempt to acquire such knowledge and experience themselves.

Estimations are useful

However, architects can, in connection with preliminary explorations of feasibility, make most useful estimations of the probable relationship between estimations of the cost of the projected physical improvements and the amount of investment justified by its earnings. Obviously, preliminary studies are needed to show how many units can be provided on the site of the types and kinds likely to have continued market acceptance at obtainable rentals. The financial objective is to create these units with the minimum invested capital that will yield a continuing and reasonably safe maximum return on that capital.

The justified cost of creating a project is, therefore, inherently related to the net income to be derived from it. The net income is, in turn, the residual amount of the entire gross income of the project less all of the vacancies, operating expenses, taxes, re-

---

Financial Analysis of Hypothetical Multifamily Project

Gross Income	$107,526
Vacancy and collection losses, 7%	7,526
Effective Gross Income	$100,000
Operating Expenses, Reserves and Taxes	40,000
Net Income	$ 60,000

Overall Capitalization Rate, 7¼%
Value of Property ($60,000=7¼% x $827,600.) $827,600
Financing, title, legal costs, etc., 35,600
Land Cost   75,000   110,600

Amount applicable to all on-site improvements and architects' and builders' fees	$717,000

The "overall capitalization rate" is before depreciation. It must, therefore, return all invested capital and provide return on the capital (interest) also. It may be capitalized in various ways. The amount available for all on-site improvements less the amount required for such improvements as landscaping and utilities other than buildings and architects' and builders' fees is the amount available for buildings.

serves, etc, arising from project operation as a going concern. If the gross rental probabilities, vacancy and operating expenses, etc, can be reasonably estimated, the resultant net income, at a required rate of return, can be projected to an estimation of the permissible cost of the project improvements and building construction.

If the construction costs, land costs (and financing, carrying charges, etc), return requirements, and operating expenses are known or assumed, the effective gross income and the gross income necessary to support a given project can be computed —as in the example on the preceding page—by a reversal of the process discussed.

The illustration in the example does not, of course, necessarily demonstrate the criteria used for the determination of a mortgage amount insured by the FHA, as this may be limited by other criteria such as loan-value ratio (involving value and cost) and statutory limitations (based on per unit or room dollar limits), debt service requirements, and so on.

Operating expenses vs net income

It will be observed that operating expenses have a direct and obvious effect on "net income." Such expenses vary from locality to locality and, more importantly, with the type of project and services rendered. As with all cost comparisons, to be valid, data should be derived from experience with similar types and sizes of projects providing similar facilities to the same general market. Data serving as a guide can be found in publications of various associations; for example, the *Journal of Property Management* published annually by the Institute of Real Estate Management, regularly publishes material on such subjects.

The area of pre-design service described here is sketchy at best and will serve only to suggest a means of minimizing much of the "cut and try" effort expended by many architects. Even if not applied to actually broaden the architect's own services, an understanding of the process and terminology of market and financial analysis should improve the quality of services and relations with realtors and sponsors. It has been said that architects are at a disadvantage in dealing with businessmen; only by learning to deal—as do businessmen—with the cold facts of the economics of building and by becoming proficient in this area can architects overcome this disadvantage.

Quantity take-offs needed

The architect can also expand his services and value within the commonly accepted area of practice in areas such as the preparation of quantity take-offs for projects designed for sponsors. The practice of obtaining bids on the basis of such take-offs would obtain better bidding for the benefit of the owner.

Services in construction stage

Strange as it may seem, many lenders see little value in the architect's supervision, due undoubtedly to certain unfortunate experiences they have had. It must be said, however, that many lenders do retain architects for supervision and these architects perform outstandingly. Further study should be given to the re-establishment of the architect as an active participating member of the building team and to removing all doubt as to his impartiality in his professional actions during construction.

Comprehensive Architectural Services: Colleges and Universities

BY ROBERT E. ALEXANDER, FAIA

For colleges and universities, especially the mushrooming community colleges, comprehensive architectural services can fulfill pressing needs of clients

College enrollment will rise to 8,616,000 students by 1975, according to US Department of Health, Education and Welfare projections; the enrollment then will be about double that of 1963 and almost four times that of 1950. From all indications, a large portion of the increasing student population will be educated in community colleges that are yet to be built

Analysis, Promotional,

Managerial Services

A community college

The potential scope of an architect's services for a college or university varies according to many factors such as the size and age of the institution and the staff and other resources available through the institution itself or state agencies. A large state university located in a populous state, founding a new campus, may have the educational planning staff, space experts, program analysts and a wealth of operating experience so that the architect's role is confined to his traditional site planning and building design functions. However, it is assumed here that a small, new community college is to be built in a state where little or no pertinent experience is available and where no strongly staffed state agency is available.

An architect's means of providing expanded services will also vary according to the size of his organization and the volume of work he produces in the subject category. A large office specializing in higher educational facilities may offer all services through employees or associates. Even the smallest office, however, can organize a group of consultants as a team specifically designed to deliver the highest quality, coordinated, comprehensive services outlined below. In areas where no "experts" are available, the problems are also simpler and the architect in even a two-man office can learn to handle most of the problems involved.

For purposes of illustration, it is assumed here that a committee of laymen has been appointed to found a community college. They are convinced of the need and desirability of the project, but they must translate their abstract enthusiasm into specific figures on need, use, cost, benefits, size, growth, orientation, etc, in order to proceed on a secure basis and to convince an electorate. The committee may engage an architect at this embryonic stage if the architect is prepared to offer educational, survey and community planning services.

The architect assembles and analyzes information on population and existing higher educational opportunities and use. He projects probable attendance estimates and recommends limits of the district. His educational consultant conducts a survey of indigenous community interests, job opportunities and aspirations. He outlines a potential curriculum and shows how it would relate to the economy of the district. He suggests certain aims and objectives.

The architect then estimates, in broad terms, the probable costs and timing of the institution before having planned any buildings. His economic consultant analyzes the tax resources and position of the community to support the project; his land planner reports on land and transportation availability in general terms.

Determination of
feasibility

At this stage if the project appears feasible to the committee, an official Board of Trustees is formed. Their first act may be to select a President of the college who thereafter directs and takes the lead in educational planning. The architect, however, may still be called upon to provide staff experts in many fields including education.

Operational Program

The operating plan and organization of the institution will be determined by the President and the Board. The architect and his educational consultant may offer valuable advice for use in the analysis of the planning and design implications of an operational idea and in suggesting alternatives for consideration.

The operating plan will state how the aims, objectives and curriculum will be carried out. Will the institution be organized along vocational or academic discipline lines? What will be group size policy? What proportions of seminars and large lectures will be sought? How will TV be used? How will language classes be conducted? How will computing machines and teaching aids be used?

Decisions on such questions will determine faculty requirements, maintenance facilities, building forms and the cost and quality of education. The interplay between educator and architect at this early stage may benefit the project profoundly.

Establishment
of basic philosophy

The basic philosophy of building design and open space relationships is determined by the Board, but the architect is best equipped to visualize the possibilities and the effect of such policy on human and operational relationships. The type, height, compactness, form and materials of construction can now be outlined. Housing relationships and functional grouping related to faculty, student courses, specialization and public use can be determined. Site, climate and soil requirements can be analyzed to determine how they may influence site selection and building design and costs. A policy determination of ultimate maximum growth will be required at this time.

Space requirements

Space requirements may be tailored to class size and number so that each student and faculty station is used efficiently. A student station that will be occupied one-third of the available time costs twice as much to the consumer as one used two-thirds of the time available. The architect, or his space-use consultant, can save many times the entire cost of his services by integrating the space program with the educational operating program plan.

Site selection

Schedule of costs

Fund raising campaigns

Operational Design Services

Equipment and furnishings

Building Design and Construction Services

The architect then may analyze various incremental development plans. Certain functions are essential before the college can open. Complete buildings may be developed to ultimate requirements and used in the interim for a combination of uses. Time schedules for design, construction and payments must be adopted.

The architect and his community planning consultant review possible sites as to location, service area, access, transportation, utilities, topography, costs, soil and esthetic features. The architect may test each suitable site against a schematic development plan based on the program. Comparable analyses of all the factors involved, rating each site, will help the Board to a rational, justifiable and secure decision.

From the space program and the incremental development plan, tested against a schematic site plan, the architect can develop a schedule of development costs. He should embrace in this the full costs of development including furnishings, technical services, inspection, tests, landscaping, utilities, roads, fund raising, etc. The development costs will usually run twenty-five per cent—or more—of the estimated building costs. A projection of a building cost index as well as contingency allowances should also be employed to avoid embarrassment to the Board and the architect. Coordinating the incremental schedule with the estimated growth of the institution, and leveling the curve of development, he may then prepare alternate financial plans based on bond issues, annual tax rate increases or fund raising campaigns. The plan may be modified by the resources of the community or political considerations.

Many architects also assist the Board in fund raising or bond campaigns, preparing special graphic material and publications and making personal appearances to answer questions at public meetings. Some architectural offices even maintain offset printing departments for the efficient conduct of their internal business and for better service to clients.

The educational purpose of an institution may be enhanced by a complete analysis of the problems of administration and maintenance that will be encountered in later years. Such a study by the architect may not only be of value to the college administration, but may also be of aid to the architect and his staff, helping to make the design of the general plan and the buildings themselves more realistic. Manufacturing "process charts" may seem incongruous in education, but the flow of students, faculty and paper, especially in a large institution, can be vital and might very well be planned in a manner similar to the flow of manufacturing production lines.

The architect can offer well-documented advice on equipment and furnishings as well as on purchasing policies and long-range maintenance policies. Few architects can offer sufficient personal experience or a laboratory of their own, but any architect can obtain information and reliable laboratory test reports for the benefit of his client. The architect's obligation is to become well informed and to develop the judgment which will make his advice valuable and therefore remunerative as he expands his services.

The traditional building design services are well understood generally, but emphasis should be placed on the relatively new distinction between schematic and preliminary design, which was developed for the security of the client and architect. Too few consulting engineers fully realize their responsibilities to join with the architect in the schematic concept and in developing a complete design during the preliminary stage.

Services during bidding and contract letting bring to mind a common misinterpretation of comprehensive services. During this period especially the client tends to ask for—and the architect may tend to give—legal advice. In expanding his services, the architect must never profess to be a lawyer or an educator. There is a fine line to be drawn between advising on the law, for instance, and citing one's own case histories in similar cases or advising on construction or design "practices of the trade." There may be planning or design or cost implications in an educational proposal, but this does not convert an architect into an educator.

Post-construction services are so seldom offered and carried out that they would appear to be expanded services and deserve special consideration. In the first place, the architect can provide a manual to the client for every building, on its completion, giving instructions on operation of equipment and maintenance of materials. On one campus these instructions, varying from building to building, were incorporated into a faculty and administration guide to the use of facilities. The collection of written guarantees and follow-up on all guarantee periods might very well be an established and valuable service performed for clients by the architect on every building he does.

Supporting Design Services

College campus planning often requires the special talents of urban planners and road and traffic designers; it always requires sanitary and utility design, landscape and site planning. Not only may fine artists be introduced for specific embellishment of projects, but often the advice of sculptors and painters may be integrated with the work of the architect's own design team in the development of the forms and colors of architectural components.

In some cases, consulting architects, who have a wealth of experience and knowledge in the special field of higher educational facilities, may be engaged. Their diverse experience and authoritative assurance may be so convincing to the Board that superior results are obtained.

A fundamental purpose of the architect's profession is to be of "ever-increasing service to society." The limits of his service are society's needs related to the development of man's environment. The architect can reach these limits of service if he attains three things:

1 Recognition of unfulfilled, related needs
2 Preparation for—or coordination of—competent services for fulfillment of these needs
3 His client's recognition of his ability to deliver and confidence in his organization

The Board and administration of a college will quickly recognize the value of comprehensive services, if they are convinced that the architect is prepared to handle such services effectively—and they will be found willing to pay for the services. The ultimate result should be better-satisfied clients and consumers and a better-served society.

15

Comprehensive Architectural Services: Bank Buildings

BY GEORGE F. PIERCE JR, FAIA

To architectural offices of all sizes—from the smallest to the largest—bank buildings present opportunities for comprehensive architectural practice, especially in such important areas as operations programming and planning

Opportunities for comprehensive services

Bank commissions offer architects, regardless of the size of their organizations, a great number of opportunities for rendering comprehensive architectural services. In the first place, a large number of banks are being constructed today; and nearly every architectural office finds itself, sooner or later, with a commission for a bank. Secondly, the bank client is not usually experienced in the coordination of design and construction of numerous projects for his institution, as an industrial or commercial corporation client might be. Hence, in a bank, there is normally no "built-in" departmental organization that may have completed economic, feasibility, financing, operational studies before the architect is called in.

Analysis, Promotional, Managerial Services

Often the architect will find himself in a position in which he can help a bank client establish whether or not a need exists for a remodeled or new bank facility. This can be accomplished by analyses of present operations, efficiency of existing methods of paper work and personnel flow, inter-relationships of departments to each other and to their present locations, adequacy of space allotted to employees and customers, the sufficiency of parking and drive-in banking facilities and of the general environment. Some architects may be astonished to discover how well qualified they are in these areas, if they will only take the time and effort to expose themselves to the realities of such problems first hand.

Establishment of needs

Economic analysis

After the completion of a thorough study of an existing banking operation, the architect will have on hand most of the information required for study and development of an economic analysis of the proposed project. He will then be in a position to advise his client on the probable costs of new or remodeled facilities and the prospect of a reasonable return on his investment. The architect should then be able to establish accurate estimates of new equipment required, personnel, the building area which will be required to operate efficiently now and in the projected future, and also the size and general type of site on which such a project should be located. From these facts, and with the assistance of qualified consultants and collaborators, an accurate projection of the scope and the cost of the entire facility can be easily completed.

Financial consultation

For a bank client, there will probably be little need for an architect to render financial advice. This is the specialty of the banker; so the architect will find the consultants for this phase built-in. Interim and long-range financing will almost certainly be smoothly organized and completed by the bank client. If not, the architect might well begin to worry about the reality of the entire business affair.

Land assembly

After feasibility studies have been completed, economic studies made and favorably considered, and financing has been assured, decisions to find and purchase a site and proceed with planning can be made. The architect, depending on the size and qualifications of his staff, can take on the responsibility of seeking for—and assembly of—the land for a site. The more usual role of the architect would probably be that of agent for his client for the purposes of retaining a qualified realtor, specifying the site qualifications required, reviewing the prospects which are available, and finally making a recommendation for purchase to the client. Certainly, the architect, in close consultation with his client, is better qualified than any other person to judge all of the many aspects of a prospective site for a specific job. This is especially true if the architect has already proceeded through the economic, feasibility and financial services previously outlined in this article.

Operational Programming

During the period of the search for—and purchase of—a proper site for a bank facility, the architect can save time by beginning the operations programming phase of his services. The results of this phase will have more to do with the eventual success or failure of the operations in a bank facility than any other responsibility the architect assumes. The results of operations programming also serve to demonstrate clearly the thorough understanding the architect has gained of a particular planning problem and its ideal functional solution—not only from the standpoint of his client's business philosophy, but from that of the personnel who will direct the bank's operations and from that of good banking practice. On the following page, typical banking operations are outlined in some detail.

Relationships between bank operations

Of course, the architect's knowledge that the functions outlined exist in most banking institutions will not, in itself, solve the problems. The architect must establish how these operations should work theoretically, before he can begin to relate the operations in their functions and before he can develop a plan concept. This requires close co-operation between architect and client.

Operational Design Services

Establishment of operational methods is best accomplished by means of diagrammatic studies of functional relationships and personnel and work flow. The operational diagram, shown on the following page, was developed for an actual bank planning project. It was finally accepted by both client and architect as the theoretical solution of the special problems of this particular bank only after a number of other such diagrams has been discussed and rejected or altered. It may be noted that both present and future personnel requirements are shown, together with the theoretical separation of floor levels dictated by site limitations. Before such a final, comprehensive diagram of a bank's operations program can be completed, the building occupancy requirements (both personnel and departmental) must be firmly established, site acquisition completed, and the basic philosophy of banking operations and building design must have been agreed upon.

If a banking institution is large enough to require it, the diagrammatic chart idea can be profitably carried a step further into studies of the theoretical functioning of each department.

After the departmental relationship and work flow diagrams have been completed and approved and a satisfactory site has been acquired, the design and construction phases of the project can be scheduled to fit the financing timetable. The architect can then proceed with the succeeding phases of his services, many of which he has performed traditionally. There should be no need to stress here the importance of recognition of the general environ-

Bank Operational Program Outline

Major banking operations can be divided into the following basic functions:

I Banking Floor
  A Public Spaces
    1 Circulation—ingress and egress
    2 Checkwriting desks, line-up space
    3 Lounge, waiting space
  B Tellers
    1 Commercial
    2 Savings
    3 Notes
  C Officers Platform
    1 Open desk space
    2 Private offices, conf. rooms
  D Access—Safe Deposit, Money vault

II Operations
  A Bookkeeping Department
  B Proof Department
  C Clerical, Mail, Record Vault

III Safe Deposit Vault
(may contain bank money vault)
  A Safe deposit boxes
  B Clerk-Receptionist
  C Coupon Booths

IV General Services
  A Toilet, Employees Lounges
  B Snack Bar
  C Mech. equip., Maintenance, PBX
  D General Storage

In addition, the following operations are often a part of the functional requirements of banks:

V Automobile Parking

VI Drive-in Tellers

VII Meeting Rooms
  A Board of Directors
  B Community
  C Employees

VIII Trust Department, Foreign Exchange, etc.

Operational plan for First National Bank, San Angelo, Texas; The Office of George Pierce—Abel Pierce, Architects and Planners; Lovett and Sellars, Associate Architects

BANK OPERATIONAL PLAN —
DEPARTMENTAL RELATIONSHIPS AND WORK FLOW

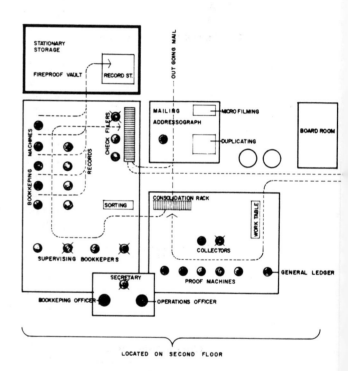

LOCATED ON SECOND FLOOR

LEGEND

ment of which the new structure will become a part, or of creating a building that will be a compatible asset to the surrounding community. And the influences of climate, materials, traffic patterns, approach vistas, effects of structures in close proximity to the site, etc, which are of such basic importance in good architectural design, probably should not even have to be mentioned. Yet only too often these factors are ignored, often resulting in a potentially good solution that has been ruined by oversight.

On the other hand, it will do no harm to re-emphasize the necessity for close cooperation and coordination of the entire

Cooperation, coordination important

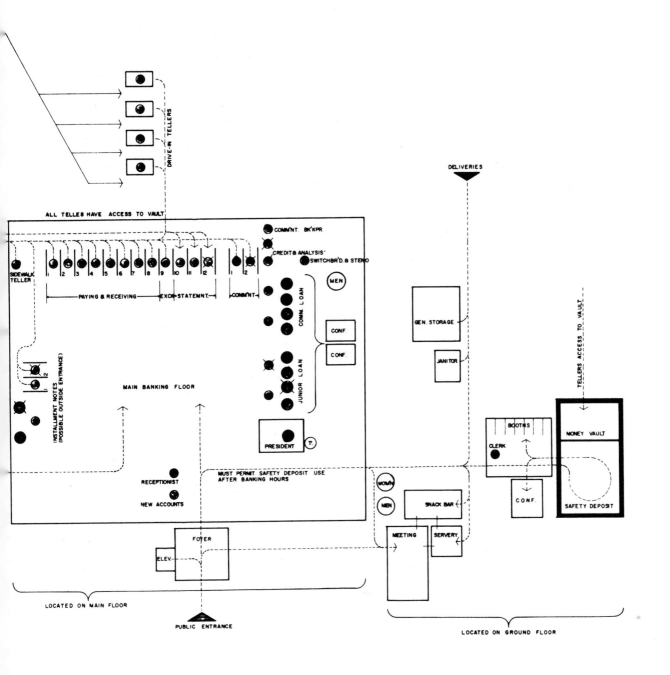

Supporting Services

design team during the development of preliminary designs, working drawings and specifications. Those professionals who are to be responsible for furnishings and furniture can—and should—contribute a great deal to the design and detailing of built-in tellers' counters, storage units, space dividers, and other bank fixtures. Architectural graphics should be integrated into the preliminary design concepts, and then followed through within the project based on the established criteria, not "stuck on" later wherever convenient locations can be found. Teller money-changing machines can be made an integral part of the counters, rather than placed on top later. Adding machines can be installed with their faces set flush in check-writing tables thereby reducing maintenance and accidental damage which may result when they are mounted in more exposed positions. File cabinets can be made into handsome space dividers through careful selection of styles and colors and by covering groups of them with smart looking and useful one-piece tops. Sculpture, murals and art work should be closely coordinated from the beginning. The potentials of architectural lighting may well be the least realized of all of the facets of good architectural design; in any case lighting is usually the last facet to be considered. And there are many ways to attain proper circulation of cooled or warmed air within building spaces, without the usual offensive and dull, symmetrical spacing of supply and return grilles on the ceiling, in the vertical enclosure surfaces, or at the window perimeter.

Construction Services

During construction, a bank project demands no unique or special services that ordinarily would not be rendered by any qualified architect on any quality building. Fine materials and finishes are usually specified for banks and can be attained only by meticulous observation of the contractor's work. However, the desire to fulfill the goal of total design of the physical banking environment requires something more than this. The purchase and installation of all fixtures and furniture should be professionally coordinated. Graphics should—and can—be controlled and well-designed, including building signs, large-scale instructional and directional materials, personnel identification markers, stationery, office forms, check books, promotional material and public advertising. It is really not impossible to carry off such a program, if the architect will make a positive effort to convince his client of the dividends he will receive at no added cost. A growing number of highly qualified independent interior consultants are currently striving for professional association with architectural firms. Capable graphic artists and designers are somewhat more difficult to find. However, the architect is better qualified than he is usually willing to admit to be a helpful advisor to his clients in their relationships with interior designers, artists and other such consultants.

Comprehensive architectural services for a banking institution, or for any number of other projects, really begin when the architect simply gets himself into the spirit of the control of total design and then does everything he can to perform effectively. Of course, this is an oversimplification of the facts. Yet architects are actually very well qualified indeed to fight for this important position at the center of things if they go on out and get their feet wet.

16

Comprehensive Architectural Services: Research & Development Buildings

BY ALBERT C. MARTIN, FAIA

Because it is one of the fastest growing fields of architectural interest and one in which original thought and pioneering are essential qualifications for success, the research and development building field offers architects unusual opportunities for the practice of comprehensive architectural services

Research and development has achieved its present high degree of significance to the public through dramatic space age endeavors such as missiles and electronics. Yet such industries as frozen foods, plastics, petroleum and medicine have long been engaged in—and heavily dependent on—research and development. In the 'thirties, about $200 million was spent annually on research and development; the present rate is about $12 billion; conservative estimates place the annual figure at about $30 billion in the 1970's

The creative mind is the cardinal determinant in designing the environment for research and development activities. Of course, for every effort such as office work, manufacturing, recreation, worship, etc, the surroundings must be created in accordance with the specific demands of the activity. But in no other phase of life are environmental necessities so exacting, so important, as they are in research and development.

It is not at all unusual to find that forty to fifty per cent of the total personnel force at a research and development facility are scientists, technicians or other highly trained professional people. The ratio of professional to semi-skilled or untrained employees rarely exceeds fifteen to one hundred in most other businesses.

Because of their background, education, social status and occupational positions, research and development personnel gravitate to stimulating surroundings, both at home and at work. This establishes three requisites for the architect: every part of the design must be of exceptional quality; buildings should be located in—and fully integrated with—a commercial area that is of comparable character; the facility should be close to residential neighborhoods that will be attractive to personnel.

New materials and techniques

Several other inherent characteristics must also guide the architect. First, the structures must be adaptable to new and unique building materials needed to facilitate scientific uses.

Importance of lighting

Another architectural characteristic of these buildings is the importance of light. Buildings must offer illumination control to eliminate glare and bring natural and artificial light into balance.

Need for flexibility

A third trait is the need for internal and external flexibility. This cannot be limited to the structural shell or the plan for interior partitioning; it must also become a part of all utility and comfort systems. By its very nature, research and development work is dynamic. Programs and projects are begun and completed within a period of a month, six months or perhaps a year or two.

Complex of buildings

Fourth on the list of characteristics is that an amalgam of structures is most practical, usually, for facilities of this type. The building complex must permit future subdivision of property. This increases the real value of the facility, eases the problems of initial financing and makes possible orderly incremental expansion. Most importantly, the scale of building masses becomes comfortable and psychologically acceptable.

Thus research and development design obviously places heavy restrictions and responsibilities on the architect. He must scrutinize sociological, topographical, scientific and labor factors, as well as construction technology and building costs. And time is often of paramount importance. In response to swiftly changing requirements, the architect must provide equally fast and flexible planning, design and engineering.

Comprehensive services required

In addition to the design of the physical structures, there are six paramount services which today's architect must be prepared to offer as an expert if he is to provide research and development clients with proper environment. He must be an evaluator of feasibility studies, a total-design consultant, an expert on space utilization, an innovator of new methods and materials, a supervisor of building economics and a participant in public relations counseling.

Analysis, Promotional, Managerial Services

A feasibility study is conducted for one infinitely significant purpose: to expose statistically—and make possible the evaluation of—factors that will affect the adjustment of an organization to its future environment. Two interrelated categories must be thoroughly explored: economics and physical planning.

Economic considerations

Economic aspects obviously include present and future land values, labor markets and zoning trends, as well as transportation facilities, peculiarities of surrounding land ownership and community relationships. For research and development clients, however, the architect is faced with obstacles not usually found in studies for a manufacturing plant or office building.

Site selection

Of first importance are the status and characteristics of the personnel who will work in the facility. Although a given site has many features perfectly suited to other types of organizations— easy accessibility, proper zoning and good community relationships potential—it will not be suitable for a research and development facility unless attractive residential areas, an appealing community, a quiet atmosphere and appropriate land-use trends are also evident. In the selection of a site, emphasis must be placed on environmental factors that will spur the creative mind.

Architect as coordinator

As the architect is the traditional designer of structures, it is only reasonable for clients to call on him to plan their immediate surroundings. Little by little, the architect has accumulated other responsibilities so that today he is involved in comprehensive services in such areas as engineering, planning, color coordination, interior design and literally anything else having to do with the physical aspects of a facility. In many of these areas, the architect's greatest value to his client and others is as a coordinator. He should not attempt to do the work of other professionals and specialists; rather he should serve as quasi-chairman of the planning team to counsel and systematize component efforts aimed at achieving a well-integrated, total result.

In coordinating total design, the architect can guide the development of the property through counsel on zone status, lease documents and community commitments for outside improvements. He might also recommend good traffic control patterns.

Expediting the work

Another contribution the architect makes as the coordinator of total design is in the encouragement of expeditious actions. In research and development work, swift technological advances, often coupled with unexpected demands for immediate solutions to pressing problems, require fast action by design and construction teams. If the architect has, in his organization, well-qualified planning and engineering groups, he will often be better able to offer expeditious—as well as thoroughly coordinated—services. Some architects may disagree with the concept of the planning-architecture-engineering organization, but considerable evidence exists of the effectiveness of such an arrangement for design, efficiency, speed and control, especially in research and development work.

Design and Planning Services

When surroundings are being designed for the creative mind, care must be taken with the relationships of one internal space to another, of internal to external spaces and of one external part to another. It must be remembered, however, that the fluctuating nature of research and development activities also demands interior and exterior flexibility. Today's satisfactory spatial criteria may not suit tomorrow's project. And esthetic appeal, a cardinal element, must come from orderly and well-proportioned space relationships in and around the buildings.

To meet these research and development stipulations, the architect should first establish a system of unit components. Beginning with careful consideration of the spatial and environmental needs of the individual man, needs will evolve into basic patterns or systems of space units. Combinations of these basic units will then evolve through further study. Finally, the complex of spaces must be organized to meet the requirements of a division; then division by division, they must be arranged to serve the whole.

Modules and clusters

If it is assumed that a module of four feet has been found most suitable for a system of given space units, a typical office might contain twelve four-by-four modules. A representative cluster might have approximately ninety modules subdivided into a number of combinations of offices. Incidentally, the space of this cluster might be the ideal size for a single laboratory should reassignment of space become necessary.

Psychological considerations

Several techniques can be employed within research and development structures to comfort the eye and mind. Mental fatigue is greatly alleviated or precluded by providing the eye with a combination of long- and short-vision ranges. Corridors or long rooms should not, if possible, terminate with a blank wall; a door, window, or stairway should punctuate the wall. Wall perforations also eliminate the closed-in, contained atmosphere which encumbers the creative mind.

Exterior glass walls might well be used generously in research and development buildings, especially for small offices and work spaces. Changing panoramas add interest and relieve boredom, mental fatigue and feelings of extreme seclusion. However, care must be exercised to avoid harsh extremes. A sea of automobiles, a blanket of concrete or a monotonous series of structures should not meet the eye which just before was focused on close work in a laboratory, drafting room or research office.

Master planning

Research and development spatial requirements can be properly met, particularly if the project is a complex which can be master planned. For example, properly spaced rectangular buildings, at right angles to each other, serve as jetties into parking lots, limit the sizes of lawns, facilitate foot and auto traffic, and add a fresh perspective to the structures. As in all architecture, each project has its own individual set of peculiarities and specifications that distinguish it from all others.

Configuration and placement

The choice of structural configurations and building placement patterns for research and development facilities depends heavily on psychological demands, but there are other requirements which must also be met. The architect must remember the kinetic nature of the activities to be housed, the usual requisite for plans that will permit future subdivision, and, of course, costs. To satisfy all of these needs, the architect might well eliminate all but linear buildings from consideration, with the exception of special-purpose structures. Circular, oval or other exotic shapes are very rarely suitable for research and development work for they make interior flexibility almost impossible to achieve, initial and maintenance costs prohibitive and land-use inefficient.

Nearly all types of building products are manufactured in linear shapes—rectangles and squares. Therefore, initial construction costs are likely to be kept at a minimum if the structure adheres to the straight-line principle, and future replacement of glass sections, wood paneling, acoustical tile and other mass-produced materials is likely to be easier and less expensive.

In a research and development complex, building duplication, when appropriate, adds cohesiveness and rhythm, but a series of look-alike buildings should be interrupted with an architectural surprise to avoid monotony. This might be achieved by introducing into the complex a taller building, a mall-pool combination, a structure offering a strong contrast of materials or shape.

New methods and materials

Research and development architecture has, in a few short years, broken many of the shackles which have bound architects and builders to accepted construction techniques and material applications. This is largely due to the leadership of the young, imaginative men and women who are engaged in research and development work. Their willingness to try new things and their recognition of the fluidity of space needs tend to overflow into their relationships with architects and builders. A notable example of this is the "concurrency approach" to design and construction, which was developed to provide high quality buildings in the least possible time. This approach calls for the architect to expand his services to a point just short of actually entering the general contracting field. In the concurrency approach, the architect and

Concurrency approach to design and construction

builder combine efforts with the client to a degree seldom witnessed in other architectural work.

Design during construction

Essentially, the concurrency approach requires crystallizing the interior arrangements of the building while the shell is being constructed. When the concurrency approach is employed for major research and development projects, design and construction programming becomes so complex that new scheduling techniques, such as the critical path method, offer attractive advantages. When using the concurrency approach, the architect must freeze the arrangements of the building step by step, during construction, usually just one or two steps ahead of the working crews. Close collaboration between the architect, general contractor and client representatives is essential. It is not at all unusual to have formal client-builder-architect conferences on the site every week to study, in minute detail, construction progress and future scheduling.

Importance of schedules

Concurrency necessitates the creation of closely-knit, perfectly calibrated schedules of building phases, to allow pre-purchase of long-lead equipment, chronological determination of specific work by trades, the time expected to be consumed by each phase, continued approval by municipal building inspectors and timely incorporation of design information.

New materials and their uses, limitations, advantages and costs must always be uppermost in the research and development architect's mind. He must search constantly for materials that will provide better control of acoustics, vibration, glare, temperature and foreign particle infiltration. He should be easily accessible to building-product suppliers who are engaged in the search for—and development of—improved materials. The architect may even find it necessary to establish his own research and development department to study potentials of untried products, or to compare the qualities of several items under consideration.

Building economics

Unlike most other projects, original costs of research and development structures should be computed per employee, not on a square foot or other basis. Since it deals solely with men and their creativity, the over-all research and development budget for operations is keyed to the cost per man. The architect must follow this line of thought when he computes building costs.

Studies indicate that the weekly payroll of a research and development facility is equal to approximately one dollar per square foot. In terms of rental, a $20 per-square-foot facility costs the employer about $12 per week for each employee, including maintenance, taxes, a reasonable return on invested capital, etc. Some companies in the research and development field estimate their costs for recruitment of qualified technical personnel at about $1,200 per employee. Therefore, the architect has a serious responsibility to his client to create a working environment which will attract and hold such high caliber people.

Need for continued cost reporting

As previously discussed, the architect, general contractor and client will ordinarily meet on the site periodically to consider research and development building progress. The agenda for such discussions should include cost reporting. Frequent appraisals of expenses will help educate the client with regard to cost factors and will preclude financial surprises upon job completion.

*Economics of
specialized requirements*

Research and development structures have special elements that are not usually found in other types of construction—huge test chambers, clean rooms, specialized laboratories and the like. These elements have resulted in a need for further expansion of architectural practice. They have also created new cost factor problems. When working on these new elements, the architect must serve as a coordinator of specialists, in fields ranging from cryogenics to thermodynamics. In addition to the scientific knowledge supplied by these consultants, the architect gains information from them that has a direct bearing on the construction costs.

Many people contend that such specialized phases of research and development planning should be entirely within the realm of company engineers. It must be remembered, however, that research and development engineers are usually too close to their own specific problems and projects to allow them to be objective about actual costs. And sometimes because of their subconscious desire to have their efforts appear to cause as little burden as possible to the firm, such engineers tend to understate the complexity of their problems. However, the architect will be in a position to evaluate specific parts of the whole project and render objective advice on budgetary allotments for each.

Public relations services

Assistance by the architect with public relations activities for a research and development project differs from that for other types of buildings primarily in degree of importance and in the speed of execution.

Drama surrounds research and development work. There is a hunger for information and interpretation. It is not a simple matter to translate the highly technical purposes and meanings of research and development work into the vernacular. Persistent and coordinated efforts by the client, with the assistance of the architect and his public relations representative, can remove much of the obscurity from these activities.

Communication with the public

The architect can help prepare a community for a new research and development facility by showing renderings and models of the physical plant, pointing out its architectural features, emphasizing the caliber of personnel to be drawn to it, noting the financial contributions to the area through taxes and pay checks, and calling attention to the community as a desirable location. Every communication medium, such as personal contacts, speeches and the printed word, should be employed even before the facility is constructed.

In public relations, the architect can increase his value to the client and the builder by recommending courses of action designed to preclude negative situations. For example, he might suggest routes trucks and construction equipment should take to avoid travel through residential neighborhoods or he might outline plans for easing traffic flow to the completed project.

Architects should contribute information for company-sponsored public announcements, groundbreaking ceremonies, dedications and open houses. This will reduce the chance for errors, by the architecturally uninformed, in descriptions of the complex—misstatements which might injure the positive climate desired for the facility, as well as the architect's own professional reputation.

Comprehensive Architectural Services for a Research, Development, Engineering, and Manufacturing Project

Space Technology Center. Owner—Space Technology Laboratories, Inc., a subsidiary of Thompson Ramo Wooldridge, Inc, Redondo Beach, California. Albert C. Martin and Associates, Architects and Engineers. Phase one, now complete, includes three "R" buildings housing research, laboratories and computer centers, an engineering building, a manufacturing plant and a cafeteria-service unit. Phase two will add two "R" buildings, office building and a library-auditorium

An abbreviated case history of a research and development facility will serve to illustrate some of the principles of comprehensive architectural services for such projects. Each research and development project will have a specific set of circumstances and requirements unlike those of any other. However, the elements and considerations faced by the architects of this project are revealing of the process involved in the creation of a proper atmosphere for the creative mind.

In close cooperation with Robert A. Burgin, director of administrative operations for Space Technology Laboratories, Inc, the architectural firm assisted with the compilation of comprehensive economic and physical feasibility studies. Ten sites were examined in the context of the client's requirements. The final choice was a 110-acre site in Redondo Beach. The site is near, but not directly adjacent to, several good residential neighborhoods, close to a new freeway and four miles from Los Angeles International Airport. Thoroughfares surrounding the land were found adequate. Zoning trends and land-use patterns promised an immediate and future environment amicable to the client's needs.

Purchase of the property was followed immediately by the preparation of a master plan for a complex of structures, which, even if future subdivision should be necessary, would be entirely autonomous. The plan provided for a set of buildings that would also satisfy the high degree of flexibility and effective space relationships required by the large number of scientists and technicians.

Analyses of Special Research, Development Building Problems

In order to define the size and configuration of typical buildings, the architects made a study (across-page, top) to evaluate the merits of various configurations and to determine the most suitable dimensions for the prototype research (R) buildings. This chart deals with efficiency of form (ratio of wall area to floor area in square feet), space relationships in terms of extreme radius, space factors and per cent of circulation.

Based on these studies, an approximate size of 125,000 square feet was selected for the "R" buildings. The architect recommended a central core of laboratories, flanked by peripheral office clusters, based on modular techniques with utility systems designed accordingly and full-height movable interior partitions. All recommendations were accepted by the client. Originally, L-shaped structures were considered but it was found that a better master plan would result with rectangular buildings.

In order to provide the best possible mixture of natural and artificial lighting, the architects consulted with Foster Sampson, a specialist in illumination techniques. In order to achieve the fourteen per cent light infiltration recommended, the architects built several scale models for testing a variety of glass types, as well as combinations of types of glass and other materials. To rate the results of these studies, the architects prepared a chart (across-page, bottom) which demonstrated that the most desirable arrangement was a window wall of gray glass with an overhang supporting panels of gray glass as shown in the diagram below.

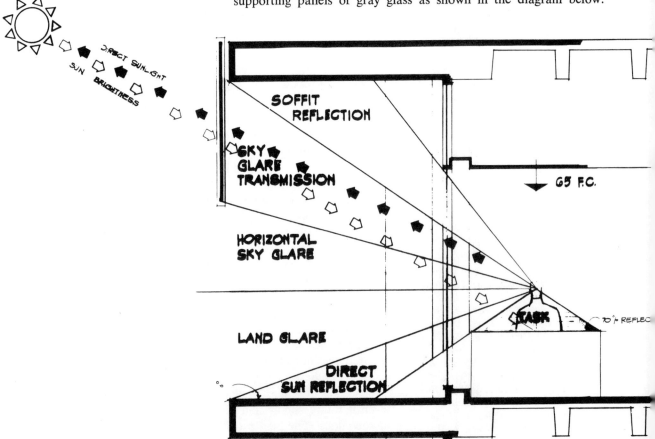

PROTOTYPE ANALYSIS—TWO STORY BUILDING

SUN SHADE STUDY

■ FIRST CHOICE

▨ SECOND CHOICE

100,000 SQ.FT.	☐	▭	8	L	T	✚
A. EFFICIENCY OF FORM SQ.FT.WALL AREA:SQ.FT.FLR.AREA	.233:1	.256:1	.385:1	.294:1	.333:1	.298:1
B. SPACE RELATIONSHIP EXTREME RADIUS (FT.)	164	172	169	250	178	156
C. SPACE FACTOR CONTIGUOUS AREAS	2×50,000	2×50,000	4×25,000	4×25,000	6×16,667	8×12,500
D. CIRCULATION %	17.8	18.0	21.3	20.5	18.7	19.7

125,000 SQ.FT.						
A. EFFICIENCY OF FORM SQ.FT.WALL AREA:SQ.FT.FLR.AREA	.218:1	.222:1	.357:1	.256:1	.270:1	.294:1
B. SPACE RELATIONSHIP EXTREME RADIUS (FT.)	176	192	192	244	178	157
C. SPACE FACTOR CONTIGUOUS AREAS	2×62,500	2×62,500	4×31,250	4×31,250	6×20,833	8×15,625
D. CIRCULATION %	26.0	18.0	18.8	23.5	18.6	21.2

SUN SHADE STUDY

SUN SHADE	WINDOW WALL	TASK FC FL		DIRECT SUN REFLECTION	LAND GLARE	HORIZONTAL SKY GLARE	SKY GLARE TRANS.	SOFFIT REFLECTION	DIRECT SUNLIGHT	SUN BRIGHTNESS
Ⓐ SOLEX 76%	CLEAR	366	256	1500 FL.	500 FL.	2500 FL.	1900 FL.	480 FL.	3040 FC	64,500 FL
Ⓑ SOLAR GREY 42%	"	324	227	1500	500	2500	1050	480	1680	35,600
Ⓒ GREY-LITE #14 14%	"	288	202	1500	500	2500	350	480	560	11,900
Ⓓ OPAQUE (WHITE BACK)	"	281	197	1500	500	2500	200	480	0	0
Ⓐ SOLEX 76%	SOLAR GREY 42%	188	132	630	210	1050	795	200	1280	27,100
Ⓑ SOLAR GREY 42%	"	170	119	630	210	1050	440	200	723	14,860
Ⓒ GREY-LITE #14 14%	"	156	109	630	210	1050	147	200	236	5,000
Ⓓ OPAQUE (WHITE BACK)	"	152	106	630	210	1050	84	200	0	0
Ⓐ SOLEX 76%	GREY-LITE #14 14%	107	75	210	70	350	266	67	425	9,020
Ⓑ SOLAR GREY 42%	"	101	71	210	70	350	147	67	235	4,980
Ⓒ GREY-LITE #14 14%	"	96	68	210	70	350	45	67	78	1,660
Ⓓ OPAQUE (WHITE BACK)	"	95	67	210	70	350	28	67	0	0
⅜" SOLEX 64%	¼" SOLEX 76%	279	202	1,140	380	1,900	1,220	365	1,970	41,300
¼" SOLEX 76%	¼" SOLEX 76%	300	210	1,140	380	1,900	1,300	365	2,330	49,020

**The Concurrency System
of Design and Construction**

Time was of the essence in the construction of this job; accordingly, the concurrency or design-during-construction technique was employed. Successful use of the technique was made possible by close cooperation between the architects, the general contractor and the client. The result was a remarkable compression of the time of conception, planning and execution of the project. Excavation was commenced while building design was still on the drawing board. As each phase was completed, drawings for the next were made available for immediate action in the field. In this manner, nearly 640,000 square feet of building space were made ready for occupancy in a total design and construction time of less than fourteen months.

Comprehensive services of the sort that has been described for the research and development industry hold many rewards for the architect, not the least of which is more complete and effective service. As the principal member of the design-construction team, the architect may reach a new peak of professional status. Relationships between architects, clients, builders, subcontractors, landscape architects, interior designers, etc, can be closer and more compatible than ever before.

Everything indicates that the architect's role in research and development projects will continue to grow in importance; and it seems reasonable to predict that the architect will become more engaged in the scientific approach in order to provide a superior environment for science and industry.

Part Three:

The Architect and His Client

17

Comprehensive Architectural Services: The Architect and His Client

BY DUDLEY HUNT JR, AIA

Comprehensive architectural practice helps make it possible for the architect to understand his newer types of clients better, to work with them more harmoniously, to satisfy their expanding and changing needs effectively

The general characteristics of many of the important clients of today are: 1) They are organizations rather than individuals; 2) They are controllers of buildings rather than owners; 3) They are providers of space for others rather than occupiers of space; 4) They tend to be big and complex; 5) They are primarily concerned with buildings that are good business. The role of the architects, when working with these clients, is to serve their needs so effectively that good design becomes good business.

Architects have a new client, or rather they have several. Of course, the old familiar client—the individual owner who builds for his own use—is still around, but with every succeeding year, he is responsible for a smaller portion of the total amount of building construction. The new clients of the architect are organizations instead of individuals; they build, not for their own use, but the use of others; and they build more and more each year.

Perhaps the most familiar of the new clients are the corporation, the government agency and the institution, but there are also the entrepreneur—speculator or investor—and the industrial producer of complete buildings or their components. The entrepreneur and the industrial producer, having come on the scene later than the others, are therefore less familiar. This does not make them any less important. Architects are finding that an increasing number of projects are initiated by entrepreneurs, and if architects are to serve such clients, it becomes necessary for them to learn the business, so to speak. Industrial production of buildings and components will surely increase in the future. If the architect is to influence the future of this field, he must learn its fundamental principles and gain an understanding of this new type of client.

Needs of the new clients

In common with all others, the new types of clients need a high level of performance in the basic design-working drawing-specifications-construction sequence of architectural services. And they want their buildings to do the jobs for which they are intended, efficiently and profitably. Often they want the buildings fast and, almost always, within strict budgets. In addition, most of these clients want—and need—some of the phases of comprehensive architectural services. Such needs vary between clients and between projects but, in general, each of the new clients needs assistance with some combination of financial, site, operational, promotional and similar problems. And they are going to get such help somewhere, if not from architects and their staffs or consultants, then from non-architectural sources.

Smaller offices can serve the new clients

In order to avoid any misunderstanding, it should be pointed out that the type of comprehensive services needed by the new clients is not the exclusive province of large, diversified architectural firms. Many of the new clients can get along very well indeed with the services of smaller offices, if they are geared to their client's needs. Perhaps the best example of this is the homebuilder market. Much of this work, when it is handled by architects at all, is performed by smaller offices. It goes without saying that the overriding task of these architects is to sell builders on the merits of good design. It is no less important for these architects to understand the business problems of builders and to assist them in every way possible to solve their problems. In fact, this might very well be the one most important avenue toward better design in houses.

Needs of the homebuilder

In the August 1963 issue of *House & Home,* the need of the homebuilder for comprehensive services is illustrated very well. While discussing the growth of "design" companies that do everything for homebuilders except construct and sell the houses, Walt Wagner points out that these companies ". . . provide not just design but land planning, feasibility studies and market analysis, design of model homes and sales offices, landscape design and coordination, color-coordination and display boards, interior decoration, financing advice, and merchandising and promotion counsel. . . ."

What is being described here sounds suspiciously like comprehensive architectural services for builders, but in this case, the services are being delivered by others, not by architects. That the need exists is demonstrated, in the same article, by the fact that one of these "design" firms has been in existence for over eighteen years and has designed over half a million houses. Another, started five years ago, has already had $380 million worth of houses built from its designs.

The other new clients also need some degree of comprehensive architectural services. This will be dealt with in detail, in other articles, by authors who have had a great deal of experience with these clients. Only an attempt to establish the general context for the details—a broad look at the whole spectrum of these clients—is in order here.

Client Characteristic No 1: Organization, Not Individual

What are these clients like? In the first place, they tend to be multiple, rather than singular, organizations rather than individuals. The architect who works with them must deal with a client group rather than an individual client. This may be a relatively homogeneous board of directors of a corporation or a corporate building department. At other times, the group may not actually be unified at all, in any real sense, but rather a loose confederation of individuals or corporations, each with its own interests to serve. In one recent project in the million-dollar class, the major interests involved were two independent developers, two real estate agencies and two investors—and a law firm apiece. Finding himself with what amounted to six clients, four of them corporations, represented by six law firms, it should come as no surprise that the architect immediately brought in an associate architect and their his attorneys, in an attempt to improve the odds. In larger projects, particularly those for sale and leaseback, the situation is often even more complex.

Client Characteristic No 2:
Not Owner, but Controller

In most cases, the new clients are not owners, in the usual sense of the word, but controllers of buildings; and this in many cases, for only short periods of time. The simple fact is that many of the projects put together by entrepreneurs, whether for themselves or for others, are sold as soon as the tax laws make their sale feasible. Some are held as investments, but the tendency even here is for such buildings to change hands often. Even corporate, institutional and government clients are controllers, not owners, of buildings since—in theory at least—they build in the name of their stockholders, their members or the public. And there is also a growing tendency for all of these clients to make use of the sale-leaseback. It should also be pointed out that all of these new clients build, not with their own, but with other people's money.

Client Characteristic No 3:
Providers, Not Occupiers

Many of the new clients are not occupants of the buildings with which they become involved; rather they are arrangers, or providers, of space to be occupied by others. It is scarcely necessary to point out that the attitudes of such clients will vary considerably from the attitudes of the older type of client who builds his own building for his own use. Of course, there is also a difference in attitude between the client who expects to hold his property as a relatively long-term investment and the one who expects to sell it as soon as he can do so profitably.

Client Characteristic No 4:
Large Size and Complexity

The new clients are apt to be characterized by such traits as bigness and complexity. And the tendency is for them to get bigger and more complex. Growth and diversification—almost synonymous with bigness and complexity—are probably the most prevalent characteristics of corporations today. This seems also to be true of the entrepreneurs, the producers (most are corporations) and the institutions (labor unions are perhaps the best example). Surely all will agree that government, on every level, is also in a period of rapid growth in size and complexity.

None of this should be taken to mean that the new clients are only concerned with buildings of great size. As has been pointed out, the homebuilder is one of the most important of these clients, especially to the smaller architectural office, exactly because he constructs a sizable number of small buildings. Furthermore, the producer of relatively large numbers of relatively small buildings, or of even smaller components, can be expected to become an increasingly important architectural client.

Client Characteristic No 5:
Concern with Business

Finally, it seems fitting to round out this general discussion of the new clients by referring to their almost universal primary concern when they engage the services of the architect—that is their concern with the business of architecture or, more properly, with the business of construction. Almost without exception, the new clients are engaged in business. Understandably, business being what these clients know best, it is also what they think is important above all other considerations. Accordingly, the new clients expect their architects, not only to "speak the language" of business, but to have a proper, that is to say "healthy," attitude toward the necessities of business. This is not to say that these clients are averse to good design, if it is also good business. It is up to the architect to prove that good design can be good business.

Necessary to prove that good design is good business

18

The Architect in the Business World

BY LEO A. DALY, AIA

In order to practice effectively today, architects must be able to perform their professional services within a business environment, for businessmen

Not less, but more

Whether he realizes it—or likes it—or not, today's effective architect is an entirely different kind of professional practitioner than he would have thought possible during his years of university training. Client needs have expanded dramatically in the past fifteen or twenty years. Because of this there is a diminishing market for the services of the architect who ignores changing trends, who fails to acquire the competence to handle new requirements or who remains unresponsive to the need for satisfying the increasingly complex demands of his clients. The plain truth is that the always challenging profession of architecture has also become a lively business. It is not that the architect need be *less* of an *artist;* rather, the challenges of his environment compel him to be *more* of a *universal man.*

Because the architect is in fact a professional, the practice of architecture tends to be held in high regard by the business community. This does not mean that all practicing architects inspire the same degree of confidence among businessmen. Clients, by and large, are business-oriented, whether they are corporation executives, institutional administrators or government officials. Such clients expect businesslike associations and reasonable returns on their investments in the architect's professional services. To win their confidence and obtain desirable commissions, the architect must share their concern for the practical considerations characteristic of the business world. The architect who yearns to live alone in a dream world unpeopled by clients who expect rigorous acceptance of the standards of modern business practice resembles a surgeon who never performs an operation or a teacher without students.

Complications in architecture parallel complications in world

As life and living, commerce and finance, education and government have become more complicated, so has the practice of architecture. Because some in the profession elect to remain aloof from the main stream of massive change, competition from nonprofessional sources has flooded into the void. Hand-wringing, brooding or expressions of bewilderment are no substitute for recognition that such competition flourishes because it provides a range of services that the businessman-client wants and finds familiar. Enterprise is a welcome talent in any marketplace. And the architect-entrepreneur wins his commissions with the services he offers.

Historically, the practice of architecture has never been without its pitfalls, but it is a good deal harder to bring an appreciative smile to the client's face today than was the case only a few years ago. A few years back it was a rare architect who even dreamed of being asked for his advice on market analysis, financing, land assembly, programming, insurance or taxation. Now this is not at all uncommon. For example, a school board has promotional problems; the board favors the design and construction of a new school. The pupil population is skyrocketing. What can·be done to obtain a favorable outcome in an upcoming vote on an enabling bond issue? The board is composed of a group of public-spirited private citizens who are convinced that the new school is a community necessity. But how, they ask, can they convince their fellow citizens that the funds should be forthcoming?

The architect can; he should; and he often does. Knowledge of school population growth projections, residential building trends, likely street construction, techniques of issuing bonds and amortizing public debts and types of structures best suited to particular communities represent part of the architectural firm's services. The architect can give professional counsel on the preparation of promotional materials that will clearly explain both the community requirement and the program for financing the project, that will contribute to the success of the bond issue and that will facilitate timely construction of the school. Residual effects of such services are the enhancement of the image of the profession and the improvement of the architect's chances of being selected for future commissions.

How architects can cope with the new needs

In order to cope successfully with the diversified demands that are commonly placed upon him today, the architect may either obtain specialized assistance from outside consultants or he may enlarge his own firm to include the increasingly comprehensive range of services that so many clients now require. It would appear that the lion's share of such work will go, more and more, to the firms which are expanding their staffs and services, especially to those firms whose personnel have learned how to talk the language of the executive or administrator with confidence born of experience. A fairly recent phenomenon seems to be that many clients prefer to turn to a single firm for services that they were once satisfied to receive from several sources. The practice of many architects has been developed accordingly. In any event, architects whose practices have survived since World War II have had to make decisions with respect to the comprehensiveness of their services.

Need for continuing attention to the market for architecture

The laws of economics apply to the architect as they do to all mankind. Consequently, the architect must keep an attentive eye upon his market if he is to make sure that his personal services remain in demand. As demand changes in scope, the architect must review the quality of his own product. Quality, however, is a product of courage, energy and aggressiveness as well as talent and good taste. The astute architect advances the interests of the architectural profession generally when, by his diligence and ingenuity, he succeeds in fulfilling his client's expectations by supplementing skill in design with whatever peripheral services may reasonably be required. The mutual respect between client and architect that can develop from comprehensive practice may, in fact, result in greater freedom for architectural design. Indeed, those architects who recognize the conditions of the times and engage in comprehensive practice find themselves better equipped to insist upon standards of esthetic excellence and, in this way, make important contributions to the restoration of quality in architecture.

The architect who understands the importance of remaining within the budgets, of controlling costs and of adhering to deadlines is not going to lose friends among his clients. If, in addition, his firm qualifies as a source of prudent advice on such matters as real estate acquisition, zoning ordinances, site planning, financial procedures, business law, economic feasibility or the engineering disciplines, the architect can earn for himself an extra measure of esteem. If a client can see in his architect a man with managerial ability, a man with esthetic values who is at home in the business world and conversant with other professional fields, the increased confidence of that client is likely to cause him to give his architect a greater degree of freedom for creative expression in design. On the other hand, the architect who expects to prosper in professional practice, without providing the broadened services that once might have been called fringe activities, is likely to find his world of design a world of continually contracting horizons.

Need for participation in the life of the community

It is mostly by the things that the individual architect says and does—and by the range of his personal participation in community life—that he and architectural practice in general become known to clients and the public. Without active participation on a broader scale than that usually expected of those in other pursuits, the architect may fail both to fulfill the role for which he was trained and to project the image of professional competence which is basic to popular confidence in architects.

Need for explanation of architecture to those outside the profession

There is much in the press and in popular literature about science, industry and government and about some of the professions. But, frankly, even the well-read executive finds little about architecture or the men of architecture in the course of his normal reading. Nor can the younger generation readily find much information about architecture. Splendid books are available about virtually everything else, but it is next to impossible to think of good books about architecture which might be appropriately recommended to an interested young man. The point is that architecture is little-known and poorly understood by most people who otherwise are literate, competent and well-informed about the world around them. This being the case, the architect has some high hurdles to overcome if he is to advance his profession and make his own practice and particular talents known to those who need his services.

*Expanded professional
responsibilities*

Most architects will readily acknowledge that they have a professional responsibility to make real contributions to the world around them. For most, this contribution is properly confined to limited geographic areas. However, if he is to be a comprehensive man truly, an architect certainly will have to participate in activities beyond the confines of his own office. He will have to undertake useful services for his community. There is little doubt that the extent of his involvement in community life will be, in a significant proportion, a measure of the effectiveness and impact of his entire career. The need for community participation is great. The opportunities are many. The work is demanding. The returns in terms of personal satisfaction and community recognition can be rewarding beyond the belief of those who have resisted taking the plunge.

Who, other than the architect, is under a greater obligation to make a generous contribution of his time and talents to his fellow citizens? With a sound academic training, a sense of good order, an intimate knowledge of the arts, expertise in design and planning and the experience of daily contact with the practical problems of private and public clients, the architect is a welcome addition—and can make important contributions—to an inviting range of activities which reflect the academic, institutional, intellectual, artistic, civic, charitable and even the financial and public service life of the community. Many thoughtful architects do involve themselves constructively in the lifestream of their communities. Too many others retire after graduation to dead-end streets where they spin dreams about clients who they are sure will inevitably learn of their unexercised architectural talents.

*Need for better
communication with the public*

There once was a day when even great kings went to their barbers for delicate and painful surgery. Today, some clients choose to assign commissions to dealers who have about as much professional relationship to architecture as does a barber to modern medicine. There were compelling reasons for an ailing king to look to his barber for relief in a time when serious surgery was an unknown element in the practice of most physicians. Today, however, when architectural practice is unequalled in its potential, when the challenges of coherent environmental design are the concern of a great many thoughtful men, it is a failure in communications, rather than deficiency in talent, that prevents the services of some segments of the architectural profession from being utilized to solve the needs of the building public.

*Role of the architect as
creator and manager*

By virtue of his training in the building arts and sciences, the architect, traditionally, has considered his role to be that of the creator of living and working environments. This tradition remains at the very heart of current practice. Responsive to the demands of changing times and new managerial practices, the architectural profession is now equipped to supplement the familiar basic services with a range of business-oriented skills. A profound respect for design and a pervasive concern for esthetic values must remain as the inspirational core of modern practice. For these are qualities that signify the professionalism of architects; and they dignify the agency relationships between clients and architects. These are qualities that responsible clients admire and need. Through comprehensive services, the architects have an unparalleled opportunity to earn the respect of clients, acquire control of projects and provide clients with quality architecture.

Need for acceptance of authority and responsibility

The new architect faces a practical problem which is not unlike that of a company executive who must somehow convince the buying public that his product now is better, that something new has been added. Clearly, the architect engaged in comprehensive practice can point with pride to the fact that—in his case—something new has been added. The market has demanded changes in architectural practice. Aggressive members of the profession are responding. To the basic services of design, production and supervision, comprehensive practice adds the managerial analytical, fiscal, promotional or operating elements that serve to satisfy the client's particular needs from conception to completion. This is the organizational pattern for which the businessman has been—haltingly, perhaps—searching. Within his own company, the businessman has become accustomed to pinpointing authority and responsibility—and he has become accustomed to control. In his agent, the architect heading a comprehensive firm, the businessman sees a professional who also can effect control. This elevates the role of the architect to a level from which he can organize and coordinate; no longer is he solely a designer railing at arbitrarily imposed limitations on his creativity. Neither will he be a broker frantically reconciling conflicting interests. Rather, through delegation, he will be the possessor of the authority of his client. Comprehensive services qualify him to be entrusted with this authority. Authority leads to control. Control gives the architect the power to administer and create.

Comprehensive architectural services must become known in the marketplace

Coordinating authority, based on client confidence, is the cornerstone of comprehensive professional practice. The major problem in this, right now, is for the effective practitioner to make the expanded character of his practice known in the marketplace. This matter is of critical importance to all, not only to the larger firms which retain permanent staffs of personnel experienced in both professional and related services, but to all architects. There never was a better public advertisement for an architect's work than a fine building set in a gracious environment. Unfortunately, the design of an admirable building is only one of the helpful ingredients of an effective practice. To keep work coming in these days, the architect must enter the marketplace and make a case for his professional talents. Even within the reasonable constraints of professional standards, too many architects fumble the opportunities they have to market their services. Otherwise, how to explain the costly buildings all over the nation which are being constructed without the services of architectural firms? How to account for the fact that some professional firms manage a full roster of clients and a high business volume while other talented practitioners have to struggle to keep themselves profitably occupied?

The architect must continue as custodian of the public's esthetic values, but if he wishes to remain solvent, he must make his new comprehensive role recognizable in the marketplace.

19

Marketing the Services
of Architects

BY D'ORSEY HURST *

How to organize basic and comprehensive architectural services for growth, profitability and efficient, stabilized practice that will meet needs of clients

*The author is a management consultant who has had broad experience with architects and others who offer services, and is president of D'Orsey Hurst & Company, Management Consultants—Business Research

Establishing a stable economic environment

Goals for practice

In order to turn out a good product you must have a stable economic environment. This is just as true when the product is architecture as when it is an automobile. Establishing a stable economic environment requires a continuity of commissions, and this continuity in turn requires that your firm be organized to compete. Without dwelling on the subject of competition, perhaps it is enough to point out that you not only compete with your fellow architects but, as you no doubt know, with the whole gamut of so-called "specialists" in everything from construction to the manufacture of building products.

Another way of saying all this is: you've got to acquire commissions; you've got to build, maintain and control an organization to execute these commissions, and finally, you must operate efficiently and at a profit. However, the main subject here is the acquisition of commissions; yet this in turn calls for review of your business development program—the "where" and "how" of selling architectural services.

Maybe it is best to begin by asking yourself some questions: Am I satisfied with my present volume of work? Am I satisfied with the composition of my current practice? With the types of projects and extent of my participation in these projects? Is my current practice stimulating to me, to my associates and to the bright, younger staff men whom my firm must attract and hold in order to prosper?

If I am not satisfied with things as they are, where do I want to be? In other words, what are my goals? It is no doubt safe to assume most architects want stability as well as growth. If this is so, then how do. I want to grow; in volume, in profitability, in terms of a more diversified practice?

Specialized or general practice

For example, growth, as a specialist in one—or a few—building types, may offer stability since specialists seem always to be in demand. This avenue may therefore satisfy growth and profitability. However, there are obvious limitations in such a practice—in terms of holding on to well-qualified staff members who demand stimulating and challenging assignments. Also there is the risk of becoming overweighted in one direction and thereby running the risk of losing the ability to provide the comprehensive services possible in a full-scale architectural firm.

Comprehensive architectural practice

The decision may be to grow in the direction of comprehensive architectural practice. This may be necessary for sheer self-preservation since more and more of the architect's work is being taken away by non-architects, many of whom specialize in some of the so-called peripheral services. Or some other growth path may be chosen. The fundamentals of the "where" and the "how" of selling architectural services apply no matter which route is taken.

Current status of practice

Now, let's examine your practice as it exists today: What are your strengths? This should be readily apparent. As part of this self-examination, you must be your own severest critic in terms of client satisfaction. Have clients been satisfied with your meeting of completion dates and budgets? Probably the most important and influential factors in the eyes of the businessman prospect are your firm's ability to control the costs of jobs and to meet deadlines.

What is the character of your repeat business? Do the same clients come back? Do they refer prospects with the same building types, or do they consider you versatile enough to do a variety of types of projects?

Let's examine the experience of your key staff members, again in terms of their abilities and experience. And, finally, it will be well to take a long look at the scope of services which you can now offer with your present organization.

Analysis of your own organization, its experience and strength, is only part of the job in developing a sales program. The next and equally important step is an analysis of the needs which exist within your community, county and state, or however you define your market area. The mechanics for determining and analyzing the types of work which presently exist and most probably will exist during the foreseeable future is a subject for an article in itself. However, your own knowledge and experience locally has no doubt given you enough insight to make such a determination for the purpose of establishing, generally, the direction you wish to take in the near future.

Practical objectives for practice

Finally, you must interpret these factors of *self-analysis* and *market analysis* in terms of a series of practical objectives. The single most important question to ask yourself at this point is:

Do I possess the experience, personnel, satisfied clients and scope of services to compete for the types of commissions which exist in my market area?

You must then pinpoint the types of commissions you wish to go after in the future.

As the last step in this self-analysis, it is then necessary to make an effort to determine the standing of your firm in the eyes of the prospects you have selected. Are you typed? If so, how? For example, if you are typed as a school architect and have selected industrial commissions as your next target, you must evaluate to what extent your "school" image is an impediment and to what extent you can relate this as strength.

Here's one approach you might take. Break down the components of work you've done for schools and relate the points of similarity to the average industrial commission. There are many similarities: in site location, cafeteria, laboratories, administrative and clerical areas, heating and ventilating, and other mechanical facilities—strengths and experience in such areas will relate to many building types.

Up to this point you've examined your experience and background, where you stand in the community and, to a degree, what types of work are open to you—based on achievements to date and building types planned in your market area.

Organization for practice

Now, it is time to take a look at how you are currently organized to sell architectural services. What sales tools do you have? Do you have an up-to-date brochure? How recent—is it designed to be updated? Or do you make up a detailed individual letter each time a new prospect comes along? Do you need separate brochures—in other words, one general brochure and one for each important category of your work?

How are you utilizing articles on the work of the firm? Do you obtain reprints of speeches and articles? Are you maintaining a mailing list of former clients and personal contacts who can represent or influence references and recommendations for future commissions?

What are your presentation practices? Do you use film strips, slides or other audio-visual presentation tools, in addition to photographs and drawings? Do you continue to document your work in a professional manner? This means using qualified architectural photographers. Since prospective clients often ask questions concerning how your firm will be organized for their project, are you prepared to make a visual presentation on how you will function if you are selected?

Organization for business development

How are you currently organized for business development? It has been our experience that the biggest single thing lacking in architectural firms is a well-defined new business function. The most successful practices in the country today—from the standpoint of stability and profitability—are those with effective, organized business development programs. These firms also know how to speak the language of their prospects, especially in terms of budget and calendar requirements. Who shares the business development responsibility? Or is it the responsibility of one individual? Or, as so often happens during busy periods, is it unassigned and based on "who has time now?" What budget in terms of time and dollars do you allocate to the business development function? How are you organized to carry out a continuing development program?

How past commissions were obtained

The best method for appraising your strengths and weaknesses in terms of development of future commisisons is an analysis of how you obtained commissions in the past. Why did clients select you? This may seem obvious in many cases, but careful investigation may reveal that the most obvious reasons do not tell the whole story. Such analysis may reveal strengths to be re-emphasized in your selling program. Any prospect faced with a choice—in products or services—wants to know the benefits or points of uniqueness that you can offer in terms of his needs. Basically, the buyer asks this question: "What makes you better than your competitors?"

Unique selling proposition (USP)

If you can provide strong answers to this question, you are well on the way to development of what is known in industry as the "Unique Selling Proposition" or USP. The answer to "why did clients select us" may provide you with the soundest possible answer to "why *should* clients select us."

Now that you have assessed "where you are, how you wish to grow, the types of commissions you want, your current business development program, strengths and weaknesses, and your "Unique Selling Proposition," you are ready to tackle the next step, planning your program.

Your program must be planned around the objectives described earlier. Which are your best prospects in terms of building classifications and past clients? What are your sources of new business?

New business targets

Who should be hearing of you and from you? Since decision-making usually involves more than one person, and fewer and fewer commissions are being awarded by a single individual, it would be well to pinpoint your new business targets by evaluating their categories in the following manner:

The Initiators These are the men in the prospective client's organization who make the initial inquiry or "feeler" to you. Obviously, in order to do this, they must have heard of you (or, *from* you), directly or indirectly.

The Influencers These are the various executives all along the line—committee members and others in staff positions—whose goodwill is important. They don't make the final decisions, but they influence it indirectly.

The Permitters These are the executives higher up the line who seemingly are not directly involved in the decision, but who can express approval or disapproval in the narrowing-down process leading to final selection of an architect.

The Deciders These are the line officers who are charged with the responsibility for making the actual decision. However, as has been pointed out in the discussion of the other three targets, the Deciders do not make their decisions in a vacuum. They are influenced all along the line—by the Influencers and the Permitters.

And, if the Initiators did not bring up your name for consideration at all—then of course the real decision-maker involvement with you will be quite simple: there will be none. As one of our recent reports to a firm of architects pointed out: "Never neglect the top officials, but never cultivate them alone. . . ." The top officials are of great importance, but not necessarily of the *greatest* importance to you in your practice.

It is an excellent idea to think of each prospect in terms of the decision-making process within the firm. Then plan your strategy to approach the appropriate individuals at the appropriate times.

Now let's look at some fundamental elements which will enable you to shore up your business development program. You may be doing all—or many—of these things now, but ask yourself if you have an organized plan or just a hit-or-miss proposition. Remember, the firms that are most successful are those which have established business development policies—and stick to them.

First—establish a budget for business development. Look at what you have spent in the past—in terms of your own experience —and consider: "Was the amount spent realistic, in terms of the materials and man-hours that are needed?" Setting a budget in terms of a percentage of gross income is difficult, since we've seen a range of from 3 to 18 per cent. Frequently, when the percentage was on the high side, the budget was a catch-all for all non-billable time. On the other hand, one particular firm with a 5 per cent budget has a far more effective sales effort, due to their organized sales approach, than another firm with an 18 per cent budget. Certain types of business development work may take more time and effort than others, due to such factors as appearances before boards rather than individuals. You may find that you have to invest considerably more than you have in the past, and this will require a basic policy decision to appropriate a larger initial fund to "position" your firm.

One firm that has considerable stature today was relatively small, a few years ago, but it had a few prestige jobs behind it and loads of ambition. The senior partner realized the firm had reached a point requiring just such a basic policy decision—whether or not to appropriate a sum, which for them was of an unusual size, for a major business development effort. Shortly before Christmas he called his key staff members together, carefully explained his point of view and gave them a choice. "We've had a good year," he said, "and X-thousands of dollars are now available for us all. Do you want to take this money as a bonus now or to invest it in our future through a major business development and public relations program?" The majority agreed with the senior partner to invest in development of the firm. This was a wise decision, since today the firm is one of the most successful in the country.

Second, assuming you have arrived at a budget, you must have proper sales tools in order to implement your business development program. These tools, referred to earlier, include an adequate brochure, reprints of speeches and articles, as well as professional documentation of your work in the form of adequate photographs and drawings. You might at this point also include the services of a professional public relations consultant.

Budgeting for business development

Proper sales tools

A workable program for business development

Now you are ready to go into action, but to be most effective you must depend for your success upon a realistic, workable—and even rather rigid—program. Your key words for this activity are continuity and control. All too often the business development function is pushed aside the moment there are increased pressures of daily production. New business becomes a sporadic function, and in short order, this leads to a complete breakdown of the program with a resultant loss of whatever momentum had been created. Again, remember that the most successful firms are those with the most consistent new business development programs, and that—in these firms—the programs continue regardless of other pressures of any kind.

Periodic review and measurement of progress

Another important ingredient in making your program work is periodic review and measurement of progress. This is essential for control. Ideally, your program should be of sufficient importance to command a formal, periodic review at predetermined intervals. If all partners and key personnel cannot be available at these times, a more informal review arrangement may be necessary. The important thing is to have a review of some kind. For this purpose, a central prospect file and progress report system is necessary. Your system should describe each prospect in terms of what is to be done next and by whom. This responsibility must be seriously assumed or the system will fail. Many techniques are available and can be tailored to the requirements of individual firms so that the people in the firm can make their plans work.

Key staff members can help

You have a basic selling resource right in your own office—no matter how you plan your business development program. This is the sum total of the potential of your key staff members. Each associate should be a representative of the firm—alert at all times to new commission possibilities in his own universe (community, classmates, fraternity brothers). Staff members cannot function effectively in this role, however, unless *properly indoctrinated* and *enthusiastic* about the strengths of the firm.

Former clients can help

Still another resource too often overlooked is past clients. How many architects, after a building has been completed, fail to make routine follow-up calls periodically to inquire about the building's condition and performance? Such continuity leads to referrals and repeat commissions and should be made a definite responsibility of the firm's principles.

The firms that represent increasing competition for architects are business and sales oriented. Such firms can advertise, use high pressure, work on speculation, and use every other device known to modern sales promotion. However, as a practical matter, these methods cannot earn the respect and dignity of an achitectural firm that sells its services within the constraints of the professional ethical code—so long as good use is made of the tools and sound sales development principles which are permitted by the code of ethics of the profession.

Principles and ethics

The operating principles and ethics expected of architects by clients and prospects seeking their services are within the bounds of respect and dignity associated with such professionals as bankers and lawyers. Departure from these constraints, in fact, creates—among clients and potential clients—a negative image.

Evaluation Criteria for the Marketing of Architectural Services*

I Review of present business development function

A Organization and Responsibility

  1 Business Development Function

    a Assigned to partners, associates

    b Assigned to specified department

    c Assigned by client, type of work, geography

    d Assigned by combinations of above

    e Sole responsibility of an an individual

    f Unassigned ("who has time now?")

  2 Chart of Responsibility and Authority

    a Individuals involved full time, part time

    b Accountability

    c Budgeting of time by individuals involved

B Business Development Budgeting and Controls

  1 Formal, informal

  2 Standards, goals, in terms of numbers of calls, proposals, timing, "markets," sources

  3 Basis for standards—past experience (how analyzed?), professional experience exchanges

C Presentation and Client Proposal Practices

  1 Screening proposals to clients and proposal possibilities

  2 Standards of time, money to be invested and policies involved

  3 Preparation of presentations and proposals—how organized and handled

  4 Pricing

D Planning and Timing

  1 Pre-expiration of job planning in relation to lead-time

  2 Goals by industries, types of work and markets, by types of skills and services (both basic and comprehensive)

E Communications

  1 Internal, sales progress meetings, other

  2 Direct contacts programmed, personal (by whom), mail, other

F Procedures

  1 Handling and referral of inquiries, old clients, new clients

  2 Client, prospect records, files, call reports

  3 Follow-up calls on current prospects

  4 Follow-up calls on dormant former clients

  5 Follow-up calls on prospects to whom proposals have been made

  6 Geographic, or type of service, limitations

  7 Call and follow-up frequency

  8 Goals by types of calls, proposals, number of sales, dollar values of fees by types of work, by sources

  9 Organized news-scan (early identification of opportunities)

  10 Presentation and proposal screening procedures, budgeting of proposal work

* Prepared by D'Orsey Hurst and Company

11 Internal participation (assigned to staff) and follow-up, contacts, speeches, articles, other activities

12 Incentives to staff for development, intelligence, interest, and/or activity

13 Budgeting for above activities

14 Training methods to maximize effectiveness of above

II Evaluation of organization for business development and utilization of business development tools

A Objective evaluation of all facets of organization for business development listed above

B Assessment of effort and effectiveness of utilization of appropriate business development tools covering (but not limited to) the following:

1 Direct contact with prospective clients

2 Follow-up contact with former clients

3 Other cultivation activities to stimulate referrals and recommendations, including financial community relationships

4 Participation in activities of associations and societies

5 Speeches at appropriate forums and conferences

6 Professional publications

7 Publicity

8 External mailings and publications (brochures, reprints, other)

9 Presentation tools (photographs, brochures, slides and films, display panels, other)

III Evaluation of attitudes and opinions: image

Confidential research by means of personal interviews (disclosed or undisclosed) among present clients and prospects, "lost" prospects and others covering (but not limited to) the following:

A Professional and competitive standing—strengths, weaknesses

B Utilization of "top level" selling approaches and methods, effectiveness, drawbacks (if any)

C How firm is "typed." Does this classification do justice to firm's capabilities? How was this "image" acquired? Growth assets and liabilities in relation to market outlook and potential

IV Planning and programming for firm's growth: the recommended program

A Market research, market outlook, apparent needs, determination of the firm's goals

B Establishing objectives, short term, long term—classifications, practice "mix," industries, geography

C Developing programs and assigning responsibilities

D Management controls to measure progress. Improvements in procedures where possible

E Outline for implementation—timing and budget

F External assistance services if needed

20

Comprehensive Architectural Services: For the Large Corporate Client

BY HOWARD E. PHILLIPS, AIA *

Because he has long recognized the need for them, the large corporate client provides for himself many of the comprehensive services architects now perform, but which were mostly neglected by the architectural profession before

This article reflects the experience of the author, who for many years was Building Engineer for A.T. & T. Company and who is now engaged in a special study for its manufacturing organization, the Western Electric Company

The general construction outlook for the future in the United States is bright; some leading economists say that the total construction volume in the next decade may exceed $600 billion. This would indicate that construction will surely continue to play a major role in the economy. This potential indicates that architects and engineers in this country have a big job to do in the years that lie ahead.

As a part of the total, the Bell Telephone System constructs more than 1,000 building projects each year. These range in size from large factories or multistory office equipment buildings in large cities to small community dial offices in villages. The buildings are dispersed widely throughout the United States and Eastern Canada. In addition to buildings, the construction program ranges from the installation of cables on the ocean floor to microwave structures on mountain peaks.

Coordinating the construction program

A.T.&T. is the parent company of the Bell System which includes the Bell operating telephone companies, Western Electric Company (the manufacturing arm) and the Bell Telephone Laboratories. As the business grows bigger and more complex, it becomes even more necessary to delegate the authority for building work to the appropriate level of supervision. In many fields, automation promises great things in easing personal physical effort, but in this particular business the individual has never been more important.

Liaison with the architect is done by a professional building specialist acting as coordinator for the telephone company. He spells out in considerable detail, in writing, the needs and objectives of the owner. The architect then translates the study plans and instructions into a finished design from which lump sum bids may be obtained from contractors.

This big construction program is carried out with relative ease because the coordinating work is handled by building engineering groups in each of the 23 associated Bell telephone companies; each group operates with a great deal of independence. Western Electric, the manufacturing organization of the Bell System, operates differently; in this company a central staff organization handles most of the construction work on manufacturing buildings, distributing houses and laboratories.

Comprehensive architectural services

In order to provide complete architectural services, the architect must be administrator, artist and engineer. He must consider the entire physical environment. In comprehensive architectural services for many clients, he may provide professional coordination and counsel on feasibility studies, operational programming and assembly of land and money. Actually, many large corporate clients do not need all of the broad services that big architectural firms are traditionally providing today. These clients have set up their own organizations to do the feasibility studies, location and site analysis and other long-range planning.

An architectural firm seems to function best when its ownership is made up entirely of professional men. There is a risk in a firm becoming so large that non-professional members of the firm jeopardize its professional standing.

Architectural services needed by large corporate clients

The architectural services generally needed by large corporate clients are often quite different from those required by small individual clients. Smaller companies may come to the architect with a "one-shot" job, but many big clients have numerous repeat jobs. These clients may come to the architect with a piece of land, money to finance the project and a sketch of a proposed building layout. They may want the architect to prepare only the working drawings and specifications. In the Bell System, much of the early and long-range planning normally performed by architects for smaller clients is done by the companies' building engineering people. Unfortunately, it may be true that, at times, the architect is not brought in soon enough. It is highly desirable for the architect to be brought in at an early stage—before the site is selected, if possible. And more workable solutions are possible when the architect is brought in for the early planning of the various departmental needs in the building.

In the Bell System, the main effort is devoted to the communications business; and now, more frequently, outside professional talent is used for the design and planning of new buildings. Most of this design work is done by the experts who are trained to do this work—the private architects and engineers throughout the country. From an over-all Bell System point of view, this pays off in the long run. It eliminates the big staffs that would be needed at many locations for varying work loads if the companies did all the work themselves. It permits a good coordination job between owner and architect.

The owner's building engineer or project engineer works with the architect much like an individual owner. He makes decisions on questions concerning the building requirements, the use of the building and the systems to be used; and he furnishes the architect the information necessary to incorporate these requirements in the building. He works with the architect to see that telephone equipment requirements are met; but does not tell the architect how to make the drawings or write the specifications.

Fitting into the community

Operating in many cities and towns over much of the country imposes a real responsibility on the large corporate owner. The Bell System companies, of necessity, are intimately associated with their neighbors; and they try to be good neighbors by using fitting and appropriate architecture. In other words, the buildings should add something to the neighborhood; they must be neither indifferent nor detracting. Generally, the buildings are made attractive through a proper study of strictly functional forms. A capable architect should produce the desired effect by suitable proportions, mass and composition, and by a successful handling of construction materials. In fact, the more attractive buildings are usually achieved this way rather than through "trimmings."

Architects need to study the communities in which these buildings are to be situated and then design structures that are compatible with the environment. They must fully recognize and accept the image the company wishes to present to the public. To assist the telephone companies in providing suitable architecture for their buildings, two New York firms of consulting architects are retained: Kahn & Jacobs and Smith, Smith, Haines, Lundberg & Waehler. Major projects are reviewed in the early planning stage, so that any useful ideas developed in this way may be incorporated into the working drawings.

Specifications

Architects are not told how to write their specifications, but the architects are expected to write them to provide effective competition between producers by specifying two or more products which will serve equally well. Good quality materials are expected but specifications should not be written so tightly as to preclude competition among suppliers. It is believed that the words "or equal" should not be used, generally. Decisions about the comparative quality of various products should be made before bids are taken. Contractors may then submit other materials for consideration, with cost differences, at the time bids are taken.

Construction contracts on competitive bidding basis

It is Bell System policy to award construction contracts solely on the basis of merit. In almost all cases, awards are made on the basis of competitive bidding by qualified contractors. Lists of eligible bidders are carefully screened in advance to insure that bidders are equals in degree of responsibility and competence. In making an award, the reputation and competence of sub-bidders are also taken into consideration; and, of course, the right to accept or reject any or all bids is reserved. In certain cases, bids on some branches of the work may be taken separately.

Advance approval for design funds on major projects

Some of the Bell companies require that study plans on projects and preliminary cost estimates be prepared before management will give an approval to retain an architect. In order to meet such a schedule, architects are often forced to begin drawings almost immediately after the contract is approved. In order to facilitate long-range planning, Western Electric Company (the manufacturing arm) and many of the telephone companies generally get advance approval from management for the design work on large projects before funds for the building itself are requested. This procedure, also used by many other large firms, not only avoids hurried planning but also provides for more realistic project schedules, more accurate cost estimates for final funds and other advantages.

Early planning

For a successful project, sufficient time must be allowed for advance planning. The client and architect should thoroughly explore the basic requirements and have a complete understanding in their contract. This contract should include the full extent of services the architect is to provide. It is the client's responsibility to state clearly all of his requirements in considerable detail and advise the architect specifically as to the maximum building costs which will be acceptable.

Scheduling

Realistic schedules for all projects should be set up by the owner to facilitate coordination and completion in an orderly manner. However, such schedules should be sufficiently flexible to permit some changes occasioned by unforeseen problems. In this way, scheduling will be a helpful tool rather than a hardship. Discussions with other client companies indicate that the most frequent problem in maintaining a realistic construction schedule has been in not starting the advanced planning early enough. The accompanying chart (page 78) for a typical telephone building shows the large number of items which must be coordinated in the development of a new project. The chart also indicates the importance of achieving the proper sequence, from long-range planning through completion of construction and installation of equipment. The Critical Path Method (CPM) is being used increasingly on major projects when completion dates are important.

In recent years, more time has been required for negotiation and purchase of land because of the widespread adoption of zoning ordinances and the increased use of planning boards and commissions even in smaller communities. The chart indicates that early studies and the search for land for a typical project are usually made more than three years before the building is to be put into service. Unusual or crash projects, of course, may not permit the use of the normal time intervals shown, but adequate advance planning should reduce the number of such rush jobs to a minimum.

Telephone company requirements

Telephone company long-range requirements are established by commercial forecasts of population growth in various areas and by subsequent plant extension studies which indicate proposed wire centers and show preferred locations for buildings. These studies also indicate the rate of growth expected in such areas, together with estimates of the building areas needed for telephone equipment for the economic building period (normally an eight-year-old building before an addition is needed). Each organization to be housed in the building determines its own floor space requirements based upon the established standards, which represent proper directives developed through experience and technological advancements in the communications business. The building engineer or project engineer acts in the role of coordinator. He refines the requirements established by various departments and develops them into basic floor plans. These study plans are given to the architect, along with written instructions and criteria for use in developing preliminary design studies. The purpose here

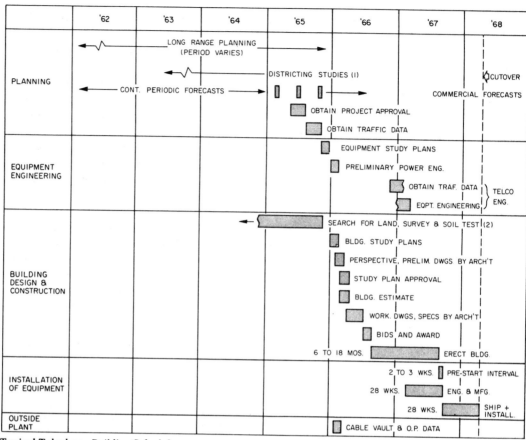

	'62	'63	'64	'65	'66	'67	'68
PLANNING							
EQUIPMENT ENGINEERING							
BUILDING DESIGN & CONSTRUCTION							
INSTALLATION OF EQUIPMENT							
OUTSIDE PLANT							

Typical Telephone Building Schedule

(1) Studies are generally made to cover over-all plans for an extended period, not for specific project except at time project is prepared for approval

(2) Period will vary depending on location. Large Buildings may require years, while small equipment buildings only a short period. Longer negotiation period is desirable in order to obtain best buy

is not to dictate to the architect concerning architectural design. However, the basic floor plans developed to meet telephone equipment needs do tend to exercise control over the dimensions and proportions of the building.

The architect usually has considerable design latitude in all telephone company structures, such as general offices and accounting buildings, that are not intended to house telephone switching equipment. Central offices and other buildings that contain switching equipment, however, must conform to certain requirements and limitations imposed by the switching equipment itself.

Some of the important features peculiar to telephone buildings designed to contain switching equipment are the unusually high ceilings (13 to 13½ ft clear), heavy floor loads, standard bay sizes for equipment areas, minimum windows, special equipment entrances, cable entrances and cable holes. Special attention must also be given to ventilation, fire, flood and earthquake protection and to adequate security and protection for equipment areas to assure continuity of telephone service.

Another problem in the architecture of telephone buildings is that the ultimate building often will be considerably larger than the initial structure. In other words, these buildings must usually be designed for expansion, either laterally or by the addition of more floors, as the telephone needs of the locality increase. The final building may well be two to four times the size of the first phase.

These varying and unusual requirements all go to make up a collection of directions and restrictions within which the architect must work. Nevertheless, since he is expected to come up with a good design, the architect must be given the freedom to do a good design job within reasonable cost limits.

The owner's organization

It has been necessary for the large corporate client to set up an organization to work with architectural and engineering firms. For this work, the Bell System usually selects people who have been trained in architecture or engineering, and, in fact, most of its building engineers are licensed architects or engineers. The size of the organization has been dependent on the type of service that has been made available by private firms. On the other hand as one large corporate client recently was quoted as saying: "If architects would do a better job, we could reduce the size of the organization we now have."

In general, the building engineer is the telephone company to the architect and almost all client contact will be through him or the project engineer. He sets company policy for the architect. He sets up schedules and objectives for the architect. He is responsible for making prompt decisions so that the architect will not be delayed in carrying out his job. The building engineer must have enough authority to make decisions, in conference with the architect, to expedite the job and to provide the best design consistent with cost objectives. In a majority of the Bell companies, the building engineer reports directly to the chief engineer (who is responsible for all telephone engineering work).

In working with the architect, the building engineer of the telephone company generally performs the following functions:

1) Does long-range planning for building projects
2) Prepares program—collection, collation and integration of data on needs, site, etc.; obtains floor space requirements from operating departments
3) Selects architect in consultation with chief engineer
4) Arranges for purchase of land
5) Arranges for land survey and furnishes survey to architect; sends survey to outside plant engineer to obtain cable entrance data
6) Prepares and transmits preliminary study plans to all operating departments for approval
7) Presents study plans to architect for preparation of more detailed study plans and cost estimates
8) Approves or disapproves perspectives of new buildings prepared by architect; also makes suggestions that lead to acceptable design
9) Presents approved study plans to architect along with outline specifications and other instructions for starting on working drawings; reaches agreements with architect on materials to be used, methods of construction and general design concept
10) Provides necessary guidance in preparation of working drawings and specifications; reviews and checks drawings periodically to see that telephone company requirements are met
11) Reviews working drawings with fire and safety inspection consultants
12) Approves contractor bid lists presented by architect
13) Holds bid openings and recommends acceptance of bids to appropriate telephone company authority
14) Advises successful and unsuccessful bidders

15) Prepares and executes contracts

16) Advises company public relations of contract award

17) Supplements architect's inspection to see that important telephone company requirements are met

18) Approves payments to contractors

19) Accepts completed buildings from contractors

20) Inspects projects near end of one-year guarantee periods.

Western Electric Company follows essentially the same pattern in the design and construction of its buildings. However, Western has a group that designs a portion of its total construction program and another group that supervises and inspects all of its construction work.

Building study plans are generally prepared by the building engineer's staff and routed to the various operating organizations for approval. These study plans, together with other instructions, are given to the architect for preparation of more detailed study plans before starting on the working drawings. The study plans presented to the architect are not necessarily final. The architect, after consultation with the owner, may make changes to provide a more suitable layout, if the fundamental telephone equipment requirements are met and consideration is given to provisions for growth, flexibility, etc.

Architect's responsibilities

The architect generally performs these services for the Bell Telephone Companies:

1) PRELIMINARY SERVICES—Conferences with owner, site reviews before actual purchase of land (if possible), preliminary study plans, rendering of exterior and estimate of cost; the owner usually prepares outline specifications and a preliminary estimate as a basis for discussions of the scope of the project with the architect

2) CONTRACT DOCUMENT SERVICES—Conferences with owner, working drawings and specifications including preparation of color scheme; bids are generally received by the owner and the owner prepares the contract

3) SERVICES DURING CONSTRUCTION—Office administration such as supplemental drawings, shop drawing review and approval of samples; field administration including inspection, issue of change orders, certificates for payment and work-as-built tracings on completion of project

4) CONSULTING OR SPECIAL SERVICES—These services are provided as the occasion requires.

In negotiations with architects, written instructions must be provided at the start of a project so there is no question about the scope of the project and requirements of the telephone business. It is also important that the building engineer or project engineer assigned to the job know the status of the job as it progresses. The architect and building engineer should work closely together on each project and should have frequent consultations. The architect should furnish progress prints of the working drawings on a major project for review at intervals (at an early stage, at about the half-way point and near completion).

Cost of construction

In the Bell System, it is recognized that quality of environment has a bearing on the quality of employees that can be attracted. Also recognized is the fact that good design is good business. However, architects must realize the necessities of business economics. Good design is required, but luxury must be avoided—even the appearance of luxury—and efficient, pleasing space need not necessarily be expensive. Experience has shown that, if careful judgment is used, the architectural ideas and materials of today lend themselves well to the practice of economy. It has also been found that good building design need not cost more than poor design—many of the best telephone buildings are the lower-cost ones. There is a big difference between an economical building and a cheap building. The economical design is the one with the optimum costs, including both first costs and maintenance for the life of the building. Equipment buildings serve as an envelope for intricate and valuable electronic and other types of communications equipment. Therefore, substantial structures must be built to protect the people who maintain and operate this equipment and to assure reliable service under all conditions.

Today a wide variety of new construction materials are available. These materials lend themselves to new concepts in design, and the Bell companies like to take advantage of them whenever possible. However, radical departures from known design principles are not acceptable when they are accompanied by difficult operating problems. In construction today every manufacturer of building products must keep pace with his competitors. However, some products are rushed to the market without adequate testing data or field experience. Such new materials are not used for large projects in the Bell System until they have been proven satisfactory. It is the building owner's responsibility, along with that of his architect, to make the final selection of materials and to maintain quality control in the building. After all, the owner pays for both the initial building and for future maintenance problems and failures.

Authority of architects   The size and basic form of a building is essentially determined by the program developed by the building engineer, but the attempt is made to give the architect the maximum possible freedom to determine its design. The architect is expected to accept the burden of responsibility for his recommendations and to be responsive to suggestions after his recommendations have been submitted. Because of the considerable building product sales efforts brought to bear on him, the corporate client needs to know the "why" of the architect's recommendations. Sometimes the architect must make comprehensive engineering studies, before the selection may be made of the various materials and systems to be used.

Through long association with many good firms, the Bell companies have become accustomed to working together with architects; the results have been good. The usual expectation is to work with a principal of the architectural firm. The association with the architectural firm should be a team effort and not one of control by the corporate client. The client must strike a delicate balance. He cannot let himself be controlled to the degree that the building no longer meets his requirements. On the other hand, he must not hamstring the architect to the point where he does not get his money's worth in terms of design quality.

Architects who are experienced in telephone buildings enjoy a relatively free hand; others require more careful and continuous supervision. When architects are given design freedom they sometimes come up with extremes in design which the company management won't buy. However, the architect deserves, and must get, sympathetic cooperation.

The telephone company will have a fixed equipment layout and a definite capital budget for each project. Therefore, it must insist on control of the budget for the over-all project and adequate control over design. These controls are exercised by means of the periodic approvals of drawings submitted. If the choice of materials and scope of the project cannot be controlled by the architect, he cannot be blamed if the project overruns the budget. Therefore, the architect should have a voice in all decisions which importantly affect the shape and function of the building. How far he goes beyond his basic services depends largely on his abilities.

Selection of architects

More than 100 architectural firms are engaged annually for the design of Bell System buildings. A great many of these are smaller firms. The Bell companies generally employ architects who are located in the geographical area where the buildings are to be built. However, if a local architect does not have a big enough staff to handle a project or is not experienced in the type of construction, then the companies go outside of the area to obtain the required services. When several buildings are to be built in an area, the companies try to use more than one architect in order to create what is believed to be a healthy competitive spirit. Choosing an architect takes time and careful thought. The architect's qualifications for a particular project are the most important consideration. Choices made on the basis of personal influence should be studiously avoided.

The factors normally considered in the selection of an architect include such items as the size of the firm in relation to the job, its history, services furnished, ability as indicated by exhibits of work, amount of work designed and constructed in the last five years, proximity to the project, current workload, estimated future workload, estimated time for completion of the project, number of technical personnel and the technical, educational and professional experience of the members of the firm. Once a firm has been found to have these qualifications, it is frequently retained on a continuing basis.

Other companies sometimes turn to package builders and other entrepreneurs. To such clients completion of the job in a very short time is extremely important, even though the cost may be increased. Because many architects will not accept the responsibility for expediting jobs, the package builder has stepped in to fill this need. Such arrangements covering both design and construction generally have not found acceptance in the Bell System. Instead, the vast majority of construction contracts are awarded on the basis of lump sum competitive bids.

Small vs large firms

Smaller architectural offices definitely have a place in the Bell System building program. For the many smaller buildings and additions erected each year, well-qualified local architects often best serve the needs. This not only makes for good public relations, but frequently for better inspection since most telephone buildings are not large enough to justify fulltime resident inspectors.

If an architect is competent and assumes responsibility for

only the number and size of projects that he can handle in a professional manner, the architect should have no problem serving this company, regardless of the size of his office. Large architectural firms often have the advantage of large staffs capable of handling large projects without delay. On the other hand, in some large offices, personal attention from firm members or top-level associates may be difficult to obtain and maintain.

Inspection

The building owner would like to depend on the architect to provide inspection during construction on all major projects —even though the owner's project engineer is on the job to see that his most important requirements are met. The Bell companies probably expect slightly better than normal quality of workmanship—but do not expect all jobs to win craftsmanship awards. If inspections were to become too rigid, the reputation for being hard to work for might soon lead to high prices for a degree of quality that is not essential for the purpose. The architect should write into the specifications the quality desired, and the field inspector should see that these requirements are met. This is a test of a field inspector's ability; and the only way to insure that the client gets what he pays for.

Fees for architects

The number of contract forms sold by The American Institute of Architects indicates that the percentage fee is favored by more than ten-to-one over cost-plus and fixed-fee arrangements. The percentage fee method is used most often by the telephone companies because of the belief that it is the most economical and equitable way. However, for manufacturing buildings, the loading on payroll (cost-plus) arrangement is frequently used.

The future

The Bell System must have buildings that are designed to meet specific equipment requirements; and they must be economical to build and maintain. Relationships with the architectural profession have been excellent. The "Checklist for Architects" that follows is intended to be "constructive criticism" of the architectural profession which is now striving to do a good job better. The checklist is included here with confidence that the kind of teamwork outlined will make Bell System buildings greater assets to the community, to the company and to the architect.

It is always easier to recognize shortcomings than good points. If the architect does a good job, it is only what is expected of him; if he fails somewhere, it is remembered. Some say that the architect needs to expand his services because he is the only individual who is concerned with the total human environment. Some say that he should be more concerned with managing and protecting the practice he has, rather than expanding his services. Others say that he needs to improve the quality of services he now renders. In doing business through the years with many architectural firms, the Bell System has generally had good service from the firms it has engaged, but no job is so well done that it cannot be improved upon. Therefore, the following points are listed as ways that may improve the already fine job.

Pointers for Better Job Coordination

1) *Single Responsibility.* Big *clients* are big *organizations,* but the architect usually does business with only *one* person in the organization. Contacts and responsibility should not be divided. The architect and the company should work through only one man in each office.

2) *Coordination of Entire Project.* On important matters the client should work directly with the principals of the architectural firm, not with the draftsmen. It is, of course, important that the owner cooperate with the architect and state his requirements clearly, including the amount he is willing to spend; and he should make prompt, understandable decisions that will result in good over-all coordination.

3) *Job Coordination.* Some prominent large architectural firms, though strong in design, are weak on follow-through coordination. Sometimes an architect may accept a commission which his firm cannot handle expeditiously because of a heavy workload.

4) *Coordination in Architect's Office.* Some architectural firms might do a better job of distributing up-to-date information within their own offices. Too often, a lack of coordination has resulted in situations such as a rearrangement of a service core that blocks the path for telephone cables. Perhaps a full-time project coordinator, with no production responsibility, at a high level in the architectural organization, would help.

5) *Coordination of All Phases of Design.* The architect should coordinate all phases of the building design to insure that mechanical and electrical work will fit with structural and architectural. Otherwise, these items must be checked by the owner's representative or costly changes made during construction when the problems are encountered.

6) *Coordination of Engineering.* In the Bell System, the architect is expected to coordinate, and be responsible for, the complete building.

Pointers for Specific Design Improvement

1) *Specialized Design Requirements.* In telephone building design, the architect must realize that he is providing space for very special requirements. The building will serve as an envelope for very intricate electronic and other telephone equipment; further, its use will have been carefully timed to fit in with the growing needs of customers.

2) *Stereotyped Design.* An architect sometimes becomes stereotyped in his thinking and fails to give his client the design he needs or expects. This is often true when the architect has done a lot of work for the client. The telephone companies have specific design requirements that must be met, not only physically but esthetically. A company awards program was instituted several years ago to encourage better architecture at reasonable costs. In the last review, 75 honor awards, merit awards and honorable mentions were presented to architects for good design of Bell System buildings. The attitude of the company toward good design is indicated by the fact that if an architect consistently fails to receive recognition in the awards program, it may have an effect on whether he obtains further contracts for services.

3) *Functional Design for Equipment Buildings.* The Bell System has updated its design concepts in recent years and opened the way for more intelligent use of newer materials and styles of architecture. For example: At one time, architects seemed to think that telephone equipment buildings should be made to look like office buildings by placing many windows in equipment areas. Actually, windows expose the equipment to greater deterioration of the wiring from the sun's rays, greater hazards from fire and less

security in wartime. The elimination of unnecessary windows also reduces building costs and maintenance costs for cleaning, glass replacement, calking, painting and shade and blind replacement. Nowadays, the use of windows in telephone equipment buildings is generally confined to lounge and lunchroom areas where employees may enjoy them while relaxing.

Of course, a different approach may be necessary for a building to be constructed in a residential area. Zoning may require that building be designed to look like a residence. In any case, the design must be such that the building will fit into the community and be accepted by its neighbors.

4) *Design of Small Buildings.* More attention should be given by the architectural profession to the design of medium-sized and small buildings. Except for an occasional large headquarters or manufacturing building, the vast majority of buildings for the Bell System might be classified as small. Too often these buildings seem not to have offered sufficient challenge to architects to produce outstanding designs. This is unfortunate. Architecturally, a modest building is just as important in its own neighborhood as a large building in a great city; and the small building is just as deserving of the architect's best efforts. Then too, the percentage fee arrangement permits the architect a proportionately higher fee on smaller buildings.

5) *Design for Future Expansion.* Almost every building for a growing company should be planned for expansion. This may only mean that the building layout must have enough flexibility to allow additions without extensive alteration of the existing building. However, in telephone buildings, a growth wall that may be easily removed is consistently provided.

6) *Provide Maintenance Space for Building Equipment.* Sometimes sufficient consideration is not given to the problems of operation and maintenance of the building equipment.

7) *Landscaping.* Frequently appearance can be more enhanced through adequate landscaping than through more costly ornament on the building. Landscaping layout should be the responsibility of the architect who designs the building.

8) *Standards.* The architect must work within carefully circumscribed limits, or standards, to meet certain equipment requirements. However, the questioning of standards is always encouraged because standards tend to become fixed and sometimes the reasoning behind them will no longer apply. Standards are too frequently used as a *solution* to a problem rather than as a *guide* to its solution. Of course, certain standards are needed in order to meet exacting equipment requirements, but the imagination and talents of architects are necessary in the solving of design problems.

9) *Practical Experience.* Every man on the drafting board, every specification writer, every architectural student would benefit from some practical on-the-job experience in building construction. Too many details on drawings are either impossible or impractical to build. This means field revision, frequently at extra cost to the owner.

10) *Cost Estimating.* Some architects have a reputation in the building industry for their poor estimating ability. Particularly lacking is knowledge of operating and maintenance costs. Yet,

good background in the cost area is necessary, if proper choices of materials and equipment are to be made.

Most architects who have a reputation for good estimating use as many sources of data for their unit costs as they can. The greatest reliance, perhaps, is placed upon records of the costs of previous projects. Such dependable cost records are a necessity for good estimating. Too many buildings have been designed, and bids taken, only to find that the lowest bid far exceeds the money available. When developing solutions for projects, architects should keep in mind any cost limitations which have been established. However, sufficient design freedom is also necessary if a solution is to be developed within the budget.

Pointers for Better Construction

1) *Field Inspection.* Some architects seem to hire a "man from the street" for field inspection. Architects who have done a good job for the Bell System have used men who are specialists in inspecting telephone work; often these men move from job to job. Many of them have exhibited a loyalty to the company similar to that of its own employees. One good man at a higher salary usually will prove to be more valuable than several less competent lower-paid men.

2) *Inspections by Designers.* It is important that those responsible for the design of heating, ventilating and airconditioning equipment inspect this work during construction to insure that it is built and will operate as designed.

Feedback — The Missing Link

A channel for communications feedback from building owners and operators to architects, builders, manufacturers and building research groups must be established so that information on performance and upkeep of buildings and building components can be made readily available. The chart shown illustrates the current situation.

There are, of course, reasons why performance in service information does not get back to the points where it can do some good—reasons for the break in the chain shown in the chart. Here are some of them:

1) Time has not been taken for intelligent study and analysis of available feedback

2) The producer very naturally wants the world to know the good points about his product

3) The architect does not want it thought that his choice of products and techniques could be improved

4) The constructor wants no reflection on the character of his work

5) The owner, especially if he rents out space, does not want anything published indicating that his building is less than superb.

And so, in the ordinary course of events, those who design and make building products often fail to hear the things that would help them to improve and perfect those products. One important step might be for architects to go back to jobs they have designed, a few years after completion, to find out how the buildings have performed in service. This would not only help to establish the feedback that is so essential, but would be a great stride toward the full meaning of what the architectural profession now calls comprehensive services.

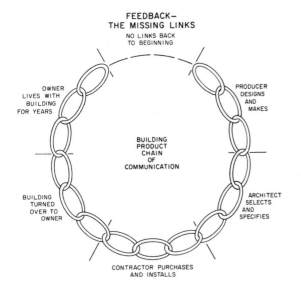

FEEDBACK—
THE MISSING LINKS
NO LINKS BACK
TO BEGINNING

OWNER
LIVES WITH
BUILDING
FOR YEARS

PRODUCER
DESIGNS
AND
MAKES

BUILDING
PRODUCT
CHAIN
OF
COMMUNICATION

ARCHITECT
SELECTS
AND
SPECIFIES

BUILDING
TURNED
OVER TO
OWNER

CONTRACTOR PURCHASES
AND INSTALLS

21

Comprehensive Architectural Services: For The Government Client

BY LEONARD L. HUNTER, AIA

The Federal government offers unmatched opportunities for accomplishment to architects who are prepared to satisfy its complex requirements

Historically the great monuments of architecture were built either by the State or the Church. In fact these great clients of the architect are as old as architecture itself.

The Church has now become almost non-existent as a client for structures that can be expected to mark an epoch in history and architecture. On the other hand, the State—that is to say the governments of the 231 nations of the world—is still, potentially, a great client of the architect.

GSA serves to demonstrate principles

To take a look at our own government and its potentials as a client, it would be necessary to examine the practices of several different agencies. However, a discussion of the General Services Administration (GSA) procedures may serve to demonstrate the principles involved in working with all government clients. Practically every department—and many of the agencies—has its own architectural-engineering staff. The size and potency of these staffs vary from the small groups which design and supervise the construction of buildings for their own agencies to the large groups that administer contracts with architect-engineers, review drawings and specifications at predetermined intervals and either supervise construction, or participate in its supervision. The General Services Administration, the Navy's Bureau of Yards and Docks and the Army's Corps of Engineers follow the latter course.

Numerous existing agencies should be unified into two

Obviously, for more efficient performance the numerous existing design and construction groups should be unified into two major groups having complete control of all design and construction falling within the two broad areas—civil and military.

The civil group could absorb into one agency or department the many construction programs of the non-military agencies. Such an organization should logically be a bureau of a new department (such as a Department of Fine Arts) which would be responsible for the sponsorship, development and guidance of all of the arts. In lieu of a new department, another possibility would be an expansion of the Department of Interior to include a Bureau of Fine Arts. Whether a bureau of a new department or a division of a bureau of an old department, the advantages of such a fine arts agency would be many. Chief among them would be representation in the Presidential Cabinet, uniformity in practices and procedures, standardization of construction without stifling ingenuity and elimination of duplicate personnel. The three benefits last-named would also reduce government expenditures.

A new Bureau of Design and Construction would administer all programs for design and construction except those significantly devoted to the military (shore installations, camps, airfields, etc). The programs of this Bureau would include those now sponsored by: Architect of the Capitol; Atomic Energy Commission; Department of Health, Education and Welfare; Department of the Interior; Department of Justice; Department of State; Federal Aviation Agency; General Services Administration; Federal Housing Administration, Public Housing Administration, Urban Renewal Administration, all under Housing and Home Finance Agency; US Post Office Department; Veterans Administration. However, since there is no such Bureau in such a Department at present, the following will demonstrate present procedures.

GSA an experienced client

GSA is not a novice architect's client, but can call upon a century and a quarter of experience encompassing many billions of dollars of construction to guide it in its multi-billion dollar programs. This vast experience has bred into the organization an understanding of the architectual profession and a degree of reasonableness that differentiates GSA from some of the less experienced agencies.

Funds and program must be procured first

The private client in many instances comes to the architect without a program. This is not the case in government. A government agency must have had sufficient funds allocated to cover an A-E contract prior to entering into such a contract. To acquire such funds, the agency must have a program for a proposed building so that an estimate can be prepared. The fiscal budget of the agency may call for an office building to house ten Federal agencies in "X" city. The specific program for this building will consist of the detailed requirements of the ten occupying agencies; their space requirements, their needs for greater-than-average floor loading, vaults, data processing equipment, etc. From this program the staff prepares an estimate which is submitted to the Bureau of Budget and, if approved, to the Congress for appropriation. The initial appropriation will probably include only those funds required for purchase of a site and for A-E fees.

Selection of architect

After the project has been authorized by the Congress and funds have been appropriated for A-E fees, the agency will then be ready to select an architect.

The procedures for the selection of architects vary widely among government agencies. For example, the system of the Foreign Buildings Operations of the State Department makes use of a committee of architects in private practice for review of the qualifications of architects on a nationwide basis. This committee then recommends to the Deputy Assistant Secretary for Foreign Buildings the architects it believes are best qualified to perform the required services. GSA also uses a committee system; but in this case, the committee is composed of staff architects and engineers. The committee reviews the qualifications of architects practicing in the vicinity of a proposed building and makes recommendations to the Commissioner of Public Buildings, who then passes the recommendations along to the Administrator of GSA for final approval. The fact that selections, made by an unbiased committee of qualified civil servants and based entirely upon the qualifications of local architects, have to be submitted to such high authority for approval indicates approval is not automatic.

Contract negotiation

Once an architect has been selected, he will receive a letter from the agency announcing his selection. This letter will request that he come to Washington on a given date to negotiate a contract for architectural services. Along with the letter will be an agenda of the proposed negotiation meeting, a brief description of the building to be designed, a preliminary estimate, several GSA handbooks and a typical A-E contract.

The purpose of the negotiation meeting is to arrive at an agreement which will be acceptable to both the architect and the government. GSA expects each architect to make a reasonable profit; long years of experience have shown that the government, like other clients, gets what it pays for.

Setting of fees

After the government's negotiation committee and the architect have reviewed the scope of the architectural services, the project program, the preliminary estimate and the status of funds, and the architect understands the proposed contract, he will be asked to name a fee which represents his best judgment as to what it would cost him to provide the required services and make a reasonable profit. The architect and the negotiating committee chairman will probably make several offers and counter-offers before they can agree upon a lump sum fee. This fee will not be adjusted up or down later if the contract price varies from the estimate which had been reviewed and agreed to at the negotiation meeting. The only cause for a change in the fee will be a change in the scope of the work.

Some agencies, particularly the Defense Department groups, use an estimated sheet count times a sheet cost factor as the basis for determining fees. However, GSA believes that a fee curve established on its long years of experience and adjusted to meet the conditions governing specific projects is more reliable.

Submissions required

At this point, the architect will have a government contract which requires him to make at least four submissions for review by the agency staff of architects and engineers. After approval of each of these submissions, a progress payment will be made to the architect. The required submissions may be supplemented with informal presentations, particularly in the earlier stages, if the architect wants to make certain that his *parti* is acceptable before going too far with it.

Submissions approval

What is acceptable and what is not acceptable? Is the government staff whimsical and capricious in making such determinations? Absolutely not. The government client demands from the architect a functional solution that will embody its program within its cost limitations; and it expects that the architect's ability as a designer will produce an imaginative concept. The demand items will be insisted upon; if the architect's *parti* does not fulfill them, the government staff will make suggestions and require resubmissions until they are fulfilled. Insofar as an imaginative concept is concerned, again the staff will make suggestions if it feels the architect has fallen short of the requirements. However, this is in the area of taste and creative concept and the final decision will usually be left to the architect.

In the two preliminary stages, the architect is expected to present a complete concept of the future building. All elements of design—both architectural and engineering—must be shown in sufficient clarity to leave no doubt as to the end product. With the submission of the second stage of preliminaries, the architect is required to present an outline specification and a detailed cost estimate. The approval of this stage is the first big milestone. Then, the architect will be directed to proceed with working drawings and specifications.

Review of government documents by architect

At this point, the architect should again review the various documents furnished him by the government. He will find most of his questions answered for him in the GSA handbooks. Periodically these handbooks are reviewed and updated by the staff, as well as by consultants in specific fields who are engaged to insure that the handbook requirements and other standards represent the latest and most acceptable construction practices; in this, cost is definitely a factor. The architect is not arbitrarily required to adhere to these handbooks; if he thinks he has developed a better way of achieving results, he should not hesitate to propose it.

What GSA expects from architect

The government client does not make a detailed check of quality of his buildings, cost again being a factor. This quality begins on the drafting boards. GSA not only demands that the architect's drawings and specifications call for quality, but also insists that these documents be complete and accurate to insure the intended quality and eliminate future change orders.

The government client constantly strives to upgrade the drawings and specifications but relies on the competence of the architect. If he is not thorough and conscientious, the architect may well be embarrassed by the change orders that ensue.

The architect's second big milestone will be the acceptance of his working drawings and specifications for bidding purposes. Now he can relax a while until the construction contract is awarded. The government takes care of reproduction and distribution of drawings and specifications, the opening of bids and the award of the construction contract.

Working drawings, specifications, construction

In some cases, the architect's contract will require of him, during construction, only the checking and approval of shop drawings and recommendations for the approval of finished building materials; in such instances, the government provides its own construction supervision. However, in recent years GSA has provided an option in its contract which permits varying degrees of supervision by the architect.

Success in GSA work

In such a large organization as GSA an architect will deal with many individuals. However, these individuals are all members of the Design and Construction team. Most of them are architects or engineers; and they have a single purpose—that of helping to produce the best buildings that can be built for the availabe funds. Design is always a factor. Architects are encouraged to be imaginative within reasonable limitations; the bizarre is not acceptable. If the architect doesn't produce an outstanding result, it will not be because his client has not given him freedom, encouragement and assistance.

22

Architectural Presentation to Clients

BY HERBERT H. SWINBURNE, FAIA

If they are to be commissioned to perform comprehensive services for buildings and their environment, architects must be capable of explaining their services to clients in terms that are completely understandable to clients

For years, the members of our firm have wondered how best to present our services to potential clients. For years we wondered what clients were. What did they all have—or need—in common? How does one reach them? How do we communicate with them? How should we organize ourselves to serve them?

What is a client? For that matter, what is architecture? What is architectural service?

Clients usually have two things in common. They don't know what an architect is. They don't know what his services should be.

Architects usually have one thing in common—they don't know how to speak a language their clients can understand.

How should one present a concept of comprehensive services to a client? Dramatically? But simply and intelligently?

How does one get a client to understand the architect? Or architecture?

Each office has its own ideas on how to go about this. We've been asked to describe ours.

The presentation we use is neither new nor novel. It is based on a concept of comprehensive services, as we see it, and as we practice it. It is intended to guide a potential client through the labyrinth of planning, design and construction, and then convince him that the services of our firm are those he should use. We speak in his language, not ours. Facts are simple—no hedging.

The client is pulled into the story by the use of two projectors and two giant screens nine feet square, saturated with full color. The client, whether one individual or a very large group, is seated in a comfortable, quiet, informal environment. He can hear well and see well. The room is dark and the sequence of information is very carefully arranged so that no questions occur until after the presentation. Pictures and language are woven together carefully to give *understanding*—full *understanding* of architectural services—full *understanding* of how one must be organized to analyze objectively, conceive creatively and build realistically.

On the pages following are shown a few examples of slides selected from the Nolen-Swinburne presentation that is made to potential clients. In the actual presentation, all slides are in color; the complete presentation includes about 75 slides. All slides are keyed to a prepared script that is read by one of the principals of the firm; all slides designated left (L) or right (R), as an indication of their positions in the left or right projector, and numbered to indicate their order in the presentation. This numbering system is used for the illustrations that follow.

125

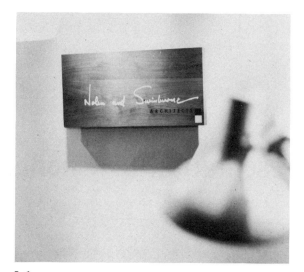

L-1

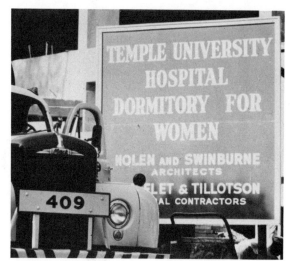

L-2

RANGE OF WORK is indicated by our planning and architectural work in the following seven fields:

Education	Religion
Government	Medicine
Recreation	Housing
Business	

Since 1950 our firm has handled 77 projects with a combined value of more than $100,000,000.

In addition we are engaged in master planning for five present and future education projects totaling almost $150,000,000.

L-3

L-4

L-6

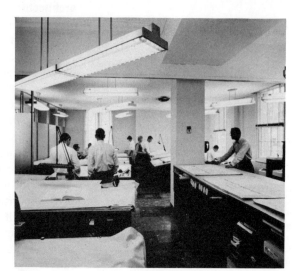

R-5

(L-1) "Let us introduce ourselves, Nolen and Swinburne, Architects & Planners. Jim Nolen and Herb Swinburne have been together since 1949 . . . in the office . . . and (L-2) in the field."

(L-3) "Since 1950, we've completed 77 projects valued at over 100 million dollars . . . (L-4) This is a $250,000 library."

(L-6) "Here are our three partners and four associates . . . (R-5) And here is one of our drafting rooms . . ."

How does one generate understanding? Here is how we go about it. But before proceeding, a bit of history is necessary.

The progress of our office toward comprehensive services and their explanation to clients has been made in five major steps, extending over the years from 1957 to the present: 1957-9—Redefinition, for ourselves, of the word architecture, 1958-61—Changing of our concept of architectural practice, in order to implement this definition, 1961—Reorganization of the office around our new concepts of service, 1959—Initiation of a research study on the art of professional communications, in order to develop better public and client understanding of our on-going projects, and 1962-3—Development of a system of professional communications, in order to reach potential clients by telling them how we practice our new concept of architecture.

Some of the results of these five steps are indicated in the illustrations shown here. The results have exceeded our most optimistic projections. Some of our thinking on the redefinition of architecture was presented in a speech made at the AIA-NSF Conference at Ann Arbor, Mich, in March 1959, as follows:

"A century and a half ago, Webster, defining the word 'architecture,' said it was the 'art of building; but in a limited and appropriate sense the art of constructing buildings for the purpose of civil life.' Today Webster defines the word in almost the same language except to say architecture is the 'art or science of building . . .' and with one word adds the effects of a century of Industrial Revolution to the concept of architecture.

"The sticks and stones of shelter, submitted to the sophisticated manipulation of science and technology, have now become the buildings, great and small, of the twentieth century. The public at large, and many architects, define architecture in terms of separate buildings. These are thought of as an assembly of materials and equipment shaped to perform some function efficiently, economically and beautifully.

"The physical aspects of architecture and its appreciation through visual perception are well understood, particularly as related to individual buildings—less so as related to groups of buildings.

"I suggest, however, that today the definition of architecture, its concept by people everywhere, and its actual practice by the professional, are too limiting, too narrow in scope—only part of a larger picture. Too much of an emphasis on concrete physical evidence; too little understanding of man and society. Too little recognition of the true role the architect should assume.

"Since man first met other forms of life and shared a natural environment with them he has been dissatisfied. He has constantly altered, changed and re-arranged his natural environment to suit his own needs and purposes. Today there are few areas in the world where man is still completely dominated by his environment. For the most part he is at least equal to it and manipulates small sections of it at will to make a more comfortable world. In the centuries ahead it is to be expected that he will eventually gain complete control over his total environment.

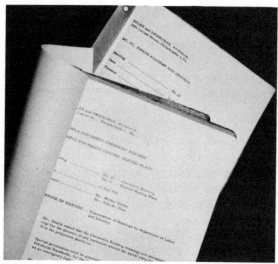

ADDED N&S CONSULTANTS

4. COST CONTROL
5. ACOUSTICAL ENG.
6. TELEVISION
7. CIVIL ENG.
   (ROADS & DRAINAGE)
8. SANITARY ENG.
   (SEWAGE DISPOSAL)
9. LANDSCAPE ARCH'T.
10. PUBLIC RELATIONS

R-6

L-9

L-11

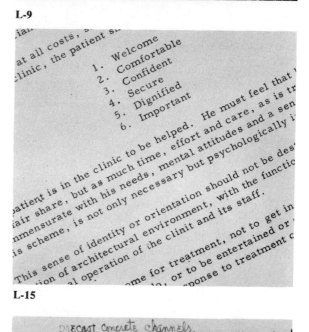

1. Welcome
2. Comfortable
3. Confident
4. Secure
5. Dignified
6. Important

L-15

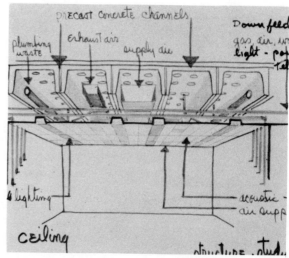

R-15

R-20

(R-6) ". . . N & S services include these added consultants whenever required . . . (L-9) Finally, we have a department of URBAN DESIGN, *and are well equipped to render Planning Services on a large scale . . ."*

"But these are physical aspects. Man must also live as an individual in groups of many sizes and as he alters the world he lives in, his needs, and the needs and purposes of the people in his society become controlling influences on the manner in which environment should be handled. New fields of thought are required here and the ultimate goals of man become a part of the picture in re-arranging the world to his liking.

"Architecture then is not just the art or science of building especially for the purposes of civil life.

"Architecture is the creation of a total environment within which can be accomplished the aspirations of man."

Further refinement of these thoughts has led us to a simpler and more succinct definition of architecture, which sums up our thoughts on the subject to date.

"Architecture is not a thing apart—beautiful for itself alone.

"Architecture is not a theory alone—of rhythmic living structure; nor of exquisite meaningful form; nor of superbly modulated space; nor of piercing intellectual synthesis; nor of totally integrated design.

"Architecture is not a study in realism exclusively—of program analysis; of functional relationships; of mathematics and law; of science and technology; of labor and business; of economics and finance.

(L-11) ". . . Information Flow insures that you will receive a full set of minutes . . . you'll always know what's going on . . . (L-15) Environmental programming is of concern to the people who will use the building . . ."

"Architecture is not the creation of a building alone; a building with all its beauty, discipline and reality. It is that building and its relation to those who will use it.

"Architecture is the creation of total environment within which can be accomplished the aspirations of man."

In order to demonstrate to clients the meaning of this definition and the methods we use to implement it, we have spent considerable time studying and arranging our client presentations. Here are some of the things we have discovered—and what we do about them.

A presentation is the method an architect uses to brief his client on how he is developing the design of the project, either in broad, sweeping principles, or in precise, minute detail. Through drawings, renderings, perspectives, models, and photographs, the architect presents a visual array of material that explains what he is doing. As he arranges this display, he describes verbally precisely what he is doing.

(R-15) ". . . accompanied with preliminary drawings, preliminary specifications, preliminary cost estimates and time schedule . . . (R-20) TECHNICAL DRAWINGS. *These begin with modular coordination . . ."*

The person, or group of people, to whom the presentation is made don't always get the full picture or explanation. As the group gets larger, several things happen. The near-sighted fellow can't see the drawings at all. The fellow with good vision can't always see what he is looking at because the drawings are too small and are rolling up at the edges; or they're too technical for him; or he doesn't understand shades and shadows. During the ordinary presentation, unless it is very carefully handled, larger groups tend to break down into smaller groups of people, each group discussing various aspects of the whole. The presentation loses continuity. There is always the fellow who doesn't hear well, or there is so much background noise that almost no one in the audience hears well.

CLASSIFICATION OF WORK	MATERIAL	LABOR
ion & Site preparation	16 235	670
rk	35 333	23357
e Work Lab & Research Unit	335 019	175 846
e Work Lecture Unit	45 944	16 049
ints & Structural	19 808	6 356
roofing & damp proofing	10 985	11 593
	58 818	74 833
rk	113 635	3 135
ne	151 724	-
Insulation & Sheet Metal	30 347	9 754
Arch.Metal	44 008	10 368
mes	9 660	7 174
	27 423	1 953
ndow & Trim Work	65 318	17 593
lass panels & doors - exterior	8 255	1 633
Lathing & Plastering	9 167	16 849
siac tile & ceramic tile	17 271	9 067
	7 821	4 326
toilet partitions	8 362	2 276
ry & mill work	13 692	1439
t Flooring	7 315	2 022
Tile	20 434	-
	13 600	

L-28

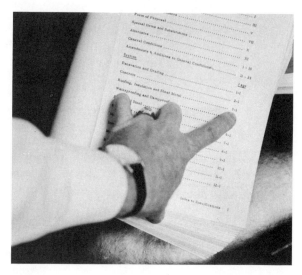

R-23

L-30

L-33

L-35

R-26

(L-28) ". . . we prepare careful and elaborate specifications . . . (R-23) You finally end up with a total cost estimate . . ."

(L-30) ". . . This owner knew the cost beforehand and decided he wanted those sunshades . . . (L-33) . . . and we will deliver to you a whole set of maintenance manuals . . ."

(L-35) "In our book 'Planning to Build,' you will be able to trace the activities you will go through . . . (R-26) The steps in building are complicated at times but management breaks them down into bite-size pieces . . ."

The proper architectural presentation should be a work of art in the same sense that the building to be shown should be a work of art.

Communication does not exist between speaker and audience, between architect and client, unless they have similar associations and interpretations of words and visual symbols. A film presentation is an audio-visual concept of word symbols and picture symbols presented in the perspective of the client's needs. It must be carefully informal. It talks about the people in the architectural office that the client will meet—the people who will be in charge of defining and solving the client's construction problems.

This requires a full command of the English language, a full command of photography, and the ability to deliver both, forcibly and with a dramatic sense of timing and direction, leaving, in the audience, a positive feeling that it has been intimately involved in a professional presentation. It should not be too slick nor too smooth. Portions of an audience can be quickly alienated by speaking down to them or speaking over their heads. No audience likes a "city slicker" approach designed to "take someone in."

Architects use the word "environment" a great deal; and the first thing they should do is provide a good one for an architectural presentation. The space should be comfortable. One should be able to see well and hear well without competition from distracting elements.

The actual presentation itself should be carefully studied and thought out beforehand. It should not be presented hurriedly, with all of the thinking ad-libbed as one goes along. For every single hour of conference time, there should be several hours of preparation time.

The sequence of drawings, data and other material should be carefully studied. The entire presentation must flow in an organized fashion. People must be led and brought along so that they see and feel the architect's reasons for each of his decisions as he moves through the creative process. People should not be allowed to splinter off into small groups to ask unrelated questions or to refuse to follow the thread of the conversation.

The material used for the conference should be specifically prepared for each conference. You need *client* drawings, not *technical* drawings; these are two different things. The drawings must speak in terms of ideas, not in terms of draftsmanship. They must make statements that can be read in the back row. Meticulous architectural drawings are not particularly useful for this kind of communication. Full and powerful use must be made of all the graphic arts. It is surprising how few architecturally-trained people are knowledgeable in this field.

In the development of a presentation we establish, first of all, a "shooting script" in which the complete scenario for the production is organized; dummies are made in which sequential information is established, the verbal accompaniment to the illustrations is outlined, and the personalities of all those attending the conference are analyzed and their likes and dislikes scrutinized. Words are carefully selected to lend power and persuasion to

This book list has been used effectively by Nolen-Swinburne in the development of its methods of communicating with clients.

COMMUNICATIONS
Howard H. Dean:
Effective Communications
Havland-Janis & Kelley:
Communications and Persuasions
Stanley L. Payne:
The Art of Asking Questions
William Strunk Jr:
The Elements of Style
Irving J. Lee:
How to Talk with People
J. Samuel Bois:
Explorations in Awareness
Harvard Business Review (Nov-Dec 1957):
Looking Around

PRESENTATIONS
Alex F. Osborne:
Applied Imagination
Stephen Baker:
Visual Persuasion
Paul Smith:
Creativity
R. R. Lutz:
Graphic Presentation Simplified
Frank Alexander Armstrong:
Idea Tracking
William Harvey:
Circulation of the Blood
Francis Bacon:
Selected Writings

PHOTOGRAPHY
Andreas Feininger:
The Creative Photographer

SEQUENCE
Disney & Thomas:
The Art of Animation
Standord L. Optner:
Systems Analysis

HUMAN UNDERSTANDING
Cartwright & Zander:
Group Dynamics
Rex F. Harlow:
Social Science in Public Relations
Gustave LeBon:
The Crowd
Ashley Montagu:
Man: His First Million Years
Wolfgang Köhler:
Gestalt Psychology

our argument and minimize unfavorable reaction in the minds of the audience. When this has been completed, the graphic and art work is then carefully selected for development.

The process now hinges on what we call "twin-screen technique of presentation." This technique requires a full knowledge of color photography and film projection. Two screens are used because we never present material in picture-for-picture sequence, but always on a comparative basis. Material on one screen is compared with material on the other screen. You go from A to B while A is still visible, or you show schematic data on one screen and you show design development data on the companion screen. The object always is to compare or to contrast ideas with design or other data.

Montages can be developed. Actual site photographs can be superimposed upon design suggestions. People and activities can be projected in such a way that they are made a part of the design concept. Above all, the impact of image size is important. People in their real roles can identify themselves with the action being shown on the screen. They feel themselves to be part of the presentation, rather than simply observers of it.

The large-screen technique and the continuity of ideas presented in a comfortable environment and darkened surroundings do not permit the audience to interrupt unless invited to do so. The audience is led on from one thought to the next, using a full presentation, and after the entire concept of an idea has been advanced for consideration, the audience may then be invited to criticize, object or approve the solutions illustrated.

Each person can see clearly and hear well, and the ideas and solutions expressed on the screen follow a very, very careful form of presentation. The weeks and months that have been spent in programming, analysis and design deserve no less than this.

The photography used must approach a level far above the amateur class. It is recommended that 2¼x2¼-inch slides be used. Enthusiasts of 35mm may object to such a statement, but slide for slide and task for task, it is our opinion that the two types of slides are not in the same class at all.

After the presentation of films, using the best automatic projectors available, you can then enter into the usual discussions back and forth with the audience, reviewing, checking and rechecking until there is full understanding and agreement among those present. Models can then be brought out and, if necessary, displayed along with the original copy from which the pictures were taken.

The use of visual symbols as a method of presentation has proven to be an exceptional method for bringing the architect's ideas into clear focus for the audience. The symbology of ideas expressed in full color, and in non-spatial diagrams and relationships explored on many alternative bases, make good arguments for convincing an audience that the architect's final concept of the proper solution is the right one. If the audience can be made to see this without interference from its own architectural prejudices, many unnecessary arguments can then be eliminated.

Part Four:

Promotional Services

23

Comprehensive Architectural Services:
Promotional

BY DUDLEY HUNT JR, AIA

Architectural services for entrepreneurs and those services related to promotion are at once one of the most promising and most neglected areas for comprehensive architectural services available to architects at the present time

One of the areas of comprehensive architectural services that holds great potential for architects, but which has often been neglected by them in the past, is in what has come to be called "promotional architectural services." By this is meant, simply, the services required by some owners in the actual acquisition of a building and its site, in the financing of the project, in the sale or rental of the completed building.

Architect resistance to promotional services

Some architects have resisted participation in such services in the past because they felt them to be undignified, unprofessional, unethical. Other architects have let promotional opportunities pass them by because they were ill-prepared to perform in this area of service. Still others have taken on promotional commissions only to find themselves out of their league when it came to dealing with entrepreneurs. For whatever reasons, architects in the past have—more often than not—found themselves either left out of promotional projects entirely or left saddened, but perhaps no wiser, when they did find themselves involved.

Clearing-up some misconceptions

It might be best to correct a few misconceptions some architects have about promotional projects immediately. First, there is nothing unethical *per se* about architect participation in promotional projects. The Standards of Professional Practice specifically state that the services of architects are based on the principle of agency. Therefore, architects are specifically allowed to act as agents for their clients in the procurement of building sites, financing of projects, etc. This is not to say that many architects will wish to get deeply involved in real estate or financing, but it certainly clears the way for architects to arrange for, and coordinate, such services for their clients. The same things might be said for public relations or other promotional activities. It goes, almost without saying, that any architect who gets into such activities in any manner had better have the background and knowledge necessary to perform such services effectively. As pointed out elsewhere, it need not even be unethical for an architect to perform some services for an entrepreneur on a contingency fee basis if the obligations of the Standards of Professional Practice are conformed with.

Promotional services not unethical

It follows then, at least as far as the Institute is concerned, that such promotional services activities can be performed by architects, ethically and professionally, if they are careful to conform to the Standards.

To participate or not?

Whether to participate in promotional ventures or not is—of course—a decision that must be made by each architect in accordance with his own motivations and goals. That some architects may find dealing with promoters undignified cannot be denied; and perhaps those architects had better avoid it. However, there are many architects in this country who find such work stimulating, creative and rewarding. For them, a fertile field beckons—a field in which there is much to be accomplished and one that a great many nonarchitectural, even antiarchitectural, interests are now performing services that architects can and should perform.

For those architects who choose to pursue the opportunities that exist in the field of promotional architectural services, knowledge and understanding of the intricacies of real estate, finance, promotion will be required. Perhaps, it might even be said that even those architects who expect to shun promotional projects would be better able to serve their non-promotional clients if they had some degree of understanding of real estate, finance and promotion. After all, is there ever an architectural project that does not require a site upon which to be built, money with which to build, promotion of some sort to the public, a board of directors, an informed client?

There is much territory to be explored by architects in the —to architects—little understood land of promotional architectural services. In the pages following, a glimpse of this area may be had. First, a discussion of the role of the architect in ventures that are strictly promotional in character, the demands for such services, what they entail, how they may be performed and charged for. Following this is a quite complete discussion of services for clients who are lessees rather than owners of their buildings. Finally, there is a two-part discussion of the role of the architect, and his relationships with others, in services for revenue-producing projects. This leaves much territory still to be covered at another time, but the present coverage does indicate the scope, and some of the details, of the field.

24

Comprehensive Architectural Services: For Promotional Ventures

BY JOHN STETSON, FAIA

The large number of buildings constructed each year that start out as promotional ventures offer a considerable opportunity to architects who would like to obtain more commissions in a wide variety of building types

Promotional opportunities

Almost every architect—at one time or another—has been approached by a promoter with an offer to include him in a venture if he will perform his services on a contingent basis. In many cases, the offer does not include an increased fee for the risk undertaken. Rarely is the architect to receive anything for his services should the project fail to develop. Conversely, the services the architect renders in such cases may not always represent everything they should.

Young practitioners, perhaps because of their understandable eagerness to be associated with a major project, are sometimes taken in by shrewd promoters seeking the most services for the least expenditure. On the other hand, untold thousands of legitimate opportunities exist for architects in the promotional field. The word "promoter" no longer necessarily carries a stigma. The legitimate promoter is apt to be a real estate broker or some other person closely associated with the selling of real property; and lawyers, accountants and contractors have found promotional ventures a lucrative means of augmenting their income.

Many architects are prepared for promotional project ventures

Most able architects have available, in their own offices and in their wide knowledge of design and construction, every weapon and all the necessary ammunition for successful forays into the promotional campaigns usually generated by real estate men or others. The man who eventually becomes the client in a promotional venture, the lending institutions and the buying public alike welcome the type of leadership a knowledgeable architect can provide.

Higher fees possible

Why are people willing to pay a greater price for the services of promoters than for basic architectural services that require more hours of work, more education and—in actuality—greater risk? Simple enough. The promoter makes money for his client in a manner he can more readily understand and in a much shorter time. Agreed that a well-designed building may well be a joy forever, in financial return, in permanence and in beauty. Yet only too many of our award-winning buildings are economic failures. Gone are the days when the wealthy supported the arts. Almost all of today's clients are businessmen who are *often* ready to enjoy the beauty of good architecture, but who are *always* looking for the greatest financial return or the most economical use of every dollar they spend.

Services for promotional projects

What clients will require for success in promotional projects—that they themselves must furnish—can most often be categorically grouped under the major classification of "money." With this consideration taken care of, what then is required of the architect? What architects must know—and be prepared to furnish—if they are to become successful "promotional architects" is outlined on the last page of this article. The first requirement is a basic and current knowledge of the available properties in the area. Vacant lots and buildings not now producing incomes proportionate to their assessed valuations are the easiest to convert to ready cash. This does not mean that architects must now start selling real estate without a license; they will sell only ideas. The architect can find out the name of the owner of the likely property or building and quietly ascertain the current market price, then let his client make a direct offer when the right time arrives. Since no selling fee need be involved, here is the first opportunity the architect has to save some money for his client-to-be.

Knowledge of available properties

This first phase of the promotional effort can be all-important. Only too often, an architect has lost a commission because some real estate salesman sold the architect's client-to-be an existing building, rather than the vacant property he was directed to show and for which he was to arrange the purchase. For success in promotional ventures, a knowledge of the needs of the community, availability of mortgage financing, availability of tenants and marketability of properties is most important. Armed with such facts, a basic knowledge of economics and architectural ability, the architect who so chooses will be able to participate in promotional ventures successfully.

Architectural and economic research

Once the property has been chosen and its best use determined, architectural and economic research become necessary. These go hand-in-hand. Too much money spent on a building, either new or remodeled, can spell defeat for a promotional venture at the start. When it has been determined that there is reasonable assurance of success, the availability of financing becomes the next step. Rough sketches and specifications, together with a reasonably accurate cost estimate, will then be required in order to interest money lenders. Along with a comparative economic study of other buildings of this type, these things are all that are usually required by lenders. If several prospective tenants can also be produced, then the success of the financing program is almost a foregone conclusion.

Role of the buyer

Next comes the buyer. If there are as yet no prospective purchasers, this is the time to bring a broker into the picture. Amazing though it may seem, bankers, stock and investment brokers, lawyers and doctors, as well as real estate men, often perform this necessary function. Once a buyer is interested and persuaded to make a written agreement, then the venture can be put together in actuality.

There are a number of ways in which architects may receive their compensation from a promotional project. Because of the

Compensation for promotional services

increased scope of the services performed, much higher fees than those usually charged for architectural services are in order. Normally there is a fee for economic research, running upwards of one per cent of the cost of the venture. Assuming a finder's fee for the mortgage, decorator's fee, landscape fee, broker's commission, architectural and engineering fees, etc, it is conceivable for a client to pay fifteen per cent for services that will be rendered in a most disorderly manner. An architect can do more for the client, in a more orderly manner, and save him money; at the same time the architect can make a higher fee and—if he chooses—end up owning part of a going venture.

Some architects take all of their fee in cash in a venture of this sort; large firms, with several partners, may find it difficult to do otherwise. Smaller firms—and particularly individual practitioners—might do very well if they took only their expenses in cash and accepted a percentage of the venture as the major part of their compensation for the services rendered. Naturally this places limits on the percentage of the total annual office output that can be devoted to promotional ventures; and it delays the return. Some architects accept their entire fee as a percentage of ownership of projects. Compensation in the form of a percentage of ownership has the advantages of tax treatment as capital gains rather than straight income and of representing a share of a profitable venture, assuming the architect has been able to put together a successful venture. The buyer, client or owner (whatever he may be called) will probably be delighted to have his architect share in the ownership, thereby assuring himself of the utmost architectural effort to turn out a building that will be successful in both esthetics and economics.

Success in promotional fields

What are the architect's chances for success in the promotional building field? Based on the facts, he can't lose, particularly if he is any kind of salesman at all. Why? Here are some of the reasons: 1) The architect will show the client how to make money. 2) He will offer the client a complete deal. If the client makes money, then he will no doubt be happy to see the architect do the same. 3) The services of the architect will be far more comprehensive than the services offered by others now trying to invade this design field. 4) There will be a smaller number of promoters on any one project. 5) The architect is trained to perform many services on projects. 6) The architect has—or should have—the respect of mortgage bankers. Capital is always available for worthy projects. 7) The client would prefer to have the architect participate in promotional projects, in order to lower costs and get a better job. 8) Idea men, if they properly sell themselves and their products, always make money. Architects are idea men or they never would have become interested in their profession to begin with.

Advantages to architect and to the buyer

The services of the architect that have been described are attractive to the buyer. And they can be of great benefit to the architect over the years. "Promotion" is not necessarily an unmentionable word. An architect's approach to the subject, the methods he uses and the manner in which he conducts his activities will be the deciding factors as to how the word will be defined in a given case. Surely, an ethical architect need fear no stigma.

Outline of Promotional Architectural Services

I Services of the Architect

A Site and Use

  1 Availability of land and/or building for project

  2 Lowest acceptable cost

  3 Best new use

    a Availability of tenants

    c Desirability to community

    d Tax advantages to investors

    e Economics of project

  4 Zoning requirements

B Economic Survey

  1 Study of similar projects in community

  2 Study of economic indicators in community

  3 Operational cost factors

  4 Income potential

  5 Chance for success

C Financing Survey

  1 Availability of money for this type project

  2 Costs of obtaining financing

  3 Construction money

  4 Interest rates and repayment plans

  5 Obtaining tentative commitment

D Design of Building

  1 Preliminaries (including outline specifications, etc, necessary for financing)

  2 Working drawings and specifications

  3 Taking of bids

E Administration of Construction

  1 As architect

  2 As agent for owner, or as owner

  3 Continuing survey of means of reducing costs to obtain best economic picture

F Decorating and furnishing

G Landscaping

II Architect's Remuneration

A Flat fee or percentage fee to be paid as project proceeds

B Fee to be paid in lump sum at completion—and sale or lease—of project

C Fee paid partly in cash and partly as percentage of ownership of project

D Fee paid entirely in percentage of ownership of project

E What are tax advantages for architect of various types of remuneration?

25

Comprehensive Architectural Services: For Industrial Lessee Clients

BY GEORGE T. HEERY, AIA

How to perform comprehensive architectural services for projects, particularly buildings in the industrial field, in which the client of the architect, in an increasing number of instances, is a lessee rather than the building owner

This article was prepared with the help of the AIA Committee on Industrial Architecture, of which the author is the Chairman, and in consultation with Frederick Blumberg, Attorney-at-Law, Philadelphia; Jere M. Mills, Mortgage Banker, Atlanta; and Gilbert H. Scribner Jr, American Society of Real Estate Counselors, Chicago

Acquisition of new facilities

For the architectural profession, comprehensive services for industrial clients who lease facilities can lead to a great increase in industrial commissions—and to the nipping in the bud of many "Package Deal" operations. To industrial clients, increased architectural activity in this often by-passed area of professional service can mean lower rents and lower operating and maintenance costs. To both architects and clients, proper handling of professional services for lessees can lead to better architecture for industry.

In addition, one mortgage banker states that the lessor will receive more favorable consideration on financing if the prospective lender knows that the lease contract is based on complete drawings and specifications prepared by the *lessee's* architect and that the construction will be properly supervised.

The six most common methods employed by industry for the acquisition of new plant facilities are:

LEASE—A company acquires a site, builds a plant using normal construction procedures (usually a general contract); the company then sells the facility to an investor-lessor and leases it back;

LEASE—A company contracts with an investor-lessor, on a stipulated rental basis, often after competitive lease proposals for one or more sites or after direct negotiation;

LEASE—A company contracts with a private investor-lessor, on a formula basis, with construction paid for by the lessor, though actually performed by a third-party-contractor on a contract resulting from competitive bidding or direct negotiation;

LEASE—A company contracts with a community or other industrial development agency, acting as lessor, on a stipulated rental or formula basis, with construction paid for by the lessor though performed by a third party as above;

OWNERSHIP—A company contracts with an independent general contractor on a contract resulting from competitive bidding or direct negotiation;

OWNERSHIP—A company contracts to make direct payments for subcontracts and/or labor and materials (without surety), with an architect, engineer, or project supervisor acting as superintendent, coordinator and expeditor.

Other variations exist, most of them involving leases, but these are the major types. Many architects are oriented only toward the owner-general contract type, and possibly, in some cases, the owner-subcontract type. Yet four of the six major methods involve leases; so it should not come as a surprise that the following scene has been enacted many times:

Architects may lose out on leasehold commissions

An architect learns that his friend's company is to build a new plant. When the architect calls on the friend and offers his services, he says he appreciates the architect's interest, but they are going to have someone build the new plant for them and lease it to the company, so he guesses they won't need their own architect. The architect is sorry to hear this, but maybe they'll keep him in mind the next time the company builds its own building, and lets it go at that. And neither party may realize that *both* have missed a good opportunity to do a *better* building with savings in original cost, maintenance and operations.

It is, of course, a truism that many companies could operate much more efficiently, control their costs better, and get better architecture by using independent architects for their leased facilities. However, architects must accept most of the blame for the fact that often this is not so—for it is the architects who have something to "sell," and it is they who must do the "selling" to potential clients.

Need for Lessee Services

On the other hand, it is fortunate for both industry and the profession that a number of architectural firms, scattered throughout the country, have made it their business to have people on their staffs who are familiar with the various problems and processes of leased industrial facilities. These firms offer a valuable professional service tailored to each industrial client's needs and specifically related to industrial, single-occupancy, leased facility acquisition.

Advantages of leasing

The following are typical of the advantages that may be gained by a given company through the leasing of plant facilities:

Conversion of Construction Cost Estimate to Rent Estimate

Estimated Project Cost:

Construction (120,000 sq ft floor area)	$560,000
Land Cost	72,000
Architectural Fees	33,600
Interest During Construction	6,800
Surveys, Tests, Legal, Reproduction, 3% Contingency	20,000
Total Project Cost	$692,400

Rules-of-Thumb for Estimating Rents:

Ten-year Lease—9% $\times$ Cost ($692,400) =
Annual Rent =
$62,316
(or $.518/sq ft)

Twenty-year Lease—8% $\times$ Cost (692,400) =
Annual Rent =
$55,392
(or $.462/sq ft)

This hypothetical example is based on a net lease for a lessee client with an AAA rating, with the lessee paying all operating and maintenance costs including taxes and insurance. Interest during construction is figured at a rate of 6% demand, on two-thirds of the total project cost, during a construction period of six months, assuming that the average loan during the period will be one-half of the total loan. The percentages used in the rent estimation rules-of-thumb will vary considerably with the money market and with the lessee's credit rating. Also, any real estate commissions or management fees must be added to the rents shown.

Capital investment in fixed assets will often be held down. This often makes possible more rapid expansion than an individual company's working capital would otherwise allow.

Rent will be an expense item and, therefore, fully deductible on income tax returns under normal circumstances. Also, leasehold improvements may be depreciated over the useful life of the improvement or the term of lease, whichever is shorter.

Credit will be less directly tied up than it would be with a loan. The balance sheet will look more favorable, since the fixed assets representing realty will be eliminated.

Mortgage or loan agreements may act to prevent additional borrowing later.

Arguments about the estimated life of the properties for depreciation purposes can be eliminated.

Stock control of a company may be retained and additional capital required for business operations secured at the same time through sale-leasebacks instead of through issuance of new stock or other means of this sort.

Problems of Leasehold Acquisition

Since World War II, there has been greatly increased activity in building construction for long-term (usually 10-20 year) leasing. It should be realized, however, that many companies find that ownership rather than leasing best fits their situations. Immediately after the end of the war, many corporations had their real estate, distribution, or purchasing departments handle leasehold acquisitions rather than their architectural or engineering departments which handled (with independent firms or their own personnel) only the company-owned facilities.

Not infrequently, the real estate, distribution, or purchasing people, having no construction background, tried to over-simplify the acquisition process and ended up with some very unpleasant surprises. It was not unusual at that time to encounter such people, armed with a one-page description of a 100,000-sq ft office and warehouse, looking for a complete "package" and firmly convinced that the requirements were so simple that only the rent and location need be considered as long as the prospective lessor agreed to meet the short list of requirements. This state of affairs still exists, and still leads to some extremely unpleasant surprises. These are usually the result of one or more of the following difficulties:

The construction proposals received may not have been readily comparable due to differences in design, drawings and specifications, or to incompleteness of these documents, or to the understandable lack of technical ability on the part of real estate, distribution or purchasing people to interpret or question the construction documents.

Very little thought may have been given to the project by the captive architect or draftsman. Consequently, the building may suffer from lack of planning that solves the lessee company's operation and maintenance problems, not to mention the fact that the appearance of the building—which bears the company's name— almost invariably suffers.

Frequently construction will not have been performed in accordance with the lessee's expectations because of a lack of adequate localized supervision, incomplete drawings and specifications or the difficulty of maintaining the type of direct control over the builder-lessor that an architect normally can exert on a contractor through his control of the purse strings.

Mechanical and electrical systems frequently may be troublesome in operation because their design was done by subcontractors rather than by an architect and his engineers, and because the main criterion in the selection of the systems was the prospect of their relatively low original cost.

Lessee Services by Architects

Just as the format for normal architectural services has evolved to satisfy the needs of owners—and as an integral part of the formal development of the construction industry over the last century—so in recent years a new architectural service—the Lessee Service as it will be referred to here—has started evolving, to satisfy the long-term lessee's needs.

The Lessee Service is—as the name indicated—a professional service provided to a *lessee* as opposed to an *owner*. Just as normal architectural services are related to an owner-contractor agreement, the Lessee Service is related to a lessee-lessor agreement. Needless to say, many architects have provided Lessee Services for years without giving them a special name, either on their own initiative or under the direction of clients.

Lessee Services may be performed by a lessee company's own architectural department, but more and more frequently they are being performed by private architectural firms because, among other reasons, of the high costs and personnel difficulties that even the largest corporations encounter in maintaining complete architectural departments.

Basic principles of lessee services

The basic—and first—principles of Lessee Services are the following:

1 The services are equal in scope to normal, complete services; they include preliminary studies, preparation of working drawings and specifications for the work, structural, mechanical and electrical engineering, and supervision (general administration) of the construction.

2 For a lessee, the contract documents must serve a dual role. They must be documents of the lease contract and also construction documents; often they become part of standard construction contract. (It would be extremely dangerous, and bad practice, to have one set of documents for the lease agreement and a different set for construction purposes.) In this work the term "Owner" is generally interchangeable with the term "Lessee" and the term "Contractor" interchangeable with "Lessor."

3 The architect who performs Lessee Services must be even more flexible than usual in order to ward off the individual problems and requirements of his lessee clients. The sort of flexibility he needs can result only from some knowledge of lease agreements and his client's tax and financial position. Some general knowledge is also required of real estate as well as of prospective investors, lessors, developers, sites and builders in the area of the project and of current conditions of the mortgage market. Established working relationships with real estate brokers and other specialists in this field will also be most valuable to the architect performing lessee services.

4 The lessee client will be able to get better terms, and possibly lower rents, if a high degree of flexibility (larger bays, higher ceilings, etc) is designed into the leased building. The financeability of a leased building is equally as important to a lessee as it is to a lessor.

Four major leasing methods are as follows:

Leasing Method No 1

A company acquires a site, builds a plant using normal construction procedures (usually a general contract); the company then sells the facility to an investor-lessor and leases it back.

This is probably the simplest method of leased facility acquisition. It is frequently employed by larger corporations; the company simply acquires the land required and builds the facility it needs, using its own capital funds or short-term financing. After the facility has been occupied and is in operating order, the entire property is then sold to an investor under the terms of a previously agreed-upon long-term leaseback to the seller-lessee (the company). Often there will be options in the contract to repurchase the property at agreed-upon prices within specified times. In such cases the architect should advise his clients to consult their attorneys regarding the possibilities of adverse tax rulings on repurchase plans. A number of insurance companies and retirement funds are very active as investor-lessors. In other instances, the lessor entity may be closely affiliated with the lessee; the lessor may be the employee retirement fund of the lessee company or a real estate holding subsidiary of the company. However, there may be some undesirable tax implications in connection with such options to purchase and in leases with affiliates.

Architect's role in sale-leaseback

In a sale-leaseback, the architect's role is not altered appreciably from its normal course. In such a case, a standard owner-architect agreement is in order, and the construction contract documents may be prepared by the architect for an "Owner" and a "Contractor" without reference to a lessee or lessor. However, an architect who wishes to make his services more valuable to an industrial client should always determine if a sale-leaseback might be under consideration by the client. If a sale-leaseback is to be considered the architect should:

1 Determine if the proposed purchaser has design criteria that must be met;

2 Obtain from the proposed purchaser a formal approval of the final contract documents prior to commencement of construction or an informal approval in states in which insurance companies are prevented by law from making firm commitments to purchase uncompleted buildings;

3 Provide Lessee Services only with the full knowledge and approval of the client and after determination of any special provisions of the sale-leaseback that may require additional services from the architects.

Leasing Method No 2

A company contracts with an investor-lessor, on a stipulated rental basis, often after competitive lease proposals for one or more sites or after direct negotiation.

Many architects, and others, mistakenly call this type of lessee service a "Package Deal," but it is not. Even though the builder-lessor, in such cases, may often control the design through his own personnel or architect, this cannot be objected to on grounds of ethics, since, after all, *the lessor is the owner.* It is true that "Package Dealers" are quite active in this field, but the transaction, in itself, is not a "Package Deal."

A definition of "Package Deal"

At least for the purposes of this article the term "Package Deal" is defined as follows: a contract between an owner and a contractor in which the contractor controls the preparation of the drawings and specifications with his own personnel, or by employing an outside architect or engineer. "Contractor" means just that; a builder is not necessarily a contractor. A contractor *contracts* to do a specific thing for a stipulated remuneration. In other words, a "Package Deal" is an agreement in which there is an identity of interest between the design entity and the contractor. Another variation of the definition: a design entity, proposing to act as contractor, would represent an unethical identity of interests and would fall into the category of "Package Deal." An architect acting as an entrepreneur or lessor is *not* acting as a "Package Dealer." A contractor acting as a lessor is *not* acting as a "Package Dealer." A negotiated contract is certainly *not* necessarily a "Package Deal"; and it may often have many advantages to the owner.

Architect-contractor ethics

Many architects are under the impression that there is a great gray zone of ethical behavior for contractors and architects in these areas. In actuality, there seems to be a clear line demarcating the proper activities of the architect and the contractor. In the author's opinion, the architect must not act as a contractor or allow himself to be employed as the architect for a project by a contractor who is acting as surety; and a contractor should not attempt to control the design. If these proprieties are observed surely both the architect and the contractor may ethically provide many services beyond the confines of the typical owner-contractor-architect relationships of the past.

Whichever department—real estate, distribution or purchasing—is in charge of a leasehold acquisition, it has quite a large task to perform and has need of the Lessee Services of the architect. The people in these departments of companies may often be the last to realize their need for such services but just as often they are the easiest to sell after having experienced some of the unpleasant surprises previously mentioned.

Competitive lease proposals or direct negotiation?

The main task of these people is to obtain the best possible deal for their company, not only on construction, but on location, site, terms, special provisions, and—of course—rent. They may find it desirable to purchase (or otherwise obtain control of) a specific site and receive competitive lease proposals—all for the same site—or negotiation directly with one prospective lessor may appear to be the better course of action.

In other instances competitive lease proposals may be obtained, each prospective lessor making a proposal for a different site, each site usually under the control of an individual prospective lessor.

Another method is direct negotiation with a prospective lessor who controls a specific site that is acceptable to the company that will lease the facilities.

Competitive lease proposals are usually best

In almost all cases, it is in the best interest of the company (lessee) to have competitive lease proposals or negotiations based on the same *complete* drawings and specifications, prepared by the *lessee's* architect. Even when competitive lease proposals for different sites are obtained this is desirable when it is possible. However, in this case, it is sometimes necessary to obtain the competitive lease proposals on diagrammatic drawings together with relatively complete preliminary specifications.

Pointers for architect

In using this approach to leasing by the client company (lessee), the architect might well keep several points in mind. First of all, the architect's specifications, in addition to covering the construction, should tie down as many variables in the lease agreement as are feasible in the individual situation. Just as it is usually desirable in receiving bids for ownership to have contractors' prices as the only variables, so is it usually desirable to have the amount of rent as the only variable in receiving lease proposals.

The architect should bear in mind that his services do not supplant the services of his client's attorney. This is *at least* as true in Lessee Services as in normal services.

Leasing requirements in specifications

After review and approval by the client's legal counsel, the architect's specifications will usually need to include the following:

1 The desired term (length) of the lease;

2 The desired provisions for options to renew the lease;

3 The desired provisions for options to purchase the property. The client's attorney will want to give particular attention to this point, for unless the transaction is properly fashioned, the lessee may lose his rent deduction and the lessor may lose his depreciation deduction, thereby defeating an important objective, and some of the advantages, of the lease;

4 The desired covenants concerning maintenance and insurance. It is not uncommon for the lessee to provide all maintenance and carry all insurance, further pointing up the necessity for the lessee to control the design and construction;

5 Desired covenants concerning real estate taxes—provisions usually written into lease specifications after local investigation and discussions with prospective lessors. In tax covenants, it is not unusual to protect the lessor with an "escalator" or tax payment limit clause. Also, in other instances, the lessee may agree to pay all real estate taxes;

6 A paragraph specifying that the lessor is to reimburse the lessee for planning costs (architect's fee, surveys, tests, document reproduction, etc) and stating the specific amount of reimbursement. The inclusion of this requirement means that even the planning costs become a part of the lease amortization program and the lessee client is saved from having to use capital funds for costs of this type;

7 Also, of course, a paragraph explaining the dual role of the contract documents and relationships, in the terminology of such interchangeable terms as "Owner" and "Lessee," as well as "Contractor" and "Lessor";

8 Statement concerning effect of property condemnation;

9 Statement concerning the right to sub-lease;

10 Statement concerning building alterations and security for the lessor against loss;

11 Statement concerning destruction of property, irrespective of insurance coverage;

12 Statement concerning restoration of property in case of casualty, and use of insurance coverage;

13 Statement concerning default and escape clauses for each party, if the other should fail to live up to the agreement.

Real estate services

Architects should recognize that their professional Lessee Services do not supplant the services of the real estate broker. A good broker provides a valuable service to his client. Usually brokers will represent prospective lessors, and their commissions will be paid by the lessors, though this point should be made clear in the architect's specifications. In other cases, the lessee client may appoint a real estate counselor to represent his interests and to work with the architect; here again the counselor's commission arrangement needs to be spelled out in the specifications.

After a lessee client has tied down a specific site, and the architect has prepared the final drawings and specifications in basically the same manner as for an owner-client, lease proposals may be received from prospective lessors or their agents. The proposals must be based on the complete documents. Having a specific site tied down has at least two advantages to a lessee and one to bidding lessors. The lessee is assured that the site is the one he wants and analysis of proposals will be easier than otherwise. To bidding lessors, it means that the land cost will be the same for all bidders. In such a case, the architect's specifications should include a paragraph covering the lessor's required purchase of the site from the lessee or others (and reimbursement for land options, if any). This paragraph must, of course, state all of the terms of the purchase including the price of the land.

Competitive proposals on several sites

When it becomes desirable—or necessary—for the client company to receive competitive proposals on different sites, it is usually desirable to have selected bidders (prospective lessors) submit sites for advance approval. If this is possible, the architect can prepare normal and complete documents with alternate site plans, foundation plans, grading requirements and the like for each site. (It may be necessary for the architect to make an additional charge for each such site after the first one.) However, time and other circumstances may not always allow the foregoing procedure to be followed. In many cases, the architect must devise methods of serving and protecting his client with bidding documents composed of diagrammatic drawings, alternate plans, drawings that would normally be considered only to be preliminary studies, site criteria documents, diagrammatic site plans and other inventions. The final working drawings and specifications will then be completed after receipt of proposals and tentative award of the lessee contract.

When the client company negotiates directly with a prospective lessor who controls a specific acceptable site, the documents may be prepared in basically the same manner as in the case of competitive bidding for a specific site. Here the architect, together with his lessee client, will negotiate and work with the specific prospective lessor.

Leasing Method No 3

A company contracts with a private investor-lessor, on a formula basis, with construction paid for by the lessor, though actually performed by a third party contractor on a contract resulting from competitive bidding or direct negotiation.

This situation is characterized, for the most part, by similarities with the method discussed immediately above. One major difference that may occur here is that the lessor's only interest may be the "paper," in other words the credit of the lessee and the terms of the lease contract. In the construction contract, the lessor's interest will probably be the same as the lessee's. In many cases the lessor may be virtually inactive insofar as the construction program itself is concerned, since the lease will be on a formula basis.

The "formula" lease

A "formula" refers to an agreement between the lessor and the lessee that states, in effect, that the periodic rent payments are simply an agreed-upon percentage of the total cost of the project. (Usually eight to twelve per cent per year, the exact rate depending on such variables as the term of the lease and the worth of the lessee.) Also, provisions for renewals and options to purchase are related to the total cost in terms of a formula. In formula leases the lessor will usually be given a maximum limitation on the total cost of the project.

A "formula" variation

One of the variations of this type of lease, that the architect should know about, is the possibility of a connection between the building contractor and the investor-lessor. This is not necessarily a bad thing; and it may even be desirable on some occasions. However, when this occurs, the architect will be dealing with a situation that has much in common with leasing method No 2, previously described.

Construction contract competition

In the straight formula situation, the lessor will ordinarily prefer to have competition for the construction contract. This fact, along with others previously discussed, means that the architect will have to provide a service to the lessor as well as to the lessee. This does not necessarily mean that the architect will be caused additional work, at least not enough to require additional charges. However, there may be situations, particularly during construction, in which the lessor will require a considerable amount of additional services and additional charges, by the architect, will be in order.

Leasing Method No 4

A company contracts with a community, or other industrial development agency, acting as lessor, on a stipulated rental or formula basis, with construction paid by the lessor though performed by a third party as in method 3 above.

In this case, the architect will perform basically the same services as in the example immediately preceding. Differences in this case are caused by the fact that the lessor will usually be even more impersonal and less active than in the other. Frequently a community group will merely act as a financing vehicle. This means the architect will have to do the same things for the lessor that he would do for any owner-group client. However, since the lessee's interests and the lessor's interests tend to be even more nearly identical in this case—for the construction program—than in the preceding case this probably will not cause the architect an appreciable amount of additional work.

Community-lease services

In serving his lessee-client in a community lease situation, the architect can be of great value to all parties concerned through such services as the following:

1 Aid in the original selection of the community;

2 Aid in selection of the site;

3 Coordination of community activities on utilities and other services, roads, etc;

4 Provision of independent and impartial influence to assure the lessee and the lessor of the best possible construction at the fairest prices.

Verbal Agreements Unsatisfactory

Many architects have had unfortunate experiences similar to the following: the architect and his client had executed a standard owner-architect agreement for an industrial building. (Or the architect proceeded on an industrial project with only a verbal agreement covering what was presumed to be a typical situation.) While the architect's work was in progress, the client found that it might be advantageous for him to lease the facility and decided that he should accept a lease "package" instead of following the original course.

The client then feels that it is to his company's advantage to terminate the architect's services. When a situation such as this occurs, the client or the architect, or both, are often dissatisfied with the termination arrangements. And worst of all, had the client had any way of knowing, he could very well have gotten the best lease deal by continuing to use the services of his own architect.

Owner-Architect Contracts

When the architect is originally commissioned for an industrial project he can easily prevent such a situation from occurring by bringing up for discussion the possibility of a leasehold acquisition. Then, if it is agreeable to the client, provisions may be made in the form of supplements to the standard agreement form that will make the document serve equally well for standard services and for Lessee Services.

While this sort of procedure holds a number of advantages to both parties, it has one big advantage for each of them. To the client, it means that project planning can proceed smoothly and with continuity even though he may not have determined which acquisition course will best serve his needs; flexibility is again the byword. For the architect, it means that the chances of the project being unexpectedly terminated are reduced.

Basically, the same form of agreement is in order in such a case, whether or not the client has definitely decided ahead of time on a leasehold acquisition. In any case, the architect's own legal counsel will be his best source of advice for modification of the standard form of agreement. However, the architect can help guide his attorney on important points to be covered. Some of these are the following:

The contract should state that the client may be either the owner or the lessee of the facility.

It should state that the client has the right to cause payments on account to be made by an owner-lessor to the architect.

The contract should also state that the original client is responsible for the architect's fee if, for any reason, a lessor does not make the payments in the proper manner.

Adaptation of Standard Contracts

Standard AIA Owner-Architect contracts may be readily adapted for use with lessee clients by the addition of two clauses such as the following:

"The term Owner as used herein refers to the Architect's Client, who may be either the actual Owner or the Lessee of the project. In either case, the Architect will provide the same services as set out herein to the Client, and the Client, whether he be Lessee or Owner, will have the same obligations to the Architect.

"AMENDMENT TO PAYMENTS ARTICLE—"If the Owner (Client) should elect to become the Lessee of the project he may cause payments to be made directly to the Architect by the Lessor or other parties. However, in so doing, the Client is not relieved of the full obligation of all payments to the Architect required in this agreement. The Architect shall continue to represent the Owner (Client) if he becomes the Lessee."

In addition, the architect may desire to extend to his client the right to delay the first payments on account of the fee to an agreed-upon date or until the commencement of construction whichever comes first. (This should apply in the case of a lease-hold acquisition only.) If the architect is in a position to grant this extension of credit, it will allow the lessee-client to see his project completed without any capital outlays.

It is hoped that some of these points will be useful to other architects. However, many practitioners will be able to add to—and improve on—the suggestions made here; and industrial clients themselves often can make valuable contributions to the leasehold acquisition process. In any case, it is important for both clients and the architectural profession to recognize this basic truth: *If a company is going to be the single occupant of an industrial facility for a relatively long term, whether as tenant or owner, that company, in its own interests, needs to exert control over the planning and construction of the facility through its own independent architect.*

Committee on Industrial Architecture
The American Institute of Architects
1735 New York Ave NW, Washington 6, DC

George T. Heery AIA, Heery and Heery, Chairman; John S. Bolles FAIA, John S. Bolles, Architects and Engineers; Louis DeMoll AIA, The Ballinger Company; CORRESPONDING MEMBERS: Alfred S. Alschuler Jr, AIA, Friedman, Alschuler and Sincere; MacDonald Becket AIA, Welton Becket and Associates; Leo A. Daly Jr, AIA, Leo A. Daly Company; Robert F. Hastings FAIA, Smith, Hinchman and Grylls Associates; Sol King AIA, Albert Kahn Associates, Inc; Harry J. Korslund AIA, Korslund, LeNormand and Quann, Inc; E. Keith Lockard AIA, Lockard, Casazza and Parsons and Associates; Donald E. McCormack AIA, Caterpillar Tractor Company; Albert C. Martin Jr, FAIA, Albert C. Martin and Associates; Louis Rossetti FAIA, Giffels and Rossetti; Arnold W. Thompson AIA, American Airlines; John L. Turner AIA, John L. Turner and Associates. CONSULTANTS: Frederick Blumberg, Attorney-at-Law, Philadelphia, Pennsylvania; Jere M. Mills, Mortgage Banker, Atlanta, Georgia; Gilbert H. Scribner Jr, American Society of Real Estate Counselors, Chicago, Illinois

26

Principles of Feasibility
For Revenue-Producing Real Estate

BY LARRY SMITH *

In order to properly serve the increasing number of clients who build for the use of others, rather than for their own use, the architect must have some understanding of real estate investment principles and be prepared to cooperate with clients and the real estate organizations that advise them

*The author's firm, Larry Smith & Company, Real Estate Consultants, has general offices in Seattle, branch offices in Washington, New York, Chicago, Beverly Hills, Toronto

Architect's guide to revenue-producing real estate

There is a significant difference between the approach to the design of real estate improvements for the use of an owner and those constructed for revenue-producing purposes.

Where real estate improvements are designed for the use of an owner—whether that use is personal, economic or institutional in nature—the judgment of the owner can be exercised freely in determining the extent to which the cost of development is a proper expression of the owner's attitude toward the suitability of the improvement for the desired use. Questions of future maintenance cost, depreciation, obsolescence, advertising value and convenience can all be answered within the framework of the owner's personal knowledge and attitude.

On the other hand, when a real estate improvement is created for revenue-producing purposes, the efficiency of the design and the cost of the total improvement must operate within a narrow and relatively rigid framework represented by the effective demand for the facilities being created, the market value expressed as rental for such facilities, and the ability of the owner and his advisors to solve the equation of costs and net return.

Therefore, in the development of revenue-producing real estate, the architect must be guided by the facts of effective market demand and must create a project design and specifications which will be capable of producing a net profit for the owner. Thus it is important in such cases to first obtain an expression of the economic elements which will control the effectiveness of the proposed project as a profit-producing investment.

The development of economically sound revenue-producing real estate is dependent upon the following factors:

a) Market demand for the facilities at a rent capable of supporting the capital investment

b) Identification of the cost structure best suited to produce the optimum net profit (the most effective combination of income and expense, including financing costs)

c) The ability of the architect to design a project consistent with the identified costs and specifications

d) The development of the project in the most effective location and the development of stores or other rental units within the project in most effective location relationships to each other

e) The ability of the owner to control the cost of construction and develop, within the budget, the project as designed

f) Ability of owner to lease or sell project efficiently

g) Ability of owner to finance project economically

h) Ability of owner to operate project efficiently.

The production of a sound piece of revenue-producing real estate therefore requires intensive efforts by the architect, by the owner and by the owner's real estate brokerage and management organization. This holds true whether there is an internal real estate organization or the owner employs outside talent for the real estate functions.

The extent to which an owner will require specialized real estate advice and talent in the execution of a project will depend largely on the owner's experience and on whether he has a competent real estate staff in his own organization. However, regardless of the source of the real estate "know-how," many of the decisions in connection with the development of revenue-producing real estate are real estate decisions; and decisions of this sort should be made against a background of real estate experience and full knowledge of current real estate techniques and market conditions.

Market Analyses

The space limitations of an article of this nature preclude the possibility of any detailed discussion of techniques of market analyses. However, many offices in the United States have had a sufficient amount of experience to provide sound analyses of the market for all types of real estate investment property—residential, commercial, industrial, entertainment and institutional.

In many of the projects that have been built by owners with unsatisfactory results, preliminary analyses of the market would have indicated that there was no reasonable possibility of obtaining tenants in sufficient quantities—and at sufficient rentals—to make the projects profitable investments.

Margins of profit limited

The margin of profit at current construction and interest costs is very limited—a typical annual return for entrepreneurial effort in office building and retail development being approximately $.50 per sq ft of rentable space. This means that the available margin of error, which would wipe out all return for the developers' risk and effort, is somewhere between 8 and 20%. Any combination of vacancy factor, rent reduction, increase in operating expenses (particularly in taxes) or increase in the cost of land or building which would total the above percentage of variation from standard operating ratios and the identified economic specifications would be likely to wipe out an owner's profit over financing costs and, conceivably, make necessary significant cash investments each year in order to maintain ownership of the property.

Unfortunately, there are many projects in which an increase of capital cost above a budget of $2 per sq ft, combined with a reduction of less than $.20 per sq ft under the anticipated rental scale, have been sufficient to put the operating results "in the red."

Therefore, before any development of a revenue-producing project is undertaken, it is imperative that a sound analysis of the available market should be made. The result should be expressed not only in terms of quantitative demand but in terms of the revenue per sq ft at which that demand can be expected to be effective, and at which the quality of development and associated

Cost Specifications

costs required can be justified by the market.

From the market analysis, the owner and his advisors should determine the cost specification for the project under consideration. Shopping centers have been developed at costs ranging all the way from $8 to $35 per sq ft including land and building. Office buildings in recent years have been developed at anything from $12 per sq ft, for construction alone, to as much as $55 per sq ft. In a given case, the expenditure required to produce the type of structure which will assure the *maximum revenue in proportion to cost* and the most effective ratio of operating expense and depreciation to income is a matter of investment decision and should be made by the owner, in discussion with his architect, before even preliminary plans are prepared.

Direct relationships between costs and income

There is not always a direct relationship between cost and income. In somes cases, improvements in the amenities and specifications are essential in order to capture the maximum income for projects. In other cases, the market will not be capable of producing rentals sufficient to justify such amenities and specifications. In many cases the relationship between landlord and tenant is such that certain costs are passed on to the tenant, when the costs are related to the *tenant's* motivations and interests. Other costs related to the *landlord's* interests are usually absorbed by the landlord.

Profitable investments can be planned if they are based on sound knowledge of the market, on predetermined specifications of costs and on planned distribution of cost between the landlord and tenant. The extent to which this is possible is not generally understood by most people. Variations, between one project and another of similar class, between the capital costs of one project and another in the same category or in the relationships between landlords and tenants with respect to division of costs and operating expenses in projects, can cause variations in income of as much as two or three times the probable net profit to the landlords. This is only one indication of the extreme care that must be exercised in the planning of any revenue-producing project. From a practical standpoint, there is little likelihood that a sound investment balance can ever be achieved unless there has been an initial determination of the cost range which must be achieved.

Project Design

In many cases, architects have demonstrated their ability to design projects within cost limitations. Too rarely is this ability used in developing projects to cost specifications that had been determined in advance. Often, the practice has been to achieve tolerable results through the process of trial and error or by the stipulation, at some point in planning, that costs "simply must be kept—or brought—down."

Too often the architect makes the assumption that a project must necessarily be developed with a certain degree of quality with little regard for the fact that a range of possibilities is open to both the architect and the owner. The selection of the standards of design and construction for a project should be based on *joint decisions* of the owner and the architect—decisions which are in harmony with the investment objectives of the owner. Rather than having decisions *presented* to him by the architect, the owner should be invited by the architect into discussions which can lead to informed decisions.

Construction Cost Control

It is well known that bidding procedures, as well as sub-contracting and material purchase techniques, can cause variations in the cost of a project of as much as 15 to 30%. When a real estate facility has been developed for *use* by the owner rather than for *investment* purposes, savings in time during construction may be of greater value to the owner than savings in costs if the latter can only be achieved by a delay in completion.

Based on the general assumption that the margin of annual profit available to a developer is likely to average $.50 per sq ft of rental area (although experience shows the range to be from an actual loss to a profit of as much as $1 per sq ft or more), a saving of thirty days in the construction process might increase the profit, before income taxes, by approximately $.04 per sq ft.

Time vs costs

In certain cases the meeting of contractual deadlines for delivery of space in a building may be important, altogether apart from the question of cost. In such circumstances the owner must be guided by his contractual obligations. In other cases, the possibility of a higher volume of retail business in space for which rent is payable as a percentage of sales (such as during the latter months of a calendar year) might increase the value to an owner of any time saved. However, speaking in general terms, a cost saving of only $.04 per sq ft of rentable area could justify an owner in *delaying* the completion of the job for thirty days, if the delay would permit greater cost savings through redesign or changes in specifications and materials after consultation with the sub-contractors actually doing the job.

Obviously, a 10% cost variation in a structure costing $20 per sq ft is an extremely important investment factor to an owner; but even minimal cost savings such as those discussed are of such importance in revenue-producing real estate that generally speaking, substantial delays of completion are justified if they result in more efficient design or more effective cost controls.

High interest rates make time-cost ratios critical

This relation between time and cost is most critical during the periods of relatively high interest rates on the first mortgage borrowing characteristically used to finance revenue-producing buildings. At present interest rates—which are very near their high point for the last twenty years—correct determination of the relative importance of time and cost controls is more essential now than at any time since the beginning of World War II. The control of cost is frequently stated to be the responsibility of the architect. If he assumes this responsibility on a project, the architect must understand that costs must be contained within the framework of the budget originally specified for investment success. This requires complete understanding of construction cost processes and the ability to foresee all variations which might occur in construction.

Many experienced owners who engage in frequent construction activities have developed their own engineering and design departments for the express purpose of cost controls even though independent architectural offices are used for project design, preparation of working drawings, etc.

Frequently the owner-developer who is developing one or two projects which represent the investment of surplus funds suffers the greatest penalty for ineffective cost control in terms of the original project specifications. The architectural offices which

Marketing

perform the greatest service to the real estate investment community are those whose knowledge of cost relationships and whose ability to exercise the required controls for owners who have no engineering departments are equal to the investment tests.

If a project under development is to be sold by the owner to a prospective user or to be leased under either gross or net lease terms, the ability of the owner to market the project effectively will be critical in determining its economic feasibility.

*The Dollars and Cents of Shopping Centers, Urban Land Institute, 1962-63

Recent studies of shopping center economics* indicate a very wide range in the rentals obtained by the owners of the project which form the base of the studies. In many cases, the variation was due to general or local market conditions beyond the control of the owner. In other cases the variations in rents represent expressions of the efficiency of the owners in negotiating with the tenants or the effectiveness of the architectural design.

Except for design, these matters are beyond the control of the architect, but knowledge of the effectiveness of an owner's marketing organization is of importance to the architect in determining the flexibility of design and cost control available.

For example, there are certain owners and leasing organizations who thoroughly understand the leasing of basement areas in shopping centers when these have been properly designed. Other owners regard basements as uneconomical—possibly due in part to the fact that they and their leasing organizations may not understand the proper utilization of basements. Architects must be aware of these strengths or weaknesses before recommending specific designs. When designing any revenue-producing structure, the architect must determine whether or not the owner is capable of efficiently marketing a specific project which may be designed.

Location

Experienced operators of real estate recognize that the location of a project and the arrangement of specific uses within the project are two of the most important concepts in the development of real estate values.

The architect may not be able to control the location of the project as a whole, but he will be responsible for the location and orientation of the project on the available land. However, the selection of the land itself is a real estate matter; as such it should be covered in the market analysis because the analysis of available uses should always be related to a specific location under consideration by the owner.

The size, shape and location of the space to be occupied by each tenant in a revenue-producing project is a matter of current real estate experience, as well as design efficiency. The best results will be achieved when the architect cooperates closely with the owner or the owner's representatives in determining the specific size, shape and location of the areas to be rented to each individual tenant.

What makes real estate parcels unique

The unique quality of real estate is that no two parcels are *identical*; the *individual location* of a parcel creates its value. Even two adjoining parcels of similar size will have different qualities of location. One of the principal differences arises from the occupancy of each parcel.

Shopping center locations

Extensive experience has been developed in recent years concerning the qualities of location as they apply to retail stores in shopping centers. For example, it was previously believed that the funneling of pedestrian traffic from the parking lot into the project would create an intensity of traffic that would attract customers to stores which normally thrive on heavy pedestrian traffic. However, experience has shown that the total amount of traffic from a shopping center parking lot entering a mall through one of several entrances is not of sufficient intensity to support stores that require pedestrian traffic for survival. Such locations have been found to be acceptable only to occupants of specific appeal, such as banks and service activities. Similarly, certain stores have been found to thrive when located adjacent to other stores handling particular types of merchandise.

Conventional retail locations

The problem of locational attraction for retail stores in conventional business centers and in central business districts was thoroughly studied several years ago at the University of Michigan. Similar studies concerning locational relationships in shopping centers have been made by several real estate management and leasing offices but so far have not been published for public distribution. Certain publications, notably those of the Urban Land Institute, have dealt with the types of tenant most frequently found in shopping centers of various sizes; but the locational relationships of these shops have not been examined in the same depth.

Whenever the revenue to be anticipated from a project depends to any extent on the locational relationship of one tenant to another, the most intensive study by both architect and real estate organization will be required.

Financing

During the last fifteen years, financing techniques for new real estate construction have expanded significantly. Among the reasons for the new techniques are the guarantees provided by the Federal government for mortgage financing of certain classes of residential and commercial structures. The exact provisions of these Federal guarantees are important in design, but they are of even more importance in the economic feasibility of the projects to which they refer.

Effects of taxes, subsidies, guarantees

Similarly, there are certain state laws which provide tax benefits or abatements for certain types of development (such as urban renewal) or certain functional uses (such as parking). These laws are of significance in the determination of economic feasibility. In addition to the government influences in the form of direct guarantees or tax subsides, the provisions of the Federal income tax laws—with reference to depreciation and to the impact of income taxation on certain types of investors such as pension funds—provide financing possibilities which go beyond the conventional investments by private individuals or corporations that are taxable on the full current income at current rates.

Effects of types of control

Capital from various organizations such as pension funds (whether corporate, union or government-controlled) and endowment funds of various types, as well as some banking and other provisional investment sources, have added not only to the total body of capital but to the multiplicity of forms of investment available to the experienced owner of real estate.

The particular forms of the investment capital do not always have a direct controlling effect upon the design or specifications for a particular project although, in the case of government-guaranteed financing, such cases of control do exist. However, the availability or non-availability of the various types of capital will have a significant bearing on the ability of developer to develop his project in its most efficient form. Also, such investors of capital may require the right to approve or disapprove the project design as well as the relationships between landlord and tenant.

Operation

After a project has been completed, there is likely to be a period, of one to four years, in which it will be critical for the owner, through his management organization, to take whatever steps are necessary in the way of promotion, cooperation with tenants and other typical management functions, in order to program the investment operation to produce the most effective investment result.

One of the most important activities during this preliminary operational period is a reconstruction of the effectiveness of the space allocation among various tenants.

Need for flexibility

In numerous cases, large and experienced organizations have soon found themselves short of space in new office buildings, even though, presumably, they had planned their operations carefully. Space must be designed, in close cooperation with real estate management organizations, to achieve the maximum flexibility that is consistent with sound economics and make possible changes for the convenience of tenants and for improved investment results for owners.

Similarly, in shopping centers, some tenants will—almost invariably—be more successful than they had anticipated; and these tenants may soon require additional space. Others will be less successful, either due to locational influences or to their inability to operate competitively.

The review of occupancy after a project has been in existence for a short time is essentially a real estate function. However, it can be successfully resolved only if the initial design was such that any necessary changes can be made economically and only if imaginative solutions were developed by the architect and real estate organization working in concert for maximum efficiency, at reasonable costs, in the relocation process.

What makes a sound real estate investment

The creation of a sound parcel of revenue-producing real estate is, therefore, not only the result of a proper combination of ownership, real estate, engineering and architectural abilities directed toward the acquisition of the land and the designing and construction of effective improvements upon it. In addition, a whole series of decisions founded on experience in real estate leasing, financing and managment must be made in such a way as to produce effective compromise within the very narrow limits that mean profit rather than loss.

In the creation of a required investment result, the most effective relationships between an architect, an owner and a real estate organization will result in a cooperative effort in which the total skills and experience of each are brought to bear on the total problem. Neither the architectural office nor the real estate office will usually have sufficient experience and skill to solve all of the problems of sound development. The most effective result will flow from proper identification of areas of responsibility of each and from the desire to work in harmony.

27

Relationships of Architects
with Real Estate Consultants and Owners

BY LARRY SMITH*

The interlocked and interdependent functions of the architect, the owner and the real estate consultant in the development of projects for investment must be correctly defined and efficiently performed with close cooperation if such projects are to result in acceptable financial returns to the owners

*The author, head of the real estate consulting firm that bears his name, continues his discussion of the principles of real estate development. Not covered in this article is the fact that comprehensive services actually include site selection, land assembly and the engagement of real estate experts by the architect as the agent of the owner

Objectives of owners

In the development of real estate, one of the significant relationships is that of the architect to the owner, or his real estate advisers, with respect to the real estate aspects of the problem.

There are situations in which the architect should adopt the position of leadership in the development process, but identification of these situations will depend largely on the objectives of the owner. However, architects must avoid taking the responsibility for advice or decisions with respect to real estate matters in which they have had neither experience nor the opportunity to maintain up-to-date contact with rapidly developing and changing real estate situations.

When real estate is being developed for use by the owner, whether that use is for industrial occupancy, a retail store, an office building or otherwise, quite likely the position of leadership should be assumed by the architect.

Under these circumstances, the amount of land required for building, service, parking and traffic purposes, and its location with reference to the adjoining street or arterial pattern, will be a function of the requirements of the owner. These requirements can be most accurately determined and fulfilled by an architectural office working directly with the operating departments or the engineering departments of the owner-occupant and with specialists such as traffic consultants. Locations of departments or functions within the building and all of the factors of space and its arrangement will be related to the owner's needs and to an appraisal of the relative value of the available alternatives. When real estate is being developed for use by the owner, the function of the real estate consultant is to advise on the availability and costs of other alternatives with respect to the main site, on any necessary additions to the site and on the possible use or disposition of surplus property.

However, when a building is being developed for investment purposes—for production of income—it is likely that real estate leadership should come from the owner or from someone in the owner's employ who has a high degree of economic "know-how" in real estate matters. This is true whether the investment is

TYPICAL REGIONAL SHOPPING CENTER

Comparison of Investment Analyses to Indicate Impact of Cost Increases Assumptions: Project Area 400,000 sq ft; Average

Description		*Base at $16.*	*Increase 3%*	*Increase 6%*
Capital Investment—Land		$ 1,000,000	$ 1,000,000	$ 1,000,000
Cost per sq ft		$16.00	$16.50	$17.00
Improvements and Buildings		6,400,000	6,600,000	6,800,000
Total Cost		$ 7,400,000	$ 7,600,000	$ 7,800,000
Income and Capitalized Value				
Income from Rents @ $2.65		$ 1,060,000	$ 1,060,000	$ 1,060,000
Less Expenses—Taxes @ 40c per sq ft	$160,000			
Insurance; vacancy; management;				
promotion. @ 25c per sq ft	$100,000	$ 260,000	$ 260,000	$ 260,000
Net Income before Depreciation		$ 800,000	$ 800,000	$ 800,000
Less Depreciation 2½+		160,000	165,000	170,000
Net Income after Depreciation		$ 640,000	$ 635,000	$ 630,000
Capitalized at 6%		$10,666,660	$10,583,333	$10,500,000
Mortgage at 66⅔%		$ 7,111,111	$ 7,055,555	$ 7,000,000
Cash Equity Required		288,880	544,445	800,000
Total Investment		$ 7,400,000	$ 7,600,000	$ 7,800,000
Equity as % of Total Cost		3.9%	7.2%	10.2%
Equity per sq ft		$.72	$1.36	$2.00
Profit Potential between Cost and above Valuation		$ 3,266,666	$ 2,983,333	$ 2,700,000
Leverage—Capital Profit Ratio		11.3	5.4	3.4

The objective of the typical developer—particularly the professional developer of real estate for income—is to develop property with the maximum earning power and the minimum equity investment. The entrepreneurial capital represented by the equity investment must earn an average rate of between 15 and 25 per cent before taxes in order to be competitively profitable. Furthermore, the probability under present tax regulations is that the property will be sold within a period of ten years, in which case the capital profit in relation to the equity becomes a key ratio in determining the quality of the investment to the developer. The above table indicates the very great swings in investment merit which will characteristically proceed from a variation of only $2.00 per sq ft increase in construction cost.

The following table indicates the earned profit before income taxes expressed as a percentage of the equity and calculated after allowing for the first year's interest on the first mortgage expressed above.

Profit—First Year Interest			
Net Income after Depreciation	$ 640,000	$ 635,000	$ 630,000
Interest on Mortgage at 6%	$ 426,666	$ 423,333	$ 420,000
Net Profit	$ 213,333	$ 211,667	$ 210,000
Profit as % of Equity	73.7%	38.7%	26.3%

The following table expresses the relationship between cash flow on the project after providing for constant payments on the mortgage at eight per cent per annum.

Cash Flow			
Net Income before Depreciation	$ 800,000	$ 800,000	$ 800,000
Payments on Mortgage at 8%	$ 568,888	$ 564,444	$ 560,000
	$ 231,111	$ 235,555	$ 240,000
Cash Flow as % of Equity	90%	43.2%	30%

It will be observed that the annual rate on the equity investment expressed either as a profit figure after depreciation, or as a cash flow after mortgage payments will decline by more than 75 per cent in the event of an increase of even $2.00 per sq ft in the capital cost.

This critical relationship between capital cost of a real estate revenue-producing project and the developer's profit is based directly upon the typically low gross income from revenue-producing real estate (generally 15 per cent per annum gross rate on the capital investment or less) and the typical high debt structure negotiated for financing in order to provide a reasonable entrepreneurial rate of profit for the development effort. The ratio of capital cost to income is sufficiently important so that every possible cooperative effort must be devoted to its realization; and the necessity for maintaining this ratio at the lowest possible figure justifies a significant expenditure of time and money—including even the postponement of construction within substantial limits.

Rent $2.65 per sq ft

Increase 12%
$ 1,000,000
$18.00
7,200,000

$ 8,200,000

$ 1,060,000

$ 260,000

$ 800,000
180,000

$ 620,000

$10,333,333

$ 6,888,888
1,211,112

$ 8,200,000

16%
$3.28
$ 2,133,333
1.6

$ 630,000
$ 413,333

$ 206,666

15.7%

$ 800,000
$ 551,111

$ 248,888

19%

Tax and cost implications

Costs vs time

for office building purposes, for industrial purposes, for retail purposes, including shopping centers, for multiple-family residential purposes or for any other revenue-producing activity.

The income tax considerations which apply, both during the period of ownership and at a time of sale, demand the intimate knowledge of a real estate expert working with a tax expert. The relationship between the cost of building and land, the relationship between the cost of the total project and income and the levels of marketability at the location and for the particular project being planned—all of these are important considerations in both taxation and real estate investment policy; thus, all may materially affect the development of the project design and specifications.

Furthermore, the market for the proposed rental space in the project, both in terms of the most efficient usable areas and in terms of rental specifications (including the allocation of work between landlord and tenant), and the precise relationships between individual tenants in terms of their interdependability in traffic are matters in which up-to-date knowledge of real estate matters is essential in the planning stages of the project. Many architects, through specialization in certain types of improvements, develop substantial knowledge of certain of these factors, particularly locational relationships and typical division of work between landlord and tenant. However, local usage in these matters, as well as changing rental terms and tenant practices on both the national and regional basis, necessitates the application of the most recent information available to any problem involving building construction for income-producing purposes. One of the most critical problems in this respect is the determination of the total cost structure, including the extent to which outlay of time and redesign money is justified in an attempt to reduce the capital cost.

In property developed by the owner for his own use, it is likely that prompt delivery and the most effective design for operational purposes will be of greater importance than the savings in capital cost, except where such costs are very large.

However, in income-producing property, the available margin of profit is so narrow that even a variation in capital cost of the project, as small as $.05 to $.10 per sq ft, will probably justify suspension of the work for as much as thirty days and justify a significant amount of redesign costs as long as the saving in total costs, after allowing for such redesign fees, is as great as the margin indicated.

In order to demonstrate the principles involved in such cost analyses, a hypothetical regional shopping center is analyzed on these pages; in this chart may be seen the effect of cost increases in a project on the investment result.

In many cases, regardless of the breadth of his experience, a developer will employ a real estate consultant or other experienced real estate adviser to assist him and his organization in making the various real estate decisions that are involved as the project moves forward.

In the case of the inexperienced developer who wishes to create a successful income-producing piece of real estate, experienced real estate advice is essential. The working team should consist of at least three permanent members: the developer, the real estate consultant and the architect. The developer will provide the initiative and be available for all major decisions; the real estate consultant will provide the market report and the economic analysis upon which the project will be based and will advise on the cost structure, rental space and terms and similar matters; the architect will create the concept from which the project will take its physical shape and form. Each member of the planning team will be supported by his own organization and will have complete knowledge in respect to some phase of the operation. In addition, each should have sufficient knowledge about all three phases to provide a basis for working harmony.

For emphasis, it should be repeated that the developer who has had broad experience in real estate improvement will, depending on the scope of the project and his past experience, ordinarily have little, if any, need for the services of a real estate consultant. This fact should be kept in mind in the discussion which follows. Under such circumstances, however, the owner will function as his own real estate expert and will provide the detailed knowledge and decisions upon which the project must depend if it is to be an investment success.

Architect-real estate consultant-owner team

The architect who understands the economic aspects of real estate development, the real estate consultant who has cooperated in the past with architectural offices and who understands the problems and planning of architecture and the owner who understands and gives careful consideration to the activities of both will make satisfactory teammates and, accordingly, their cooperative effort should be fruitful.

The size and complexity of income-producing real estate projects are increasing steadily with the rapid increase in population and with the increase in both privately sponsored and government sponsored urban renewal. Many projects in both suburban areas and in central business districts now contain, in a single development, many building types such as office buildings, hotels, public buildings, medical and dental buildings, department stores and other retail and service businesses, transportation terminals, central power plants, restaurants, theaters and other amusement facilities and residential structures of every variety. The qualifications demanded of the architect and of all other organizations participating in the project are dependent upon the size and complexity of the project under consideration. The larger the size and complexity of the project, the higher must be the qualifications.

The architect must understand—and coordinate his work with—the many specialists who will participate in the planning of the large and complex projects. The architectural organization should have trained and experienced staff members in every necessary branch of planning, design and engineering so that suitable concepts may be developed and the work with the various specialists coordinated smoothly.

Similarly, the real estate consultant's organization, or that of the owner, must be of wide scope and experience. It must include a research staff, market analysts, financing and leasing specialists and men experienced in real estate negotiation and management. In some of these fields, specialist organizations may be called in; however, people with basic broad experience must be part

Timing the employment of the planning team

of the owner's or of the real estate consultant's organization.

The planning team should be established at the inception of the project and should work together continuously throughout the planning and construction period. However, the first steps toward creating the project may be taken by one or another member of the team, depending upon the objectives of the owner.

The final determination of the economic feasibility of a project must be based on a specific plan of development from which basic costs—at least—can be estimated, and upon which income can be predicated on the specific locational relationships of the various income-producing elements. On the other hand, an experienced real estate owner, or his advisers, should have had sufficient previous experience so that their preliminary consideration of the economic soundness of the project can be predicated on assumed costs and on assumed income and expense relationships based upon experience in similar projects.

In such cases, the assumed capital costs, modified to whatever extent appears advisable after development of the full feasibility report, will become cost specifications for the project. Therefore, these costs can be used as specifications upon which the architect can base his development of the physical plan, as well as the general concept of the project.

It is probable that the architect should begin work on the development of a project in advance of the real estate expert in all projects where the development is to be used by the owner. It is also probable that the real estate expert should undertake work somewhat in advance of the architect on projects that are being developed for revenue-producing purposes.

In both cases, however, it would seem desirable for the two offices to be brought into the project at approximately the same time—during the preliminary stage of the examination—and that they should work in the closest harmony while the preliminary program and plans are being developed for the investment decision.

Coordinators needed

Since each of the participants in the planning activity will probably represent a sizeable organization, it would be well for each—the owner, the architect and the real estate consultant—to nominate a coordinator within his organization who will be responsible for the particular project. Such coordinators should be in almost constant touch with each other. Regular meetings should be held at least monthly and in times of great activity at shorter intervals. All significant decisions and reports should be recorded.

During the period of cooperative effort, the committee members should state their individual and independent viewpoints strongly, because it is only in an atmosphere of mutual respect that the proper development of judgment and review can develop.

Relationships with the owner

In the past, in a limited number of cases, the real estate expert has been retained by the architect; in an even more limited number of cases, the architect has been retained by the real estate consultant. Neither of these relationships is likely to be satisfactory to either party or to the owner as any lack of experience on the part of the architect or the real estate consultant, with respect to the type of work being done by the other, is likely to result in a subordination of the recommendations of one party to the convictions and interests of the other.

Similarly, it usually has proved unsatisfactory to create a joint account between an architect and a real estate consultant. Such joint relationships have usually resulted in an attempt to provide a compromise report and recommendation to the owner. The effect of such compromise reports is to deny the owner, throughout the planning process, the opportunity of making, with wisdom, the significant decisions which will have a permanent bearing on the investment quality of the development. Many of these judgments are so related to the specific position and interests of the owner that it is unlikely that a joint resolution by an architect and a real estate consultant will produce the most effective solution for the owner. Frequently an owner will request such a joint operation and a single recommendation, but such a request by the owner should be resisted—in the best interest of the owner himself. When, after separate deliberation, the architect and real estate consultant do find themselves in complete harmony with respect to their recommendations to the owner, there is every opportunity for each to concur in the other's report. Obviously, each should have the opportunity of examining the other's report prior to any presentation so that, in the event of disagreement, each will be able to present the nature of the disagreement in the most direct form possible. Then the owner will be in the best position to make a selection from the various alternatives.

It would seem best for the architect and consultant to be employed separately and for each to have a direct relationship to the owner. They should, of course, work in close harmony; and each should be in a position to present the various investment alternatives clearly so that the owner will have the greatest possible opportunity to make a sound investment decision.

Coordination of the work

It is of the utmost importance that the work of the various offices should be closely coordinated. Therefore, one of the functions typically performed by the architectural office is to work out, with the real estate expert, a schedule of development activities. In this way, the allocation of the responsibilities for all of the functions together with their time schedules, will be efficiently developed so that the closest possible coordination will be achieved and the most effective solution found for the total project.

An example of such a schedule, developed for a hypothetical regional shopping center, is shown on pages 166-7. From this schedule, a bar chart may be drawn for use in the actual coordination of the project work.

Efficiency of design

One of the truisms that applies to real estate is that no two parcels are identical; therefore, the value of one parcel, even one immediately adjoining another, may be totally different from the other. For retail purposes in central business districts or suburban shopping areas, the value of an inside lot will be significantly different from that of a corner property. In fact, in the development of all real estate for income purposes, location is the most significant, critical factor. This is true not only for the location of a complete development, but for individual locations within the development.

Locations within shopping centers

For example, in the design of shopping centers, a process of review and rearrangement of building areas and of the location of individual retail units within the buildings will frequently raise the budgeted rent for the project as much as $.20 to $.30 per sq ft. Data recently compiled by the Urban Land Institute of Washington, DC, indicates an $.80 per sq ft variation of average rentals in shopping centers of the same size. (Rentals ranged from a minimum of $1.40 to a maximum of $2.20 for centers of the same size.) Such a variation is caused by a composite of several factors including the rental rates typical in various parts of the country, the effectiveness of the leasing organization and the extent to which space was actually finished for the tenants' use, among other things. However, a significant factor in many cases was the efficiency of the design and the locational arrangements.

Tenant attitudes   Business philosophy varies widely from one tenant to another. While many tenants who are strong creators of pedestrian traffic recognize the importance of locating their stores in such a way that all tenants in the project are successful, other traffic-producing tenants insist upon premium locations for themselves. Tenants adopting the first attitude believe that they are most successful when located in a successful project even through they may not have the 100 per cent location. The second tenant uses his bargaining power to negotiate for the best location for his own store, believing that by doing so he gets the most profitable location for himself.

Tenant and owner   It is not the purpose here to demonstrate which attitude is correct, either from the standpoint of the individual tenant or from the standpoint of the project. However, it is important to recognize that the best interests of the project owner under these circumstances are at variance with those of the traffic-producing tenants. Architectural offices are rarely in a position, at any particular moment, to determine the extent to which this attitude on the part of the traffic-producing tenants is subject to negotiation. Furthermore, the most profitable use of the traffic created by these traffic generators depends upon the location of the satellite tenants and the particular rental terms which can be negotiated for the satellite space.

Therefore, the possible locations for the traffic-producing tenants, as well as for the satellite tenants, is closely related to real estate judgment and negotiation. It follows that the closest possible coordination between the architect and the real estate expert in terms of building shape, dimensions and the size and location of the individual stores is required if the project is to be economically sound.

The same factors apply, to a greater or lesser extent, to all classes of revenue producing real estate, especially those of multiple occupancy.

Effects of local conditions   The extent to which the maximum income can be derived from any type of revenue-producing real estate will depend upon the specific local market for the classes and quality of space being produced in the project.

Rental rates and space preferences vary significantly from one part of the country to another. In the case of a relatively unimportant new project it probably will not be possible to change the rental pattern from existing usage, but in major projects where a new standard of design—or where a dramatic location—is being developed it may be possible to establish new rental patterns

DEVELOPMENT OF A REGIONAL SHOPPING CENTER

Month Activity Undtkn	Time Required (Weeks)	Description of Work	Participants	Economic Consultant	Owner	Architect	Traffic Consultant	Legal Contractor
1	13	Economic analysis of trade area		X				
4		Review of economic analysis			X			
	8	Establish size, characteristics of project; size, number of dept stores		X	X	X		
5	4	Preliminary analysis of road conditions, access, ingress and egress					X	
6	8	Site analysis; development of preliminary alternate land use plans				X		
8	4	Review alternate land use plans; determine most satisfactory		X	X	X		
	4	Merchandise plan; general location, size of stores by type		X				
9	2	Refine site plan; incorporate merchandising plan				X		
	4	Utility analysis; metering proposal				X		
		Report on project traffic, parking requirements				X		
	8	Traffic analysis; report on parking traffic; recommendations					X	
		Begin negotiations, as necessary, with local state officials on access, road improvements, alteration of municipal traffic plan		X	X			
	4	Prepare sales brochure for use in contacting department store		X				
	2	Recommendations regarding dept store lease provisions, terms		X				
	2	Recommendations regarding prospective dept store tenants		X				
9		Initial contact with prospective dept store tenant		X				
	8	Preparation of dept store lease						X
10	2	Review utility analysis; make recommendation to owner on utilities		X				
		Review utility analysis; recommendations; make utilities decision			X			
		Begin dept store negotiations		X	X			
	2	Determine owner-tenant work, allowances				X		
	2	Recommendations on provisions of general tenant lease form		X				
		Review owner-tenant work		X				
		Review specifications, allowances, recommendations regarding general tenant lease form; instruct legal			X			
	4	Prepare general tenant lease form						X
	4	Refine merchandising plan		X				
	6	Coordinate structural, mechanical, electrical, etc, with architectural; incorporate refined merchandising plan				X		
	6	Preliminary capital cost estimate				X		

All managerial duties have been listed under the owner function. However, the owner may hire a manager at any time that he wishes to be relieved of managerial duties. Though not included in this time schedule, some promotional activity should be under way throughout the development program.

if existing rents are inadequate for investment support. In this area of judgment, the experience and intimate knowledge of a thoroughly competent owner or real estate adviser can be of great importance.

This principle applies to multi-family residential real estate in which the quantity of space in an apartment building must be correlated with the market in terms of the floor area of the units being created, the location within the building and the specifications or amenities to be developed.

The floor areas of typical rental apartments of the same general quality and rental may vary 100 sq ft or more between two cities in different parts of the country. This difference in floor

Month Activity Undtkn	Time Required (Weeks)	Description of Work	Economic Consultant	Owner	Architect	Traffic Consultant	Legal Contractor
11	2	Recommendations regarding prospective major tenants	X				
	4	Prepare architectural plan to accompany mortgage brochure			X		
	2	Review capital cost estimates; recommendations to owner	X				
		Review traffic analysis	X	X	X		
		Review cost estimates; recommendations; cost decisions		X			
	6	Prepare model, drawings for leasing program			X		
	4	Financial analysis of project	X				
	4	Review general tenant lease and dept store lease forms; recommendations to owner	X				
12	4	Mortgage application brochure	X				
	2	Recommendations regarding prospective mortgagees	X				
		Sales brochures as required for use in leasing program	X				
		Execute preliminary building agreement for lease with dept store		X			
		Review and approve general tenant and dept store lease forms		X			
13		Review, approve mortgage application, sales brochure		X			
		Begin mortgage negotiations	X	X			
	28-36(1)	Begin major tenant leasing program		X			
		Assist in leasing program					
		Revisions of architectural necessitated by leasing			X		
15		Secure mortgage commitment (2)	X	X			
16		Authorize working drawings		X			
	32	Prepare working drawings			X		
		Consideration of tax situation and contact with local authorities	X	X			
17		Review, revise financial analysis; changes necessitated by leasing, revised cost estimates, etc.	X				
	28	Management training program	X	X			
		Occasional review by owner and advisors on leasing program, other phases of project		X			
	4	Revision of merchandising plan necessitated by requirements of dept store, major tenants	X				
22	8	Prepare construction contract		X	X		
24		Review, approve working drawings, specifications		X			
	52	Construction					X
		Supervise construction			X		
		Prepare tenant working drawings			X		
		Approve tenant work		X			
		Periodic financial analysis	X				
28		Arrange for consumer survey		X			
36		Opening of center		X			

(1) Leasing may be handled by the owner, project manager or broker. (2) A typical requirement of mortgagee is that a specified amount and type of tenant space be signed prior to its commitment of funds; this may necessitate a rearrangement in the leasing schedule.

area and its relation to the local competitive rental situation may spell the difference between profit and loss to the owner.

Sometimes, in buildings designed by competent architects, both higher and lower rental apartments fail to rent within a reasonable period after the project is ready for occupancy. In some cases the operating losses due to the creation of such unmarketable space run into very substantial figures before sufficient space is rented to permit a break-even position. In extreme cases a condition is created in which the project is totally uneconomic.

Unmarketable space may be due to a fundamental misjudgment of the market by the owner, but in many cases it is due to a lack of correlation of the cost of the space as designed by the architect with the realities of the rental market on which the space must be offered.

The rental market for office building space may range from $2.50 per sq ft to as much as $8.00 per sq ft, or more, depending, in part, on the type of building structure, but more importantly, in all probability, upon the rental negotiations and the location of the building, on the location of particular space within the building, and especially on the local conditions in the city in which the project is located. Furthermore, the division of costs between the owner and tenant in these buildings may be of controlling importance in determining the economic return to the owner; and this may be dependent upon competitive conditions or local practice.

Therefore, the architect must work in the closest possible harmony with a real estate expert who is familiar with the local market and the possibility of improving it. And the architect and real estate consultant must be aware of the combination of individual tenant location, size of unit and specifications, and division of work between landlord and tenant which will provide the greatest net economic return.

Perhaps the modern shopping center provides the best illustration of the opportunities for cooperation between the architect and real estate expert—whether the expert is the owner himself, a man in his employ or an independent consultant. Rental conditions in shopping centers are particularly sensitive to the classes of tenants; and they vary widely from one part of the country to another. Efficient store sizes for various classes of tenants vary not only from one part of the country to another but between specific tenants operating in the same field and market.

The wishes of the tenant can rarely be taken as a guide to efficient planning from the landlord's standpoint. It is almost characteristic of shopping center experience that certain tenants will ask for larger space than they can economically use, provided they can bargain with the owner for a low enough rent per sq ft to maintain a reserve capacity at the owner's expense. The percentage rent characteristic of present-day shopping center leases is not the answer to this situation because many lines of retail business can operate profitably at a level of productivity per sq ft at which the landlord will experience loss; and the estimate of percentage rent is effective only to a limited extent in providing a basis for satisfactory mortgage loans. A proper balance in area and location of traffic-producing tenants and higher rent-paying tenants who thrive on induced traffic is essential to the economic health of a shopping center project. The relative rent which can be accepted from each class of tenant and the locational arrangements which will provide the most effective compromise between capital cost and income can best be worked out through cooperation between architect and real estate expert.

Therefore, it appears that the architect can best assure the development of economically sound projects for his clients through close cooperation with the owner and his real estate department or advisers, especially in structures which are designed for the production of income as opposed to those designed for the use of the owner.

Part Five:

Project Analysis Services

28

Comprehensive Architectural Services: Project Analysis

BY DUDLEY HUNT JR, AIA

Before the design phases of an architectural project can logically begin, analyses must be made of factors such as location, the site and feasibility; then programs must be prepared for the project and operations to be housed

Architectural problems contain their own solutions

In the definition of the problem is the germ of its solution. Like many truisms that are often dismissed as being trite, this one states a basic principle that might better be clung to than dismissed. Architects engaged in the vast and complex areas of design and construction of the environment might be well advised not only to cling to such a principle but to cherish it. For here is the most logical, and probably the most useful, starting place for comprehensive architectural practice.

For some time now, the basic services of architects have been generally considered to begin with schematic design and then to proceed through design development, production and construction administration. Of late, it has become increasingly apparent that if they are not intimately involved with the programming of projects, very likely architects will find themselves, at worst, prevented from arriving at the best solutions to problems by previous decisions over which they had no control. At best, programming previously done by others can only lead architects into frustrating and unnecessary effort to overcome the built-in deficiencies of the program—effort that might more properly be applied to the *actual* problems rather than *artificial* ones.

So it might be said that programming—at least of buildings

*Project analysis a
basic service*

*Need for operational
programming*

themselves—ought to be made an integral part of the basic and central services performed by architects. This would be a useful step, but what is truly needed is a Gargantuan stride.

Programming of the building alone is hardly enough in a time when the operations that take place within and around the building determine, to a large degree, the final architectural solution. It would seem patently impossible for an architect to solve the overall problem of a shopping center without having been deeply involved in the operational programming of its merchandizing principles. Who are its customers? What income brackets? How do they get to the center? How do they buy? Such considerations are basic to the design of a shopping center. If he is simply presented with a ready-made program from which he must then somehow extract a building solution, the architect can scarcely expect to solve more than the piece of the total problem. Nor can his client reasonably expect more than this.

The same thing would appear to be true for most, if not all, other building types.

*Need for creative
analysis*

Actually the needs seem to go even deeper than the programming of buildings and their operations. Writing a program for a project is one thing; deep analysis of its basic problems is something else again. Without the latter, the former cannot be accomplished with any degree of efficiency or creativity. If a program, operational or otherwise, can be considered as an exposition of the broad principles upon which design is to be based, then the program must necessarily derive from an adequate body of facts relating to the problem—facts that have been gathered with a high degree of enthusiasm and perceptivity, facts that have been creatively analyzed individually and as they relate to each other and to the whole problem.

Not only does a need exist for this sort of analysis and programming, but it is a type of need most easily recognized by clients. Proof of this is the increasing demand of clients for feasibility studies, financial analyses, master programming, and location and site analyses. Further proof is furnished by the proliferation of new types of consultants, many of whom are concerned with such functions. Unfortunately, many of these consultants, though they perform useful, even necessary, functions, somehow insert themselves in between the architect and his client, thereby sometimes erecting an unscalable wall that effectively separates the architect from his client and his client's problems.

*Role of architects
and their collaborators*

A number of architects presently perform project analysis and programming services with a high degree of competence. The architectural profession as a whole must be equally well prepared to perform such services, not as the masters of all things, but as creative coordinators of the total environmental design and construction process. In services of this scope, the architectural profession certainly needs the help of talented specialists and professionals of many kinds—individuals who can make creative contributions to the over-all process and who can expect to receive just rewards for their contributions.

29

Location Analysis and Site Selection

BY MATTHEW L. ROCKWELL, AIA, AIP

For an increasing number of architectural projects, analysis of potential building locations—and site analysis and selection—have become essential phases of comprehensive architectural services to meet the needs of clients

Architectural analysis comes first

A previous introduction to the concept of the architect's expanding practice describes the services which constitute comprehensive practice. In chronological sequence, the earliest of these services is concerned with the analysis of the project. Within the area of architectural analysis there may be identified several functions, some business in nature, others professional. One of these that relates specifically to an extension of the basic professional interests and abilities of the architect deals with project location analysis and site selection.

The extension of the architect's traditional services has been questioned by some on the basis that no *one* individual can hope to perform—competently—other services in addition to the traditional services of the architect. Actually larger offices can, and have for many years in some cases, perform comprehensive services with the support of specialists of various types. But for the practitioner with a small office to feel that "this is not for him" is for him not to understand the potential workings of the process.

Whether large or small, every architectural office has traditionally offered some form of site services as a part of its regular commission. Usually restricted, in the past, to the planning of the

Site selection by architects

site itself, it is not unreasonable today to extend this function to include the selection of the site as well. Because of the increasing complexity of the factors bearing upon the site, such as traffic patterns which affect access to and egress from sites or unchangeable zoning restrictions, it is almost imperative that the architect become involved in the project before the purchase of a site. Site selection derives naturally from site planning. The architect is, or *can become,* as well qualified to *select* sites and to organize the analysis which should precede the construction of any but the most routine buildings, as he is now qualified in the *planning* of the sites.

Real estate activities

In this area of practice, a large part of the architect's activity will be in the field of real estate. The comprehensive services concept does not mean that the architect should supplant other professionals in any respect, or in this case that he should became a real estate broker. It does mean that architects should work directly with other professionals and should act as a correlator between these interests and his client. The time has passed when the best interests of the client are likely to be served by purchase of a site offered by a speculative interest without first making an architectural consideration of that particular site's appropriateness to the needs of the client.

Other chapters in this book have explained the principles of some of the many types of studies which are necessary in architectural practice today. For example, in the chapter on industrial buildings, it was pointed out that a study of potential markets for the industry should be made, along with studies of existing sources of supplies, and that many other considerations are in order. In the chapter on shopping centers, it was noted that driving time or transportation time of potential customers to the site was a part of the preliminary analysis. All of these considerations and many others may be handled by the architect either through an extension of his own natural planning abilities or through association with appropriate specialists. It is the purpose of this chapter to examine a specific project, in order to demonstrate some of the principles of architectural practice in the areas of location analysis and site selection.

Location analysis case study

In brief the study, in this case, involved consideration of the relocation of the general offices of a major food company in Chicago. At the outset of the study these general offices were located on several floors of an office building in the central business district where rentals were comparatively high. The problem posed was threefold: 1) Was a relocation of the offices to a company-owned building in the suburbs justified? 2) Was the purchase of a building elsewhere in the central district justified? 3) Was the rental of other space in the central district more favorable for the company than for it to remain where it was? The problem obviously promised only a chance that a traditional architectural commission would result.

Yet it was also obvious that the problem, as posed, could be best answered in a correlated manner by an architect. A fee arrangement was reached with the client, setting up a charge for the location and site research, this charge to be separate from the

Special fees necessary

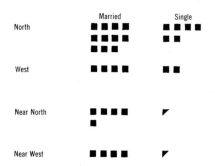

Six Year Employees—N to W Sector

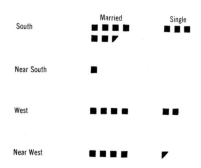

Six Year Employees—S to W Sector

*Preparation
of study maps*

fees for any future architectural commission. It is very important that this feature of the client architect arrangement be made perfectly clear. There should be no reluctance on the part of the architect to request special fees for such special work. In numerous other similar relationships, our firm never found a reluctance on the part of the client to enter into special fee agreements for this type of work.

Before considering phase one of the problem of relocation of this company, it was essential to know where company employees lived. In the Greater Chicago area, any drastic change in well-established commuter patterns was certain to have an effect upon personnel roles. The study made was simple. The Chicago metropolitan area was divided into geographic sectors and the labor forces pinpointed and tabulated.

Over three-quarters of the force lived in easily identifiable neighborhood clusters on the north, west, and south of the region, there being no eastern area because of the location of Lake Michigan. On the theory that those living in the western area could, and probably would, move into either the north or south if necessary, this group was added to both of these clusters. The result was that 68 per cent of the total favored the east-to-north areas; 57 per cent, the west-to-south areas.

These figures were inconclusive. Therefore, in order to make the study more deliberate, two assumptions were made: 1) that the long-term worker of six years or over was more important than the short-term worker for reasons of loyalty, experience and ability, and 2) that, of these, the married worker was more important than the single worker because of family and property ties. This group proved to be the most numerous as well. The north area, with 123 married, long-term workers as against 80 for the south area, showed an advantage of 50 per cent over the south. This fact led to the decision that, in the further course of the study, all sites to be considered should be located in the north-to-west sector. Obviously, the ratio of male to female employees had to be considered and the relative need and availability of each; also a measurement, even though rough, of near retirement age workers and their home locations. The details of these studies are omitted here, but perhaps enough of the character of the study is now apparent to indicate that an architect can master the details of such studies with ease.

Continuing the first phase, a study in minute detail was made of the several hundred square miles of the northwest sector of the Chicago region. The obvious influences of high land values, tax rate and the generally crowded traffic and land conditions almost automatically caused the study to begin beyond the northern city limits of Chicago. A number of maps were made, the most important and costly being a map showing all zoning districts for every community in the defined study area. That such maps are not yet available publicly is surprising and lamentable. Such a map in the hands of able architect-cartographers is a tool of tremendous advantage, as well as prestige. Other useful maps were

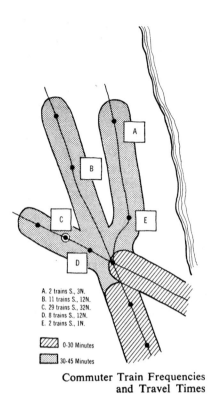

A. 2 trains S., 3N.
B. 11 trains S., 12N.
C. 29 trains S., 32N.
D. 8 trains S., 12N.
E. 2 trains S., 1N.

▨ 0-30 Minutes
▦ 30-45 Minutes

**Commuter Train Frequencies
and Travel Times**

*Considerations of
rural locations*

commutation diagrams showing areas of accessibility, in 15-minute increments, to 90 minutes' distance from the site area. A multitude of information can be shown on such maps, in a manner that will make the meaning obvious to almost any reader, of material ranging from land use to nearby labor force.

In a project such as a general office building, as opposed to a facility such as a warehouse, the distance of the site from the bulk of the working population (the source of labor) is of major importance. But the "auto-mobility" of employees should not be underrated; for example, one suburban company never had to repay an employee for more than a single day's travel before the new employee became a part of a car pool. Talks with the State Department of Labor will uncover, as was true in this subject case, hidden pools of female labor where children of school age have left unoccupied hands.

In the present case, the site to be chosen was expected to be immediately accessible to at least one of the following: a bus route, a railroad station or a main highway. Further, it was considered important that the site have a positive value for advertising to the general public—not for advertising messages themselves, but for the prestige value of the structure.

As might be expected, the land values of potential properties decreased in proportion to increased distance from Chicago; at the time of research, the range was from 60 cents to 15 cents per square foot in the suburban areas and from $4,000 to $1,500 an acre in the rural areas. For purposes of this study, a total building floor area of 75,000 sq ft was assumed, with a ground floor area of 25,000 sq ft, on the basis of two stories and a basement. Making allowances for setbacks and parking spaces, a minimum of three acres was determined to be necessary. In practice, parking requirements are often underestimated; this shortcoming includes needs for truck loading, standing and unloading, and also visitor's parking spaces. While a 20 per cent building coverage may seem abnormally conservative, the figure is actually very reasonable for structures housing any degree of activity. Of course, once the designation of a parcel size for a project has been made, the number of sites available is immediately restricted.

In the case of the particular project under discussion, only twelve possibilities were found within the "close-in" suburban area. Of these, four were superior and had comparable physical advantages, but only two of these appealed to the company officials. However, figures for one site showed 1½ times as many job applications as for the other site. Moreover, while female applications for the second site almost equalled the openings, for the first site there were 4½ times as many female applications as openings. This factor brought the search for sites in the suburban area to an end.

A location in the rural area as opposed to the suburban calls for the consideration of a different set of criteria. Here existing sources of labor are of much less importance. The decision by management to move farther afield into a rural area implies the

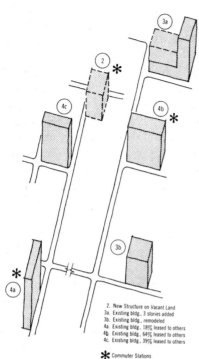

2. New Structure on Vacant Land
3a. Existing bldg., 3 stories added
3b. Existing bldg., remodeled
4a. Existing bldg., 18% leased to others
4b. Existing bldg., 64% leased to others
4c. Existing bldg., 39% leased to others

✱ Commuter Stations

Alternate Solutions Considered

*Transportation
methods compared*

*Consultation
with specialists*

concept that all aspects of the new site must have true mobility in the fullest sense. Aside from the structure, the one fixed and important feature is the rural community itself and the advantages which it offers, or fails to offer, to the project. Of the 27 rural sites considered in this case, 22 lay within, or immediately adjacent to, nine separate villages. Each village had its own background. In some instances, the national origin of the population within the area was important. In other cases, the attitude of village officials toward rezoning attempts gave an indication of either a dangerous or favorable local political climate.

While the supply of public facilities in every village was critical, each village presented different problems to consider. Of particular concern was the impact which *other* industry might have on the community at a later date. For example, one village of 2400 persons could support the 500 employees of the present company with service facilities (gas stations, drug store, beauty parlors, etc), but a second or third company following the first would soon disrupt the facilities for all. Seven sites were ultimately given preferred rank and a final choice made on the basis of two advantages: 1) the convenience of the site by rail to Chicago in an emergency, and 2) the general amenities of the village itself.

In arriving at the final decision as to the relocation of the offices, it was felt that the basic consideration must be a measurement of the comparative costs involved. Accordingly, five alternate cost possibilities were studied: 1) the cost of continuing to lease space, 2) the purchase of vacant downtown property and the erection of a new building, 3) the purchase of existing buildings for remodeling, 4) the purchase and use of existing buildings, and 5) the purchase of vacant suburban land for building purposes. Only vacant downtown property located in the near north and west fringes were studied since the future of the south area, with its tangle of railroads, was considered too uncertain.

At the time of survey, the use of automobiles and railroads was about 20 per cent each, and subway and bus lines about 25 per cent each. However, the use of private automobiles was growing constantly and west and northwest expressways were to be opened in the near future. A fringe location accessible to these two highways was thus heavily favored.

At this point it was necessary to consult with experts in building management. From them, accurate costs of both raw cleaning materials and maintenance charges were obtained. These costs included such items as window cleaning charges and polishing equipment so that a fair comparison could be made between company-accomplished maintenance as opposed to contract maintenance. Other real estate experts were consulted in order to determine costs to the company of vacancies which might result in a company-owned building in which space was leased to others. Reasonable rental income was estimated; interest charges on construction loans were studied; remodeling expense for both company and tenant use was calculated; taxes were considered. All calculable items of cost were matched to an arbitrary period of occupancy and measured on the basis of the following comparative values, related to the cost to the company of remaining in the leased space occupied by the company at the time of the study:

Alternate 1 Continuance of leased space . . . . Basic Cost (X)

Alternate 2 Purchase of vacant central property & cost of building . . . . 60% of X

Alternate 3 Purchase of existing buildings and remodeling cost

Possibility a . . . . 57% of X

Possibility b . . . . 56% of X

Alternate 4 Purchase of existing buildings and use as is

Possibility a . . . . 32% of X

Possibility b . . . . 46% of X

Possibility c . . . . 48% of X

Alternate 5 Purchase of vacant rural property & cost of building . . . . 34% of X

With one exception, Alternate 4a, the cost figures were heavily in favor of the outlying location, Alternate 5, which could be occupied at 34 per cent of the cost of remaining in the location occupied at the time. After considering the unknown expansion needs of the remote future, not to mention the prestige values of a new modern building, the outlying location was chosen.

In moving to purchase the selected property, the company felt it would be wise not to disclose its identity until after purchase. One reason was that should there be local opposition to the invasion of industry into the village, any negative effects upon the goodwill of the company could be avoided. Also while that portion of the property under consideration was properly zoned, there were points still to be settled which could be accomplished best by a third party.

Architects as agents for property purchases

Accordingly our firm understood this phase of the commission, as the agent of the owners, and proceeded to meet with local realtors and village officials to determine their requirements. This required a period of negotiation which heavily involved the company legal counsel. There was a contract stipulation that disclosure of the company identity would be withheld until the last possible moment. This feature requires that the agent be well known locally and have a degree of confidence and integrity commensurate with the serious position of trust in which he functions as the agent of his principal.

The advantage of using an architect as an agent in this manner is that the owner is represented by an expert who is qualified to advise on the various physical problems which arise during negotiation. Other than the financial aspects, these include factors relating to entrance and exit provisions, off-street parking provisions, height and sign restrictions, coverage and setback restrictions, and aspects relating to water supply, sanitary and storm sewerage, and fire protection.

Favorable results of services

The outcome in the present case was completely favorable. The land purchase ultimately made was greatly in excess of requirements, and purposely so, for protection against possible negative growth nearby whether residential or commercial.

The accomplishment of the studies described seems so natural an extension of the architect's other services as to make it seem obligatory that "site selection" become a normal service performed by architects.

30

Principles of Economic Feasibility
For Architectural Projects

BY WILLIAM G. LYLES, FAIA

Through systematic application of a few simple principles of economic analysis, architects can determine the degree of financial soundness of construction projects—as an important and necessary phase of comprehensive architectural practice—before beginning design and other phases

Architect's responsibilities for economics of projects

Whatever responsibility does an architect have to his client or prospective client to advise him concerning his need for architectural and related services? Should an architect knowingly accept a commission for an unsound project or venture?

Certainly architects, both for themselves and their clients, should know at least enough about the financial aspects of projects to recognize one that is obviously unsound financially and to recommend against services that do not appear warranted or to advise their clients when additional professional studies appear to be needed.

Most "seasoned" practitioners will agree that usually little is to be gained—and very often much to be lost—by encouraging or pursuing a project that is likely to prove economically unsound for a client. The most beautiful design usually loses its luster when the owner discovers that he can borrow only half as much as he expected, when he experiences a loss, or when he fails to make a reasonable return on his investment. If architecture is to expand as a profession, it will most likely be through the performance of services that result in tangible profits of one sort of another to clients—profits greater than could be realized without the use of architectural services—and by avoiding all situations where the architect's services are likely to prove a liability. This premise would seem to be fundamental to the whole question of comprehensive architectural services.

Clients want tangible profits

Obviously these principles are more directly applicable to commercial and industrial work than other kinds. But in most cases, in all types of work, it is usually worthwhile to give at least some degree of objective consideration to the cost of projects and their justification prior to proceeding too far with design.

There are perhaps few, if any, architects who accept a commission without giving some thought to the question of whether the project is sensible or feasible, or who fail to make diagnoses of one sort or another. However, all too often such diagnoses are superficial, framed to fit what the client wants to hear or thinks he wants to hear and are made without objective analysis.

Need for financial feasibility

The economic soundness or *feasibility* of a project or venture can only be determined by some form of *financial analysis*. As commonly used, these terms imply studies in great detail involving taxes, depreciation and many other areas in which the average architect generally is not well versed. However, some architects are presently equipped to offer very competent services in these fields, usually for a separate or additional fee. If competently performed, such studies certainly should be considered as extra services because a thorough job usually involves professional knowledge

Financial analysis by architects

in the fields of economics, accounting and law. The present chapter is not concerned with *financial analysis* and *feasibility* from the viewpoint of an economist or accountant. Instead, it is concerned with a simplified form of preliminary appraisal of economic feasibility which most architects should be able to master with a little study and help from readily available sources. Such a preliminary appraisal should be expected only to reveal glaring economic deficiencies or to place the architect in a position to recommend a more detailed professional study wiith some degree of intelligence.

Except in the simplest cases, and these are rare, quite a bit of work is necessary to make even a preliminary economic analysis. This fact should be explained to the client, together with the fact that he should be prepared to pay for this work along with other preliminary services, even though the project might be subsequently abandoned. The amounts of special charges, if any, for the preliminary analysis should be governed by the depth of the analysis and whether or not it is being made as a special service for the owner.

Feasibility determined by project cost, financing and return on investment

The economic feasibility of a project is usually determined by three things: project cost, financing and return on investment. The last named, of course, involves the other two.

Project cost not the same as construction costs

There is an inclination sometimes to consider the project cost and the construction cost as synonymous, particularly since architects often refer to the building itself as the project. This is actually far from the case when the financial aspects of a project are being considered. In addition to the construction cost of a building, the project cost includes a number of other factors. These are usually land, equipment, professional fees (architects, engineers, consultants, attorneys, etc), taxes and insurance during construction, interest during construction (i e, interest on capital advanced or invested during construction) and any other items that will be required to place the building in use. An allowance for unforeseen contingencies must always be included.

With the exception of construction cost, these items can usually be determined, or reasonably approximated, by discussion with either the owner or a reputable real estate agent or with both. The items named are ones with which almost everyone is familiar but which are often overlooked in the early stages of a project.

Estimating construction costs

A reasonable estimate of construction cost is usually the largest and most important item. The architect is the only person who can judge how and when a reasonable determination of probable construction cost can be made. And unless the architect is extremely familiar with the problem at hand, it will usually be necessary to formulate a program and the basic schematic plans, at least, before attempting even a first preliminary estimate. Perhaps more problems for owners and the architectural profession are caused by immature, ill-considered estimates of construction costs than any other aspect of practice.

Need for reliability in cost estimating

Improvement of the reliability of architects' cost estimates would do much to improve the standing of, and respect for, the profession. Experienced owners sometimes hold back a hidden reserve to make up for anticipated deficiencies in architectural estimates because they believe, and with good cause in some cases, that architects habitually underestimate construction costs. Estimates must be realistic. However, there should be no hestitation in recommending and making special charges for quantity surveys and detailed preliminary estimates when they appear to be needed.

At any rate, if even the most preliminary kind of analysis of economic feasibility is to be made, all items that make up the total project must be considered in the degree of detail that would appear to be warranted in the individual case.

Construction financing

The financing of construction projects is a technical field which is always in a continual state of change like all other markets. This is not a field for novices, nor one in which the average architect can reasonably be expected to be expert. However, there are a few simple indicators which architects can use in order to intelligently examine the broader aspects of financing.

Need for equity or long-term leases

In almost every case, the owner must have a substantial equity to invest in a project—usually somewhere in the neighborhood of a third of the cost—and sometimes considerably more. This equity may be in land value, in cash, or in other tangible assets committed to the project. There is only one substitute for equity: strong financial commitments through responsible long-term leases or otherwise so that the lender is fully protected against loss. However, such instances are rare. The owner who is expecting to "mortgage out" (i e, finance his operations completely on borrowed money) should be considered questionable, at best. Mortgaging-out may have been possible at one time, but this is almost never the case today, even in programs underwritten by the government.

Sources of information on financing

On the subject of the financing of projects, a number of sources of information are readily available to the architect. A great deal can be learned through discussion with local lenders: mortgage brokers, building and loan associations, banks and other investors. And of course, there is much to be learned from owners themselves. The financial aspect of construction projects is a field which an architect may explore to such depths as he may desire, usually to the benefit of his clients and himself. But whether he is financially inclined or not, the average architect should know enough about the broad principles to be able to tell whether or not the proposed financing of a venture makes sense and to find sources of professional help when needed.

Return on investments

The return on the investment is the most difficult facet of an economic analysis. Generally an economist—or at least an accountant—is needed to do a proper job and even then there are often many questions that are difficult, if not impossible, to answer. So many assumptions and long-range projections are involved that sometimes the whole process looks like simply a guess. But the return on investment is obviously the "meat in the coconut." And even a preliminary analysis based on perceptive observations and reasonable assumptions is far better than what would actually be a blind guess.

Analysis of financial return

Basically the process involved in analyzing financial returns is quite simple. The gross income from the project in a given period is calculated; all expenses during that period are subtracted, and what is left, if anything, is profit. Of course, income taxes, depreciation and a great number of other things come into play in the determination of the true final profits. In this case, the relationship between the profit and invested capital, or equity, is usually considered as the "return." The return from the project and its security compared with returns from other possible investments of comparable security will generally determine whether or not the project will be an attractive investment.

Analysis of leased or rental projects

The assumptions required for an analysis of a leased or rental project usually involve, among other things, knowledge of such variables as the market for the space, rentals that can be anticipated, allowances for vacancies, operational and maintenance expenses, and taxes and insurance. These factors are averaged or projected over a long period of time, generally the life of the mortgage. Projects constructed for the use of the owner himself usually involve other considerations but are generally comparable with rental projects because the most important question in such cases is usually whether it would be more advantageous to own or to rent.

Taxes and other considerations

Analysis of income taxes and other considerations that have a bearing on the relative attraction of an investment to an owner require an intimate knowledge of the owner's financial position and his other operations and expectations. Obviously, on most projects, the architect cannot be expected to have all of the necessary background and knowledge required for detailed analyses of all of these factors. However, through discussion with the owner, real estate brokers or managers of comparable buildings and a sensible accountant, the architect should be able to make a reasonably reliable decision on whether the project is a lemon or not; whether some specialist is needed to evaluate the project further; and, if so, where such an expert may be found.

An economic feasibility study

Once an architect follows this procedure on a few projects, the principles will begin to make sense, and facts will be learned that will simplify the process when it is used in the future.

In the case that follows, the owners wished to consider the feasibility of improving and expanding an existing printing plant as compared to replacing the plant with a new office building. As it turned out, four economic feasibility studies were made: one of a projected new office building and three different versions of remodeling and expansion of the existing facilities. In each case, diagrammatic plans were made for the sole purpose of approximation of areas in order to arrive at estimated costs and rentals. The expectation was that if the project should materialize after the feasibility studies were completed, the diagrammatic plans would be used only to set the general limits of areas and costs for the actual design of the project.

The actual figures for each of the four schemes, along with the applicable diagrammatic plans, are reproduced in the pages following. After a review of the alternatives and upon the recommendation of the architects, the owners went ahead with one of the remodeling jobs studied rather than the new office building. The relatively large equity required and relatively low return indicated in the office building analysis, combined with some questions on the market for office space, were the basis for the decision. Thus, the architects ended up with a rather small remodeling job (Scheme D on p186) rather than a commission for a new building (Scheme A below). But in this particular case, the analyses pointed toward this particular decision.

Scheme A—Office Building

As in diagrams, next page, ground floor and half of basement—commercial, three loft floors with approx 7,300 sq ft net rentable each; eight office floors, subdivided with 6,500 sq ft net rentable each; first class building, though not elaborate; maximum flexibility of use; rental per sq ft $3.25 for loft space and $3.75 for suites with full services but parking extra; land value of $150,000 for building proper, exclusive of parking

1 Building Areas

a Gross incl. mechanical, service (sq ft)	105,000
b Net rentable (sq ft)	
Commercial—first floor	6,000
Commercial—basement	3,000
Offices—loft	22,000
Offices—suites	52,000
Total net rentable area (sq ft)	83,000

2 Estimated Project Cost

Land	$ 150,000
Construction (105,000 sq ft @ $15.25)	1,600,000
Movable part. (eight floors @ 600 lin ft)	150,000
Architectural and engineering fees	110,000
Interest during construction	45,000
Taxes and insurance during construction	4,000
Legal	1,000
Miscellaneous and contingencies	25,000
Total estimated project cost	$2,085,000

SCHEME A—OFFICE BUILDING (Cont'd)

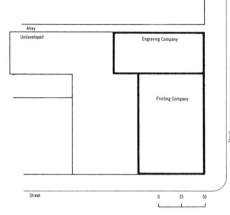

Existing Property

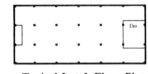

Typical Lot & Floor Plan
(7,300 sq ft net; 8,800 sq ft gross)

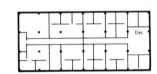

Typical Suite Floor Plan
(6,500 sq ft net; 8,800 sq ft gross)

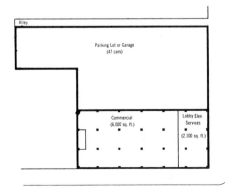

First Floor Plan

3 Possible Financing

Project cost	$2,085,000
Mortgage at 60%	1,250,000
Equity required	$ 835,000
Land	150,000
Cash required	$ 685,000

5¾%—20-yr mortgage of above amount assumed.

Annual amortization, interest	$105,300

4 Estimated Annual Gross Income

Commercial—6,000 sq ft @ $2.25	$ 13,500
3,000 sq ft @ $1.00	3,000
Loft space—22,000 sq ft @ $3.25	71,500
Suites—52,000 sq ft @ $3.75	195,000
	$283,000
Less 5% vacancy	14,000
Est annual gross income	$269,000

5 Estimated Annual Operating Cost

Operating expenses (including all services—$1.00 per sq ft rentable)	$ 83,000
Property tax	21,500
Insurance	5,000
Replacement reserve and miscellaneous	6,000
Total annual operating cost	$115,500

6 Amortization, Depreciation, Income Taxes, Profit

Annual gross income	$269,000
Less annual operating costs	115,500
Annual net income	$153,500

7 Possible Return

a If mortgaged: Annual net income	$153,500
Annual amortization, interest	105,300
For annual income taxes and return—first 20 yrs	$ 48,200

After debt service, this amount equals 5.77% of equity of $835,000 during first 20 years; $153,500 annual net income equals 18.38% on $835,000 equity after 20 years.

If owner financed, annual net income of $153,500 equals 7.36% return on $2,085,000 project cost or would amortize cost with return of 6% for 28 yrs 3 mos.

Scheme B—Remodeling, Expansion

As shown in diagrams, development of three floors commercial space on corner; removal of engraving building; remaining space on lot for printing plant

Third Floor Plan

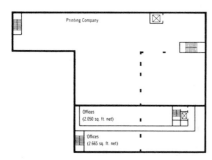

Second Floor Plan

First Floor Plan

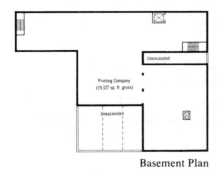

Basement Plan

1 Allocation of Space (sq ft)

Printing (gross areas)

Basement	19,327
First floor (including offices, etc)	16,616
Second floor	16,616
Total (sq ft)	52,559

Commercial	Net	Gross
Basement	—	—
First floor	5,765	7,125
Second floor	4,715	7,125
Third floor	4,715	7,125
Totals	15,195	21,375

2 Estimated Construction Cost

Space occupied by printing co	$313,000
Space occupied by commercial	300,000
Total	$613,000

3 Economic Analysis of Commercial Space

a Development cost:

Construction	$300,000
Movable partitions	20,000
Architectural and engineering fees	19,000
Interest during construction	9,000
Legal and incidentals	5,000
	$353,000
Value of land	50,000
Total project cost	$403,000

b Estimated annual gross income

Ground floor—corner 2,750 sq ft @ $3.50, services	$ 9,620
Ground floor—3 shops 3,015 sq ft, without services	6,600
Second floor—2,665 sq ft @ $3.25, services	8,660
Second floor—2,050 sq ft @ $3.00, services	6,150
Third floor—same as second	14,810
	$45,840
Less 5% vacancies	2,290
Approx annual gross income	$43,500

c Estimated annual operating cost

Operating expense—12,445 sq ft @ $1.00	$12,500
Property tax	3,500
Insurance	1,000
Replacement reserve	1,000
Total annual operating costs	$18,000

d Amortization, depreciation, income taxes, profit

Annual gross income	$43,500
Less operating costs	18,000
Annual net income	$25,500

e Possible return on investment

$25,500 for $403,000 project cost = 6.33%

Scheme C—Remodeling, Expansion

As shown in diagrams, development of existing printing building; rebuilding of engraving building with first floor for commercial, second for printing and photographer

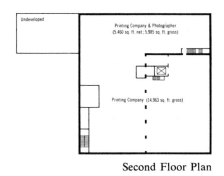

Second Floor Plan

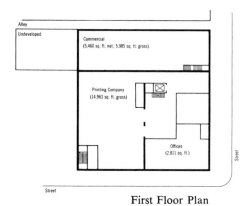

First Floor Plan

1 Allocation of Space (sq ft)

Printing co (gross areas)

Basement		14,017
First floor (including offices, etc)		14,963
Second floor (including photographer)		20,948
Total (sq ft)		49,928
Commercial	*Net* (sq ft)	*Gross* (sq ft)
First floor	5,460	5,985

2 Estimated Construction Cost

Space occupied by printing co	$275,000
Space occupied by commercial	90,000
Total	$365,000

3 Economic Analysis of Commercial Space

a Development cost

Construction	$ 85,000
Movable partitions	5,000
Architectural and engineering fees	5,700
Interest during construction	2,300
Legal and incidentals	1,000
	$ 99,000
Land value (divided with printing co)	21,000
Total project cost	$120,000

b Estimated annual gross income

5,460 sq ft @ $3.00 (with services)	$16,380
Less 5% vacancies	820
Est annual gross income	$15,560

c Estimated annual operating cost

Operating expenses 5,460 sq ft @ $1.00	$5,500
Property tax	1,000
Insurance	300
Replacement reserve	200
Total	$7,000

d Available for amortization, depreciation, income taxes and profit

Annual gross income	$15,560
Less operating expenses	7,000
Annual net income	$ 8,560

e Possible return on investment
$8,560 for $120,000 project cost = 7.19%

Scheme D—Remodeling, Expansion

As shown in diagrams, development of existing printing building and adjacent lot; engraving building unimproved

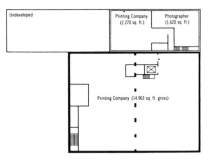

Second Floor Plan

First Floor Plan

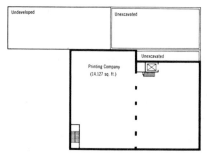

Basement Plan

1 Allocation of Space (sq ft)

Printing co (gross areas)

Basement	14,017
First floor (including offices, etc)	14,963
Second floor (printing co building)	14,963
Second floor (engraving building)	2,270
	46,213
Photographer-engraving building	1,620
Total (sq ft)	47,833
Commercial	
Engraving and florist	3,890

2 Estimated Construction Cost

Space occupied by printing co	$225,000
Commercial (existing)	—
Total	$225,000
Gross rental from existing commercial space	$4,460

Some architects or others may say that the simplified approach to the analysis of economic feasibility of construction projects described here has inherent dangers. Certainly this would be true if the procedures discussed were not used with discretion and judgment. However, the procedures described have proved to be extremely helpful in the practice carried on in the author's own office.

Of course, it would be even better if all offices were equipped to perform even more detailed economic analyses. It is to be hoped that as time goes on a number of architectural offices will prepare themselves to perform such studies in greater depth than has been discussed, with the aid of specialists on their staffs or with outside consultants. However, it would seem doubtful that this will ever be the case with the average practitioner. Perhaps it would be enough for most practitioners if they were well enough informed to understand and use the kinds of broad economic principles described here, if only for reaching reasonable preliminary conclusions on the feasibility of projects. This degree of understanding would do much to expand the usefulness of the architectural profession.

The important thing in the economic areas of practice, as well as in all of the other phases of comprehensive services, is that architects recognize their limitations and avoid getting into fields in which they are not fully qualified. Economists, accountants and the other professionals with whom architects must work in the accomplishment of comprehensive services deserve to have recognition of the full status of their own professions, just as do architects. The architectural profession must seek increasingly fruitful methods of working with these other professionals if its services are to be expanded toward comprehensive architectural practice.

31

Budget Estimating and Cost Control

BY CHARLES LUCKMAN, FAIA

In order to take full advantage of the expanding challenges and opportunities of today, architects must be able not only to control construction costs but to cause cost controls to become useful tools for the shaping of better buildings by the means of comprehensive architectural services

Purpose:

An analysis of the major elements of costs in building construction; subject— a 200,000 sq ft office building

Procedure:

A study of ways and means of enclosing the required space; a study of alternate structural systems; development of a building structure that achieves the optimum in economy by combining the most efficient means of constructing the first two factors

Approach:

Evaluation of costs of elements of a building—the shape, number and arrangement of levels, structural systems, elevator core location, vertical transportation, exterior treatment, airconditioning electrical, interior architectural treatment, space division. Consideration of the influence of use and maintenance

Architects have a moral and ethical responsibility to stay within their clients' budgets. On numerous occasions, the courts have ruled that architects also have a legal responsibility regarding construction costs. Most government agencies, at all levels, stipulate in their contracts with architects that drawings must be re-done at the architects' own expense if bids do not come in within budgets. For these reasons alone, it is necessary for architects to be knowledgeable and efficient in budget estimating and cost controls. With such knowledge comes an important added benefit—the ability to handle the costs of construction, not as obstacles, but rather as useful tools of creative design.

The cost system described here is the result of a year-long study. While it is based on an analysis of the costs of an office building, the principles can easily be applied to other building types. In the study, there are a number of places which might seem to warrant greater detail. In individual cases, this might well be so. At the present time, it seems better to concentrate on the important principles of cost controls rather than risk the confusion that often results from minute detail. In any case, the study should have value for architects who are determined to control construction costs not only in order to avoid legal tangles but to make cost controls a creative element of comprehensive practice. The system can contribute to better understanding between architects and clients.

Clients today want design that fits into their budgets, as well as design for the other values architects can provide. Clients expect their buildings to "be right." Architects can make them so, but only if they remember that to clients this means the costs of buildings as well as the other elements of architecture. Only too often, clients bypass architects for the services of package dealers or others because they believe architects to be "creative but expensive."

Good architecture and reasonable budgets are not necessarily incompatible. If cost analyses indicate that a change must be made in a wall finish from marble to plaster, this may be regrettable but scarcely a serious problem. On the other hand, if it should become necessary to shrink the building 10 per cent to bring it within the budget, the problem is not only serious but one that could be financially disastrous to the architect.

The most important thing is that architects must know how to control costs; they must be able to base their controls on knowledge—facts and figures. The system discussed here provides a framework for acquiring such knowledge and applying it to building construction. The approach used is an evaluation of the elements of a building based on costs, along with the factors that all clients seem to want—flexibility and efficient maintenance. The report deals with the usual considerations in the design of a building, with the emphasis on procedures for better cost analysis.

The present study is based on an office building containing 200,000 sq ft. First, one level of the building was studied to obtain a comparison of the costs of walls to enclose each of several shapes. In the illustration may be seen some of the facts that can be learned from such a study. A circle can enclose 200,000 sq ft with 1,578 lineal feet of wall while a square requires 1,792 lineal feet, and a simple L-shape, 2,200 lineal feet. A number of comparisons of the various shapes can be made; for example, the difference between the walls for the square and those of the L-shape is over 400 lineal feet. Thus the L-shape requires about 25 per cent more wall area than the square to enclose the same amount of area. Of course, the circle requires the least wall area, but because of the great cost of constructing curvilinear walls, this shape was discounted for the purposes of this study.

Other than the circle, hexagon, or square, the rectangular shape encloses the required area with less wall than any other shape. The rectangle is less costly to build than the L-shape or hexagon because it has fewer corners, less costly than the circle because of the problem of curvilinear walls, and has the added advantage of lending itself to the best ratio obtainable between gross and net floor area. It goes without saying that a rectangular shape seems more normal than some others to most clients. For these reasons, a rectilinear plan was chosen to illustrate the costs of constructing the office building in this study.

The next step was to decide on the arrangement of levels to develop the 200,000 sq ft. Obviously, this area can be placed on one floor, on ten levels of 20,000 sq ft each, on fifteen levels of 13,333 sq ft each, or any of a number of other combinations. In order to achieve the maximum net to gross area ratio for maximum leasing potential, and for the best utilization of the site, the decision

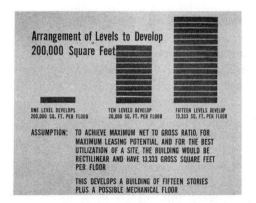

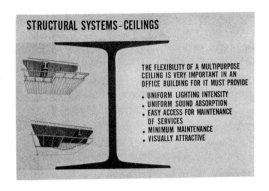

STRUCTURAL SYSTEMS-CEILINGS

THE FLEXIBILITY OF A MULTIPURPOSE CEILING IS VERY IMPORTANT IN AN OFFICE BUILDING FOR IT MUST PROVIDE
- UNIFORM LIGHTING INTENSITY
- UNIFORM SOUND ABSORPTION
- EASY ACCESS FOR MAINTENANCE OF SERVICES
- MINIMUM MAINTENANCE
- VISUALLY ATTRACTIVE

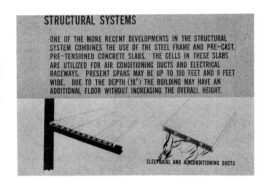

STRUCTURAL SYSTEMS

ONE OF THE MORE RECENT DEVELOPMENTS IN THE STRUCTURAL SYSTEM COMBINES THE USE OF THE STEEL FRAME AND PRE-CAST, PRE-TENSIONED CONCRETE SLABS. THE CELLS IN THESE SLABS ARE UTILIZED FOR AIR CONDITIONING DUCTS AND ELECTRICAL RACEWAYS. PRESENT SPANS MAY BE UP TO 100 FEET AND 8 FEET WIDE. DUE TO THE DEPTH (18") THE BUILDING MAY HAVE AN ADDITIONAL FLOOR WITHOUT INCREASING THE OVERALL HEIGHT.

ELECTRICAL AND AIRCONDITIONING DUCTS

STRUCTURAL SYSTEMS - STEEL DECK FLOORS
MATERIAL: STEEL DECK. 2 1/2" LIGHTWEIGHT CONCRETE

BAY SIZE	DIAGRAM	BEAM	GIRDER	AVG. COLUMN	COST PER SQ. FT.
20' X 30'		18 WF 45	18WF 45	14 WF 119	$3.53
		14 B 22	21WF 55	14WF 119	$3.14
25' X 30'		18 WF 45	21 WF 62	14 WF 150	$3.71
		16 B 26	24 WF 68	14 WF 150	$3.23
30' x 40'		24 WF 68	27 WF 94 / 24 WF100	14 WF 228	$4.23 / $4.25
		18 WF 45	30 WF 116 / 24 WF 130	14 WF 228	$3.97 / $4.05

STRUCTURAL SYSTEMS - CONCRETE SLAB FLOORS
MATERIAL: 4 1/2" CONCRETE SLAB

BAY SIZE	DIAGRAM	BEAM	GIRDER	AVG. COLUMN	COST PER SQ. FT.
20' X 30'		18 WF 45	18 WF 55	14 WF 158	$3.21
		14 B 26	21WF 62	14WF 158	$3.08
25' X 30'		18 WF 50	21WF 73	14 WF 176	$3.30
		16 WF 36	24 WF68	14WF 176	$3.21
30' X 40'		24 WF 76	24 WF 100	14 WF 287	$3.99
		18 WF 45	33 WF 118 / 24 WF 145	14 WF 287	$3.83 / $3.81

was to make the building rectilinear with 13,333 sq ft per floor. This means a fifteen-story building, possibly with an additional floor for mechanical equipment, as shown in the illustration.

Following this, studies must be made of the structure. As an example, the flexibility obtainable with multi-purpose ceilings is most important in office buildings, since they provide uniform lighting intensities, uniform sound absorption, easy access for maintenance of services, minimum over-all maintenance, and attractive appearance. The illustration shows some of the types of ceilings now available. Some of these ceilings have chambers above for air-conditioning. In order to prevent the airconditioning space above the ceiling from becoming an echo chamber, it is necessary to extend partitioning up through the chamber itself.

A further example of the considerations that must be made in the study of structure is the growing use of precast, pretensioned concrete floor slabs in steel frame buildings. These slabs may be utilized for airconditioning ducts and for electrical raceways. The slabs can be made to span up to 100 ft, in up to 8 ft widths. Since the slab depth is not over 18 in, a building can often have an additional floor without increasing its over-all height. The illustration shows a slab system in which pretensioning permits the upper and lower areas of concrete to be only 3 in thick, or a total of 6 in, leaving a full 12 in inside for electrical and airconditioning ducts.

Next comes an investigation of floor systems of various kinds. In the first instance, the assumption is that steel decking with a 2½ in slab of lightweight concrete will be used. Since much discussion with clients seems to be concerned with bay spacing, a breakdown is made of three different bay schemes—20 by 30 ft, 25 by 30 ft, and 30 by 40 ft. For the 200,000 sq ft, fifteen-story building of this example, the average beam, girder, and column sizes were computed and priced, for spans in both directions. From this information, it is possible to compute the cost per sq ft for each situation, and tabulate the costs as shown in the illustration.

With such information in hand, it is possible to answer the client who says, "Wouldn't it be nice to have a 25 by 30 ft bay . . ." with, "Yes, but that size will cost $3.23 per sq ft for the structure as compared to $3.14 for the 20 by 30 ft bay." This principle might well be extended to all of the other component parts of the building.

In the next part of the study, information similar to that for the steel deck and slab floor structure was developed for a building with 4½ in concrete slabs without steel decking. The same bay spacings were studied, structural members were sized, and the costs per sq ft of floor area developed. As may be seen by a comparison of the two illustrations, the costs of the all-concrete floor system average below the costs of the steel deck and concrete system.

Information of this sort is readily available in the experienced architectural office, but it is well worth the digging-out and tabulation. When arranged in some form similar to that of the illustrations, the information may prove invaluable not only in analysis of costs, but in working with clients. While such information may be a little harder to develop for the architect who is just beginning to

ALTERNATE ELEVATOR CORE LOCATIONS CIRCULATION LAYOUTS

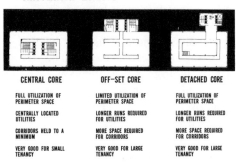

CENTRAL CORE	OFF—SET CORE	DETACHED CORE
FULL UTILIZATION OF PERIMETER SPACE	LIMITED UTILIZATION OF PERIMETER SPACE	FULL UTILIZATION OF PERIMETER SPACE
CENTRALLY LOCATED UTILITIES	LONGER RUNS REQUIRED FOR UTILITIES	LONGER RUNS REQUIRED FOR UTILITIES
CORRIDORS HELD TO A MINIMUM	MORE SPACE REQUIRED FOR CORRIDORS	MORE SPACE REQUIRED FOR CORRIDORS
VERY GOOD FOR SMALL TENANCY	VERY GOOD FOR LARGE TENANCY	VERY GOOD FOR LARGE TENANCY

VERTICAL TRANSPORTATION

	MIN. QUALITY INSTALLATION	AVERAGE QUALITY INSTALLATION		EXCELLENT QUALITY INSTALLATION	
FLOORS SERVED	1 - 15	1 - 15		1 - 15	
SPEED - FEET / MINUTE	500	500		700	
CAPACITY - POUNDS	2500	3000		3000	
NUMBER OF CARS	5	5	6	6	7
INTERVAL IN SECONDS	28	32	26	26	22
APPROXIMATE COST	$425,000	$450,000	$530,000	$600,000	$700,000

ADDITIVE ALTERNATES:	
ESCALATORS—PER FLOOR	$81,250
FREIGHT ELEVATOR	$35,000
BASEMENT ELEVATOR WHEN PARKING REQUIRED	$54,000

work with office buildings, it should prove to be of even greater value to him.

The next consideration in the study of the office building was that of vertical transportation. First established were what appeared to be the three basic elevator core locations—central, offset, and detached. The central core allows full utilization of perimeter space on all floors, and makes it possible to centrally locate utilities. With this scheme, corridors are held to a minimum and the plan lends itself to subdivision of floors into areas for small occupancies.

The offset core limits the utilization of perimeter space, since the core itself occupies a part of the perimeter. Longer runs for utilities are necessary with the offset core; more space is required for corridors. This scheme lends itself best to large occupancies.

The detached core, which has come into some favor in certain instances in recent years, requires even longer utility runs than the offset core, and more space for corridors. However, the detached core does allow almost full utilization of the perimeter of the building, and it works well for large occupancies.

After the consideration of various elevator core locations came a study of the basic differences between elevator systems of varying degrees of quality. Assuming three degrees of quality—minimum, average and excellent—the figures shown in the illustration were derived. The factors considered in the comparison of quality included speed permitted, passenger capacities per car, and number of cars required. Another important factor is the interval, in seconds, of response to the control system. For each of these three degrees of quality, approximate costs were determined.

It is not easy to convince clients or others not familiar with office building work that within the same fifteen-story building, there can be a range of costs for elevators between $425,000 and $700,000, as shown in the illustration.

To these costs can be added certain alternates such as escalators at $81,000 per floor, a freight elevator at $35,000, or a basement elevator, when parking is required on that level, for $54,000. The last-named figure is an answer to the not unusual question, "Wouldn't it be just as well to have the elevators run down to the basement to take care of the parking under the building?" With the aid of this study, it is possible to answer this question with, "Yes, it would be fine, but it will cost $54,000."

One recent development in vertical transportation that should be considered in cost studies of office buildings is the computer controlled elevator. These units are equipped to scan calls for elevator service and direct the nearest cab to respond. This advance in technology can actually reduce the number of cabs required in an office building.

At this point, the exterior walls of the office building were studied. Exterior wall treatment, of course, holds very exciting possibilities for design today. With reinforced concrete and steel construction, very light exterior curtain walls are possible. As is well known, these walls can be constructed of virtually any material. They are frequently prefabricated to reduce on-site construction time and costs.

In studying the costs of exterior walls, attention must be paid to all of the details of construction—glazing, gaskets, panel-edge sealing, insulation, drainage and vents, and the inner skin as a possible interior finish. All of these factors have a bearing on the total cost of the wall. As elsewhere in the building, costs of exterior walls need not inhibit good design.

After the walls, the airconditioning of the office building was studied. There are two basic systems in use today—the perimeter system and the interior system. The perimeter system handles the heat loads generated on the outside of the building at the same point at which the loads are generated. This system offers the maximum degree of individual control, but it requires additional supply for interior areas. On the other hand, the interior airconditioning system has the maximum degree of flexibility and is lower in installation cost. With this system, more space is required for fan rooms, and, of course, there is a higher maintenance factor due to the need for an additional amount of servicing of fans and filters.

Here, when working with clients, it is usually necessary to clarify the relationships between esthetics and standardization, and point out how the two can be effectively blended. The questions of curtains and their effect on airconditioning, the possibility of using combination light fixture-diffusers, tube type diffusers, exterior sun controls—all of these relate both to appearance and function.

Lighting systems were next studied. Some of the types in existence are shown in the illustration, along with their major characteristics. The costs of these systems vary greatly.

Then studies were made of various methods of partitioning. All of the problems and costs of the many systems possible must be taken into consideration—fixed vs movable, full-height vs medium- or low-height, baffle or screen partitions, the many materials available, the possibilities for decorative design.

At this point, in the study of the office building, it becomes possible to begin putting the information developed heretofore to work for constructive purposes. Accordingly, a table was compiled showing cost analysis summaries for three degrees of quality—minimum, average and excellent. This table reflects the information contained in three complete outline specification forms prepared at this time—one for each of the three degrees of quality. The preparation of these specifications was necessary in order to avoid confusion as to exactly what kind of building was being analyzed in each of the three cases. Also the specifications, along with the cost analyses, make it possible to demonstrate to clients that in building construction they get exactly what they pay for.

In all three grades of quality, the office building would have approximately the same basic structure. It is well known that costs in this area of construction vary only in a limited way. In the case of the minimum quality building, the outline specifications show it to have exterior walls with standard aluminum frames, painted concrete or rigid asbestos spandrels, surface-mounted light fixtures, minimum elevator service, one electrical outlet per 1000 sq ft, and standard packaged airconditioning units with one zone per 1000 sq ft of floor space.

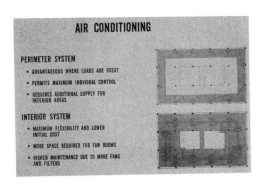

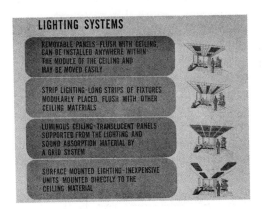

COST ANALYSIS SUMMARY

15 STORY BUILDING 200,000 SQ. FT.

	MINIMUM QUALITY	AVERAGE QUALITY	EXCELLENT QUALITY
BASIC STRUCTURE	$1,120,000	$1,120,000	$1,120,000
EXTERIOR WALLS	348,000	380,000	420,000
INTERIORS	126,000	139,000	150,000
CEILINGS	46,000	58,000	68,000
FLOORS	16,000	18,000	20,000
LIGHTS	32,000	38,000	44,000
SUN CONTROL	108,000	199,000	266,000
ELEVATORS	395,000	495,000	615,000
PLUMBING & SPRINKLERS	81,000	112,000	146,000
HEATING, VENTILATING & AIR CONDITIONING	356,000	398,000	552,000
ELECTRICAL	107,000	268,000	388,000
SITE WORK	85,000	100,000	177,000
BASIC BUILDING COST PER SQ. FT.	$14.10	$16.63	$19.83

TYPICAL TENANT FINISH ALLOWANCES

MINIMUM QUALITY

	QUANTITY	UNITS	UNIT COST	TOTAL COST
PARTITIONS	14,170	LINEAL FT.	$12.13	$171,908
DOORS, FRAMES & HARDWARE	750	UNITS	106.66	80,000
CEILING	170,000	SQ. FT.	.56	95,000
LIGHTING – 50 FOOT CANDLES	2,000	FIXTURES	31.00	62,000
TELEPHONE OUTLETS – 1/1000 SQ. FT.	170	UNITS	13.00	2,210
CONVENIENCE OUTLETS – 1/1000 SQ. FT.	170	UNITS	13.00	2,210
AIR CONDITIONING – 1 ZONE / 1000 SQ. FT.	170	ZONES	95.00	16,150
PAINTING	226,720	SQ. FT.	.08	18,137
FLOORING	170,000	SQ. FT.	.25	42,400
VENETIAN BLINDS	170,000	SQ. FT.	.18	30,600
LIGHT SWITCHES	515	UNITS	19.00	9,785
COST OF FINISH PER SQ. FT.			$ 3.12	$530,400

TYPICAL TENANT FINISH ALLOWANCES

AVERAGE QUALITY

	QUANTITY	UNITS	UNIT COST	TOTAL COST
PARTITIONS	14,170	LINEAL FT.	$13.26	$187,954
DOORS, FRAMES & HARDWARE	750	UNITS	135.00	101,250
CEILING	170,000	SQ. FT.	.75	127,500
LIGHTING – 65 FOOT CANDLES	2,425	FIXTURES	34.50	83,662
TELEPHONE OUTLETS – 1/500 SQ. FT.	340	UNITS	13.00	4,420
CONVENIENCE OUTLETS – 1/500 SQ. FT.	340	UNITS	13.00	4,420
AIR CONDITIONING – 1 ZONE / 750 SQ. FT.	230	ZONES	120.00	27,600
PAINTING	226,720	SQ. FT.	.09	20,404
FLOORING	170,000	SQ. FT.	.28	47,600
VENETIAN BLINDS	170,000	SQ. FT.	.22	37,400
LIGHT SWITCHES	700	UNITS	20.00	14,000
COST OF FINISH PER SQ. FT.			$3.86	$656,210

TYPICAL TENANT FINISH ALLOWANCES

EXCELLENT QUALITY

	QUANTITY	UNITS	UNIT COST	TOTAL COST
PARTITIONS	14,170	LINEAL FT.	$ 14.92	$ 201,416
DOORS, FRAMES & HARDWARE	750	UNITS	150.00	112,500
CEILING	170,000	SQ. FT.	.80	136,000
LIGHTING – 80 FOOT CANDLES	2,840	FIXTURES	34.21	97,167
TELEPHONE OUTLETS – 1/350 SQ. FT.	490	UNITS	13.00	6,370
CONVENIENCE OUTLETS – 1/350 SQ. FT.	490	UNITS	13.00	6,370
AIR CONDITIONING – 1 ZONE/500 SQ. FT.	340	ZONES	125.00	42,500
PAINTING	226,720	SQ. FT.	.10	22,672
FLOORING	170,000	SQ. FT.	.31	52,700
VENETIAN BLINDS	170,000	SQ. FT.	.23	39,100
LIGHT SWITCHES	1,000	UNITS	21.00	21,000
COST OF FINISH PER SQ. FT.			$ 4.34	$ 737,795

In the average quality office building, the specifications show anodized aluminum exterior wall frames with porcelain enamel panels, flush-mounted light fixtures, average elevator service, one electrical outlet per 500 sq ft, and a high velocity airconditioning system with one zone per 750 sq ft.

The excellent quality building has special anodized exterior wall frames with choice of colors and spandrel panel materials, flush-mounted light fixtures and luminous ceilings, excellent elevator service, electrical outlets—one per 350 sq ft, and a double-duct high velocity airconditioning system with one zone per 500 sq ft of area.

In all other respects, the quality of materials, equipment, and finishes varies in more or less direct proportion with the quality of the building.

In the cost analysis summary illustration may be seen a tabulation of the various cost items for buildings of all three qualities. The basic structure is the same for all three; therefore these costs are the same. There are some differences in the costs of exterior walls, but within a reasonably modest range. These costs might actually show less or more variation depending on the particular building being studied. Interior costs vary within a modest range. The range of costs of ceilings is quite large between the minimum and excellent qualities. However, the quality of the ceilings seems to be quite important to the client.

Floor costs vary only slightly. Lighting costs vary considerably, from a low of $32,000 to a high of $44,000. Sun controls, depending on the location of the building, can be a very important cost factor. Elevators show a great range from $395,000 to $615,000. Plumbing and sprinklers show a very substantial range, as do heating, ventilating, and airconditioning. Electrical work ranges from a low of $107,000 to a high of $388,000. Site work has a considerable range from the minimum to the excellent building. The basic costs per sq ft give the picture of building costs, but the figures from which these are derived tell *why* costs range so far. And the breakdowns enable architects to gain control of these various costs and explain them to their clients.

After developing the basic building costs, studies were made of the costs of typical tenant finish allowances. Again the costs for minimum, average, and excellent quality buildings were determined. For all three qualities, the quantities of materials are the same except in the case of telephone and electrical convenience outlets and the number of airconditioning zones provided. In the illustrations may be seen the tabulations of the tenant finish costs for the three qualities of buildings.

In the minimum building, the total tenant finish costs for the fifteen-story office building are $530,400 or $3.12 per sq ft; in the average quality, $656,210 and $3.86, and in the excellent quality $737,795 and $4.34. As over-all quality moves up from the minimum building through the average to the excellent, the quality of all elements of the construction is improved. The numbers of telephone and electrical convenience outlets provided in the minimum building is doubled in the average building, and almost tripled in the excellent quality building. Airconditioning costs range from

$16,150 in the minimum building, through $27,600 in the average, to $42,500 in the excellent building, a staggering increase of 160 per cent over the cost of the minimum quality system.

As has been shown, there are significant differences in the costs of both the basic building and tenant finishes when similar buildings of varying quality are compared. To complete the analysis of the office building used as an example in this study, it was then necessary to prepare a tabulation of the total costs of construction of buildings of the minimum, average and excellent qualities and an analysis of how these costs break down according to the types of work involved.

The illustrations show the result of this tabulation and analysis. The total building cost illustration effectively demonstrates the vast differences in costs—the great per sq ft price-spread between various qualities of the same basic office building. In the improvement of the quality of this building from the minimum to the excellent, it may be seen that the cost per sq ft has risen from a low of $17.22 to a high of $24.17, the one building costing almost 1½ times the price of the other.

In the cost analysis illustration may be seen the relative amounts of the total building costs attributable to various portions of the work. One of the most critical areas is the cost of electrical work. These costs range from 3.8 per cent of the total for the minimum building up to 9.8 per cent of the cost of the excellent building. Another area of surprise for most clients—and possibly for some architects—is the range of costs of the elevators. Here, the excellent building requires an expenditure of 15.5 per cent of its budget for elevators, while the minimum building requires only 14 per cent.

It may also come as somewhat of a surprise that the costs of the basic structure and site work range downward as the quality of the building is improved, from a high of 43 per cent of the total cost of the minimum building to a low of 32.6 per cent for the excellent quality building. This is the usual case. However, it should be remembered that these are percentages of the total costs; the actual dollar costs would remain approximately constant for buildings of all three qualities.

In the case of the present office building study, it would seem to have been adequately demonstrated that the quality of certain elements of construction determines in large degree the total cost of the building. Certain other facts have been uncovered in the course of the study—facts that are useful in the control of construction costs and useful in the design of buildings. Similar information can—and should—be developed by architects for their other buildings, both as an invaluable aid in their own work, and as an aid in explaining their work to their clients.

The next logical step might be that the architectural profession, as the leaders or coordinators of the design and construction team effort, should take the lead in establishing some sort of co-ordinating council on costs among all of the design and construction professions and businesses. Such an organization could collect and disseminate information not only on *what* makes buildings cost what they do but *why*.

TOTAL BUILDING COST

	MINIMUM	AVERAGE	EXCELLENT
BASIC STRUCTURE	$ 14.10	$ 16.63	$ 19.83
TENANT FINISH	3.12	3.86	4.34
TOTAL COST PER SQ. FT.	$ 17.22	$ 20.49	$ 24.17

BUILDING COST ANALYSIS

	MINIMUM	AVERAGE	EXCELLENT
LIGHTS CEILINGS FLOORS INTERIORS	7.7%	7.5%	7.2%
ELECTRICAL	3.8%	8.0%	9.8%
EXTERIOR WALLS SUN CONTROL	16.1%	17.2%	17.3%
ELEVATORS	14.0%	15.0%	15.5%
AIR CONDITIONING HEAT VENTILATION PLUMBING	15.4%	15.3%	17.6%
BASIC STRUCTURE SITE WORK	43.0%	37.0%	32.6%

32

Human Factors Analysis

BY LAWRENCE WHEELER, PH D* AND EWING H. MILLER, AIA

By means of human factors analysis, based on the principles of the relatively new science of human engineering, architects—with the help of industrial psychologists and mathematicians—are able to analyze thoroughly, accurately and in an orderly manner the design factors that relate to people at work

* Instructor of Psychology, Consulting Industrial Psychologist and Adviser to Miller, Miller & Associates Architects and Engineers, Dr. Wheeler is currently working on a study of color and the human eye on a grant from the Carnegie Foundation

The management of modern industrial and business systems requires understanding, coordination and control of men, machinery, work-environments and work-processes. The efficiency of these complex operations depends upon how well management understands each factor—its capabilities, limitations and effects upon the others. Today the architect can—and should—aid management in the solution of these complex problems. To accomplish this, architectural firms can benefit from the methods and information available in the field of *human engineering,* a professional area of research concerned with increasing human efficiency through analysis of human factors in relation to machines, work environments and work processes. Human engineering deals with communications patterns, motivation, status, trainability and other characteristics of men at work; thus, it can be part of a modern, scientific approach to the development of architecture designed to suit the needs of management.

Forward-looking architectural firms will, no doubt, increasingly endeavour to join human engineering and architecture for the purpose of solving the design problems of modern industry. By means of such services, management will be able to benefit from applied research concerning the effects of their surroundings upon people at work.

Up to the present time, the experience of the authors with these new services has been primarily concerned with the development and design of a series of trucking terminals for a top-rated national freight carrier. The approach has been found to be especially valuable in areas where communications and paper work are involved—areas in which human behavior patterns are extremely important. The sample data in this article have been drawn from one such analysis.

Human factors analysis uses straightforward, scientific techniques to give rapid, practical and profitable results that an architectural firm can use in designing new industrial—or other—buildings or in modifying old ones. Three steps are usually taken: the collection of information, the analysis of information and the evaluation of the analysis.

A Brief Outline of Human Factors Analysis

Collecting data is done in several ways: 1) *Interviews and questionnaires,* to find out where people in an organization get their operating information and where they send it. 2) *Random-time observational sampling* (watching what happens), a method that reduces the bias that often creeps into interview situations. 3) *Motion picture observation,* a technique used only for highly complex, rapidly moving systems.

Information analysis

Analysis of information requires the development of *link values* (quantitative statements showing the frequency and importance of information as it moves among work groups). Then *vector analysis* (a mathematical procedure that gives a geometric layout in which job groups are shown as related points on a plane surface) is applied. The vector plot is modified according to such psychological factors as the motivation of employees and the status of supervisors and executives. Finally, a floor plan is developed, on a trial basis, with the modified vector plot as a starting point.

Evaluation

Evaluation of results is the next step. To find out whether a new plan, procedure or system is any better than an old one, indices are developed for average distances walked, ease of voice or visual communication, crowding, accessibility, human traffic crossovers and other factors. These indices permit comparison of an existing office or industrial building with the design for a new one. Definite, quantitive predictions as to increased efficiency can be made on this basis. If the new plan is not an improvement, changes can be made until the indices of efficiency become higher for the new, than for the old, arrangement. Ordinarily, however, vector analysis will make this step unnecessary.

Trial floor plan

In doing an analysis of this kind, the psychologist and architect first make a rough floor plan of the existing building. Then all jobs are listed by title, along with the names of the current job-holders. These people are then located on the floor plan. A list of all equipment is drawn up and each item indicated on the plan. Then the people are interviewed, random-time sampling observations are made of each job group, or questionnaires are prepared; or all of these things may be done. What is required is a complete picture of the information flow through the system.

Interactions among job functions

Human factors analysis for architectural purposes, based on the foregoing methods, leads to a set of data representing *interactions* among job *functions* within the space to be designed. These interactions have two characteristics, *frequency* and *importance,* neither of which may safely be neglected by the conscientious designer. The data describing the interactions usually come from observations of a functioning plant. Frequency of contact is estimated by random-time sampling of employee activities. Interviews or questionnaires are the chief means used for estimating importance. Terms employed in this type of analysis may be defined as follows:

Interaction, contact between points in a system, if the contact results in movement of information between the points (people or machines);

Function, a job group or job activity (often this means the things one person does, but sometimes it means the similar, or highly related things, two or more people do);

Type of communication, basically there are four types of communications or movements of information, each type giving rise to a separate *"matrix"* (definition below) of data; a) *transport* (a person and/or material moves within the system), direct voice contacts are also included in this category; b) *signals,* information goes from one center to another within the system by mechanical or electronic devices (eg intercom., phone, closed-circuit TV or other signal devices) but no material, such as paperwork, moves; c) *external,* information leaves the system, either as a signal or in material form (eg mail, teletype, to files—other than those within separate functions, storage); d) *no movement,* information stays within the job function and there is no movement between elements of the system (eg control of operation of a machine not directly sending messages, data recording, or visual contact only).

Link value, whenever there is a flow of information between two points in the system, a link value is assigned to the interaction. A link value is an index based on: 1) frequency of the interaction, and 2) importance of the interaction. Frequency may be directly observed and evaluated, while importance is usually estimated on the basis of the expense resulting from lost or inaccurate transmission of each message. Where both I (Importance) and F (Frequency) have been reduced to quantitative values of appropriate kinds, usually by means of rating scales, then it can be said that I $\times$ F = LV (link value).

Matrix, link values are placed in a rectangular table that has all the functions listed, in the same order, along the top and one side of the table. Where *n* is the number of functions, the cells representing interactions may be represented as equal to:

$$\frac{n\,(n-1)}{2}$$

The sum of link values for all cells of the matrix having to do with a given function may then be examined; these sums indicate the importance, or *"rank order"* (definition below) of each function in terms of its general strength of interaction with *all* other functions. The sum of the link values between any two functions (a single matrix cell sum or inter-function sum) may also be examined and will show the strength of the connection between the two functions.

Finally, the inter-function sums may be used to perform a minimizing operation by means of vector analysis. This produces a set of points, in a plane coordinate system, with each point at the minimum, weighted distance from all other points. A "weighted distance" bears a known and specified relationship to the link values, as indicated in the paragraphs on the Vector Analysis Process, pages 197-8. The set of points is a mathematical solution to the problem set into the matrix, but it will not ordinarily be subject to immediate translation into architectural floor plans. This is because design factors and certain matters of employee psychology cannot be set directly into the matrix data. Nevertheless, the vector solution provides an optimum geometric arrangement of job functions and forms a precise starting point for architectural planning.

Rank order, job functions may be arranged according to their matrix sums of link values and the resulting list numbered from 1 through any required number (*n*) giving 1 to the job having the largest total link value. The rank order numbers form a convenient index for use in planning and should be listed wherever functions are named. The rank order number gives an immediate, abbreviated indication of the importance of the function in the overall communication network, as shown on page 199, at the top, in the Link Value Matrix Table.

Link Value Matrix

In summary, human factors analysis requires *collection of data* on information flow, *application of mathematical procedures* leading to trial floor plans and *evaluation* of the new floor plans relative to existing ones. The method is an application of standard, scientific procedures to architectural design problems wherever people must communicate in order to get a job done.

Vector Analysis Process

The method of vector analysis employed by the firm of the architect-author of the present article was designed by Dr Cletus

COLLECTION FORM: COMMUNICATIONS DATA FOR HUMAN FACTORS ANALYSIS

Date: Place: For: Analyst:

Communication Type: (place letter within symbol)

△ Transport	○ Signal	□ External	◇ No Movement
a auditory	i intercom	m mail	c control machine
w walk	p phone	x TWX, phone	r record data
t transport	s signal system	f file	v visual contact only
Person &/or material moves	Signal by wire within system	No interaction within system	No movement within system

Link Values: I × F = LV I = Importance* F = Frequency**	Make entries that will aid in analysis of: Design Factors, Status & Motivation
4 very 4 more than daily 3 considerable 3 daily 2 somewhat 2 weekly & monthly 1 slight 1 rare	*Estimate by cost of lost or inaccurate message. **Estimate by type of message, if frequency data not available.

Functions: list all internal first, then external; number serially; locate incumbents on floor plan.

Equipment: list all types; assign lower-case letter to each; locate on floor plan.

T#	R#	CT	I	F	LV	Description of Operation or Interaction

J. Burke, California State College at Hayward. The procedures are generally as follows:

1) Set up the matrix of link values based upon quantified observational and interview data, as shown in the Link Value Matrix Table;

2) Select three job functions that show minimum sums of link values, but are associated with each other to some extent (eg, garage, sales, dock);

3) Establish these three as a triangle in a coordinate system by giving each one a location (a pair of numbers);

4) Mathematical procedures, which involve minimizing a weighted, quasi-distance function, are then applied to the remaining job functions; each is weighted according to its relationship (link value) with every other function, and according to its own importance (sum of link values) in the total matrix. (For the mathematically inclined reader, a summary of this procedure is reproduced below);

SUMMARY OF MATHEMATICAL PROCESSES OF VECTOR ANALYSIS

1 Let: $\phi = \sum_i \sum_j w_{ij}(x_{ik} - x_{jk})^2$, where ϕ is the desired value,

2 Then: $\dfrac{d\phi}{dx_{sk}} = \sum_i \sum_j \dfrac{d}{dx_{sk}} w_{ij}(x_{ik} - x_{jk})^2$

3 And: $\sum_{j \neq s} w_{sj}x_{jk} - x_{sk} \sum_{j \neq s} w_{sj} = 0$

Where: i and j are the different objects; $k = 1$ and $k = 2$ are the first and second coordinates; w_{ij} is the weight associated with the pair of objects; and s is the object with respect to which we differentiate, and where: unless $i = s$ or $j = s$ we get zero; $w_{ij} = w_{ji}$ is true; $w_{js} = w_{sj}$ is true; and when $j = s$ we get zero,

4 Then: $\sum_{\substack{j=1 \\ j \neq s}}^{m} w_{sj}x_{jk} - x_{sk} \sum_{\substack{j=1 \\ j \neq s}}^{m+3} w_{sj} = -\alpha_{sk}$

Where: The three values $m + 1$, $m + 2$, and $m + 3$ are already selected,

For these three: $\sum_{j=m+1}^{m+3} w_{sj}x_{jk} = $ a constant $= \alpha_{sk}$ (for each coordinate separately),

5 Then: Letting $k = 1$, $s = 1$,

$-x_{11} \sum_{j=2}^{m+3} \sum (w_{ij}) + w_{12}x_{21} + w_{13}x_{31} + \cdots w_{im}x_{mi} = \alpha_{11}$

6 And: Letting $k = 1$, $s = 2$,

$w_{12}x_{11} - x_{21} \sum_{\substack{j=1 \\ j \neq 2}}^{m+3} w_{2j} + w_{23}x_{31} + \cdots w_{2m}x_{mi} = \alpha_{21}$

Equations 5 and 6 are solved by the Doolittle multiple regression system (described in J. P. Guilford, "Psychometric Methods," McGraw-Hill Book Co Inc, New York, 1936), to obtain the weighted values that represent the vertical and horizontal coordinates of the m variables not previously located.

LINK VALUE MATRIX
Shows Strength of Relationships Among Job Groups

1	2	3	4	5	6	7	8	9	10	Job Group Title	Rank Order of Over-All Link Values
	37.5	100.0	40.0	42.5	13.3	35.0	00.0	01.7	07.5	1 Dispatchers	1
		26.3	16.7	05.8	00.0	51.3	01.7	02.5	04.2	2 Operations	4
			10.0	03.3	06.7	48.7	07.5	02.5	03.3	3 Communications	3
				11.7	00.4	01.7	00.4	05.0	04.2	4 Dock	8
					00.4	32.1	00.0	28.7	00.4	5 Drivers	5
						06.2	00.4	06.7	16.3	6 Garage	9
							13.3	22.1	61.2	7 Accounting	2
								00.8	02.5	8 Sales	10
									17.1	9 Safety	7
										10 Management	6

Job Groups or Functions:

All link values expressed as percentages of largest single link value (between Job Groups 3 and 1).

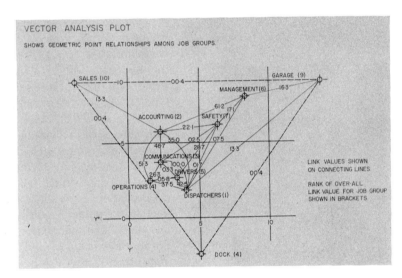

VECTOR ANALYSIS PLOT

SHOWS GEOMETRIC POINT RELATIONSHIPS AMONG JOB GROUPS.

LINK VALUES SHOWN ON CONNECTING LINES

RANK OF OVER-ALL LINK VALUE FOR JOB GROUP SHOWN IN BRACKETS

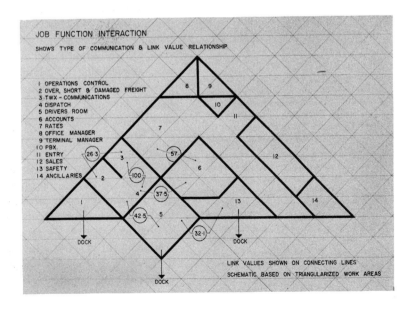

JOB FUNCTION INTERACTION

SHOWS TYPE OF COMMUNICATION & LINK VALUE RELATIONSHIP.

1 OPERATIONS CONTROL
2 OVER, SHORT & DAMAGED FREIGHT
3 TWX - COMMUNICATIONS
4 DISPATCH
5 DRIVERS ROOM
6 ACCOUNTS
7 RATES
8 OFFICE MANAGER
9 TERMINAL MANAGER
10 PBX
11 ENTRY
12 SALES
13 SAFETY
14 ANCILLARIES

LINK VALUES SHOWN ON CONNECTING LINES

SCHEMATIC BASED ON TRIANGULARIZED WORK AREAS

Vector Analysis Plot

Vector Floor Plan and Data Collection Form

Architect and psychologist

The authors acknowledge their debt to Ernest J. McCormick, upon whose discussion of methodology in "Human Engineering," McGraw-Hill Book Company, Inc., 1957, much of the present material is based.

Two other recent references that provide detailed descriptions of some of the methods of human engineering are: Robert M. Gagne and others, "Psychological Principles in System Development," Holt, Rinehart & Winston, New York, 1962, and Arthur D. Hall, "A Methodology for Systems Engineering," D. Van Nostrand Co., Inc., Princeton, 1962

5) The results of the analysis are expressed as coordinates (vertical and horizontal) for each job function; when plotted, the locations of the functions are now optimal (in accordance with the frequency and importance of interactions between and among groups) for the given set of data.

The Vector Analysis Plot, middle of page 199, is a graphic representation of the data developed in a calculation such as is shown on page 198. It should be noted that function No 6 (management) falls well away from the routine job functions and that this is in accordance with the idea that the locations of managers' offices need to be determined by factors that cannot easily be quantified (such as status, motivation of employees, non-routine nature of activities, etc).

Bottom of page 199, is an example of a floor plan illustrating a Vector Analysis Plot. Because of its practical value, an example of the Data Collection Form employed by the office of the architect-author of the present article is shown on page 197. This form gives the scales for estimating the I (importance) and the F (frequency) values for each link value. One entry shows where information comes from (R#), where it goes (T#), the communication type by symbol (CT), the information value (I), the frequency value (F), and the computed link value (LV). From such data sheets as these, the matrix of link values for each type of communication can be developed.

It should be noted that the Data Collection Form specifically directs the recording of data in a form that will aid in decisions concerning problems of status, motivation and design factors. Design factors are the special province of the architect, but status and motivation fall within the human engineer's area of specialization. Is an office window merely a window? Indeed not; it is also a potent factor in the motivation of employees, if they feel that their supervisor may be watching them through it. Furthermore, such a window may have either positive or negative motivating effects. Psychological analysis, by means of questionnaires and interviews, will permit the human engineer to advise the architect concerning such problems.

Should the manager's office be located "up front," to enhance his status, or should it be near his main work-contact areas? Again the question is not simple; status *may* be enhanced, in some cases, by putting an administrator in or near the working plant, *away* from the front office "showcase." An appropriate psychological survey could throw much light on this matter, for given supervisors in given organizational contexts; however, the results may be expected to vary from man to man and from one company to another.

Similar problems, bearing heavily upon the final operating efficiency of work environments, could be listed by the dozen. Often, both management and the architect are equally insensitive to the psychological effects of decisions in matters such as these, yet methods for obtaining systematic, objective solutions do exist. Architectural firms require the skills of human engineers in order to have these methods adequately applied on behalf of the programs of their clients.

33

Operations Programming and Planning

BY LOUIS DEMOLL, AIA

Because function is one of the most important determinants of architectural solutions—in schools, the educational process; in hospitals, patient care; in stores, marketing; in factories, production—the programming and planning of operations within buildings are integral parts of comprehensive services

Processes in building are architectural determinants

No architect—not even Louis Sullivan himself, judging from his work and writings—ever seriously took the position that "form follows function" *alone.* At least not for very long. And not if the word "function" refers only to the processes that take place in and around buildings. On the other hand, it is probably safe to say that architects are generally agreed that such processes constitute *one* of the essential determinants of architectural solutions. In many cases, they constitute a *major* determinant; and in some buildings, such as those for industrial production, the processes often constitute the *main* determinant.

If such is the case, the building program must surely grow out of the process program, and the building design out of the design of the process. It then surely follows that if the architect is to control the architectural solution effectively, he must first control—or at least be involved in—the process solution. This is true of many building types—schools, hospitals, shopping centers, laboratories, etc. As an illustration, perhaps it will be sufficient to describe here how these services are performed for one building type—industrial.

Operations programming and planning defined

In industrial architecture, the definition, analysis and solution of process problems have come to be called "operations (or operational) programming and planning." In other fields, the same terms are sometimes used to mean something quite different. For building types other than industrial, even the terms used may be different; for example, in office buildings, similar activities are often called "space analysis" and "space planning."

While operations programming may mean different things in different fields, in industrial architecture it has come to be a term applied to the analysis and programming of the operations to take place within the building and on the site which are necessary to the processing and manufacture of the products which the facility is to produce.

Operations programming, then, involves detailed study of the entire manufacturing process and its requirements; this is absolutely necessary before the programming of the building itself can be accomplished effectively. There is no reason why the knowledgeable architect cannot include work of this sort in his services —if he prepares for it.

Operations programming for new or expanded facilities for industrial manufacturing may be handled in any of several ways. Larger industrial clients, in many cases, have engineering departments that perform such work. Other companies retain outside consultants whose services are used whenever there is a need to rearrange or expand their facilities.

Many smaller concerns, however, in spite of their managers', or even their plant engineers', apparent knowledge of manufacturing processes, do not have the know-how or ability (or time) to adequately program their operations. In some cases this is because the manufacturer and his staff have never found the opportunity or time to think in terms of ideal process layouts. Often the manufacturing process will have grown haphazardly over a period of years with the result that the processes will have been squeezed into spaces which actually are neither adequate nor suitable. The operation may be housed in a building which does not have sufficient clear height, one that has been chopped up into segmented sections or one in which receiving and shipping facilities are not adequate. Haphazard growth can even lead to a process flow that is exactly backwards.

*Disorderly growth
of plant operations*

Our firm was recently called in on one project in which all material, after having been received at one end of the plant, was lifted by an overhead crane, carried over the processing area the full length of the plant and stored at the opposite end. From there materials flowed back in the other direction, through the manufacturing process, only to be lifted again to be carried back across the plant to shipping. The plant engineer of this company

Operations programming to complete design

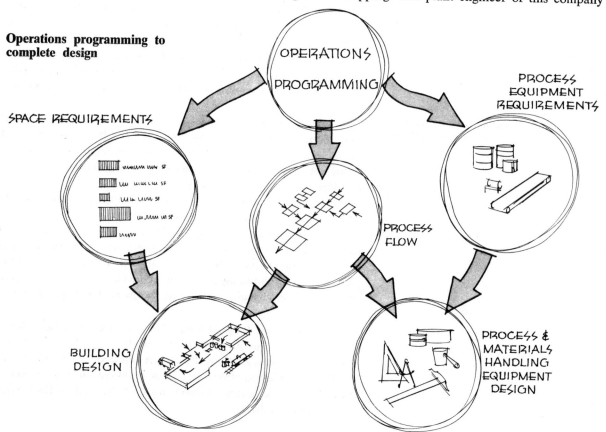

SPACE REQUIREMENTS

OPERATIONS PROGRAMMING

PROCESS EQUIPMENT REQUIREMENTS

PROCESS FLOW

BUILDING DESIGN

PROCESS & MATERIALS HANDLING EQUIPMENT DESIGN

realized that this was a complicated arrangement and that labor-saving improvements were possible. But the plant had been this way when the plant engineer first came to work with the company. Additions to the building had subsequently been made at various locations, and the engineer had never found an opportunity to conceive of a better arrangement. The current problem was that the plant was running out of space. Several thousand square feet were needed at one end of the building, the only place to add because of site limitations. At this point the company decided that before investing in additional building construction, it needed to know if there were any better way of rearranging the existing facilities. The problem of building design was a very simple one. There was only one place to locate the addition and, since it would fill the remainder of the site, only one shape was possible. The client's real problem was one of operations programming and planning.

Four methods for solving operations problems

In many cases, small industrial clients, such as the one mentioned above, will not know which way to turn in order to obtain good advice on such a problem. Actually, there are four paths that may be followed by such a manufacturing client. He may engage the services of an architect who has had a degree of industrial experience; he may contact equipment manufacturers who offer advice on equipment layout; he may hire a special industrial engineering consultant; or he may use the design and construction firms (often called "package dealers") that offer services of this type.

Past experience has shown that usually none of these methods is completely successful. The architect, in many cases, will not devote the time necessary for thorough analysis of the complete processing arrangement. The equipment manufacturer will ordinarily have only a limited understanding of the processes other than the applications of his own equipment. The special consultant, although he may be quite capable of analyzing the processes and making good recommendations, probably will not have sufficient knowledge of building construction, code requirements, etc, to do an effective over-all planning job. In addition, his fees will often be quite high, and it will still be necessary for the manufacturer to utilize the services of an architect for the design of the building and a builder for its construction.

For the reasons named, the services of a design and construction firm may often seem to the manufacturer to be just what the doctor ordered. Among the advantages often cited in its own favor by such a firm are apparently capable staff of engineering specialists, knowledge of construction problems, costs and scheduling and experience on similar projects. On top of all this, the design and construction firm often offers programming and layout services at a low fee as a "come-on" in order to obtain the later construction contract with which it is actually most concerned, and in which it expects to make sufficient profit to enable it to cover any losses on the programming and planning work.

It is interesting to note that the operations programming and planning done by outside consultants or by the engineering departments of large corporations are often boons to the design and construction companies. Once a manufacturer has a final process layout in hand, his attention will be almost completely focussed on the total costs of the equipment and of the building shell which must protect the equipment. At this point, he may be strongly tempted to turn to a design and construction concern from which he can obtain a complete firm proposal for the design and construction of the project. Then, with operational layout and schematic building plans in hand, a guaranteed maximum price for design and construction and a firm construction schedule, he is ready to go to his board of directors for prompt approval of the project.

Role of the architect

If they are to avoid being supplanted by such design and construction firms, architects must be prepared to offer similar services, with similar guarantees and *perform the services better*. And architects must be prepared to convince such industrial clients of the dangers of the conflict of interest present when the design and construction functions are performed by a single organization.

If an owner turns to an equipment manufacturer or special consultant for operations programming and layout before going to an architect, the final building may be harmed in one of two major ways. The layouts produced in this way are often so fixed and detailed that they are essentially schematic plans of the proposed buildings. If this is the case, the architect will be so rigidly controlled that the architecture will suffer. Even though the architect may develop ways of improving the layout as the design of the building proceeds, he ordinarily will not have an allowance in his fee—or the time—to go back and redo or even question any of the operations programming or planning that will have gone before.

The second harmful result of an owner having operations programming and planning performed before hiring an architect is that the schematic plans prepared will often be so carefully laid out that the owner will feel that he is then in a position to go directly to a builder for construction of the building. With a schematic plan in hand, which indicates the layout and shape of the building and the mechanical requirements, the owner may well assume that the building design is now simply a case of final design of structure, walls, floors etc. To the unknowing manufacturing client it may appear that, at this stage, he already has an architectural solution. Therefore, why should he bother with the services of an architect, especially when great numbers of builders are telling him that they can readily develop final drawings and proceed immediately with the construction?

How need for operations services can be met

Surely, at this point, it has been demonstrated that there is a need for architects to become involved in operations programming and planning of industrial plants. How can architects meet this need? For highly complex projects, certainly most architectural firms are not equipped to undertake, without the use of special consultants, services in operations programming and planning. Far more harm to the profession can result from architects undertaking such services for complex projects that are beyond their capabilities than from frankly telling prospective clients that their firms are not prepared to offer services in these areas. However, there seems to be no apparent reason why an architect cannot undertake such a commission, even if he feels it to be somewhat beyond his own personal capabilities, if he advises his

Some processes are relatively simple, though apparently complex

Basic elements of operations programming and planning

client in advance that he will use qualified special consultants where required.

In spite of the fact that many industrial processes appear, on the surface, to be highly complex, in a surprisingly large number of cases architects can perform operations programming and planning services very well if they will devote the necessary time to work closely enough with their clients to develop a knowledge of the processes involved. For many of the simpler manufacturing processes, this can be done without any prior knowledge of the methods of manufacture of the particular product.

Operations programming and planning services, no matter how complicated the manufacturing process or what type of product is being processed or assembled, are composed of certain basic elements which vary only in detail. The three basic elements or phases are: 1) receipt of the raw materials or parts, 2) processing or assembly operations and 3) distribution of the finished product. Sandwiched in between each of these three basic elements there is always storage in some form. Such storage varies from simple surge areas at the end of processing lines to vast warehouses for finished products.

The receiving phase of a manufacturing operation may require space for the storage of raw materials in liquid, bulk or bags, or space for parts packaged in large or small quantities. Receipt of material may be by rail or truck or some combination of these.

Processing or assembly areas, elements of every manufacturing operation, vary widely in their requirements, depending on the types of operations to be performed. Such operations may

Basic phases of manufacturing processes

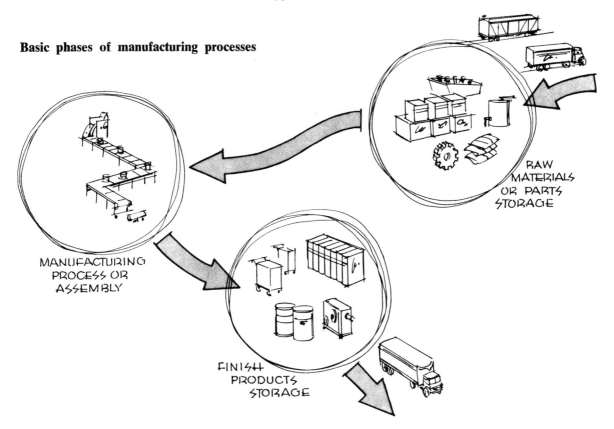

RAW MATERIALS OR PARTS STORAGE

MANUFACTURING PROCESS OR ASSEMBLY

FINISH PRODUCTS STORAGE

involve light assembly, complicated heat treatment or processing. The operation may be noisy or it may involve only the quiet assembly of small parts. The operation may be a combination of any of these types of processing or of others.

The shipping phase of the operation may require a considerable amount of storage for finished products in the form of packaged light parts, heavy equipment or bulk products in tanks or large drums. But no matter how widely the operations vary from plant to plant, each of the three phases—receipt, processing and distribution—will always be present in some form. Operations programming, then, is involved with detailed analysis of methods required for the flow of material from one of the phases to the other. Operations planning is involved with the layout of the phases and flow.

Operations services for a paint company

As an example of how these services are performed, it may be helpful to take a look at the operations programming and planning of a recently completed paint manufacturing plant. The basic requirement of the company was that it wished to manufacture two lines of paint in the proposed plant. Through a series of meetings with the project engineer of the client, the architect developed a complete program of the processes involved. Two types of materials were to be received and would go into the end product. These consisted of certain types of liquid vehicles and dry pigments. With the help of the client the volumes of finished paint to be produced were established. Next, the architect determined the number, size and variety of batches that had to be

Process layout of paint manufacturing plant

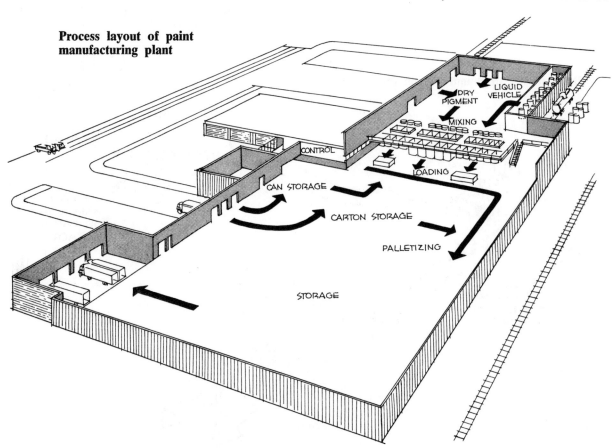

mixed, the production time required and the frequency of mixes. This information made possible a determination of the volumes of raw materials—liquid vehicles and dry pigments—required. First, the liquid vehicles, the method of their storage and the number, size and types of tanks required had to be established. In order to determine pumping and heating requirements, the viscosity of the liquid had to be known. Also affecting the operation was the method and frequency of receipts of the liquid raw material and the fire hazards involved in the receiving and storage of the materials. From analysis of such data, the optimum spacing, size and arrangement of tanks were established, as well as the building requirements for the liquid storage phase of the operation.

In the case of the dry pigments storage area, the number, size and variety of batches determined the quantities of raw materials that required storage. The quantities, type of packaging, methods of stacking and handling of the materials and method and frequency of receipts were then analyzed. Similar analyses were then made for all other phases of the operation.

Building requirements must follow from operations requirements

Only after operations analysis and programming of each of the individual parts of the total operation can the building requirements of each be determined. Only then is it possible to establish required floor areas, optimum building shape, clear heights, column spacing, and lighting and heating requirements. In the case of the paint manufacturing plant discussed above, it proved to be possible for the architects to establish criteria such as those listed without a detailed knowledge of the actual chemical process involved in the manufacturing of paint and, as a matter of fact, without even a detailed knowledge of the actual operation of all of the machinery. Of course, it was necessary for the architects to understand and analyze the basic steps in production: receiving, processing or assembly and distribution.

Contributions of the architect

Undoubtedly the plant engineer, in this case, or a specialist in process layout, working independently, could have come up with an acceptable operations program and plan for this manufacturer. However, the architect, in guiding the program with his own process engineering specialists and materials handling consultants, offered many advantages to the client. Architectural disciplines, which might otherwise have been overlooked, were considered during the initial operations programming phase of the project. The transition from operations programming to the final plant layout and design was handled without lost motion. In fact, it would be almost impossible to determine the exact point where one phase of the services changed to another. It was particularly important to the client in this case that the project proceed smoothly and without interruption, since the schedule allowed only ten months from the start of the operations programming phase to partial occupancy of the finished building. At the time the building program had been established, schematics had already been developed to a point that allowed a preliminary contract to be let for site grading. Construction, including excavation, pouring of foundations and ordering of structural steel, was started while the building details were still being ironed out. Construction continued while mechanical, electrical and process equipment designs were getting underway.

How to promote their services in industrial operations programming and planning is, at best, a difficult problem for architects. This is particularly true because many manufacturers are not convinced that architects are capable in such areas. It is doubly hard for architects to convince manufacturers that they can perform such work when they have no examples to show of similar completed commissions. Architects can, however, team up with consultant-specialists to offer prospective clients combined proposals for more rounded and complete services in such areas. Of course, larger architect-engineer firms often have staff specialists for such services; and these people work closely with the architectural staff members.

Fees for operations services

It is sometimes difficult to establish proper fees for operations programming and planning services. Quite often, the time spent in these phases, particularly when rearrangement of existing facilities is involved, will be quite expensive, proportionately, when compared to other phases of the design and construction. As a consequence, it is often preferable for the architect to work on a cost-plus basis. In such cases, the client will be charged for the architect's direct salary costs plus a percentage or multiplier to cover overhead and profit. A prospective client, however, invariably demands a guaranteed maximum cost or, at least, an estimate of total charges. At the same time, the architect must keep in mind that his competition in this field almost always comes from design and construction firms and special engineering consultants. To make things even more difficult, design and construction firms as mentioned earlier often offer such programming and planning services at a very low fee as a "come-on" in order to obtain profitable construction contracts.

Fees are related to scope of work

As an example, of what is involved in the establishment of fees for operations programming and planning services, it should be useful to describe the scope of such work for one project. In this particular project, a study is to be made of an existing soap manufacturing facility in order to establish future expansion requirements. The layout of the existing plant must be analyzed and programmed. The final report to the client must contain recommendations on relocation of equipment and departments within the existing building, production-cost comparisons of various types and layouts of equipment and recommendations for new building areas that will be required to meet anticipated production goals. Although up to 100,000 square feet of new construction may be recommended, the actual design of new buildings is not a part of this particular study. In a case of this sort, it is obvious that the professional fees can only be set by estimating the time required for the study. It is beside the point, but interesting nevertheless, that the competition for services on this project involved only a single architectural firm, but two design and construction firms.

In operations programming and planning work, the scope of services varies considerably with each project. Therefore the establishment of any type of standard agreement for services would appear to be impractical. Further, in order to avoid later misunderstandings, the architect, in his proposals, should be quite explicit about all of the services which he intends to perform.

At the same time, he should clearly define the responsibilities of his client as well as his own.

In summary, programming and planning of the operations of industrial facilities is a fascinating, but complex, study. In these phases of a total project, many of the major decisions that affect the final outcome of the building are made. In order to properly relate the building design and construction phases to the operations decisions, the architect must be deeply involved in the making of these decisions. Only in this way can architects assure their clients of completely successful—and total—solutions to their problems.

Operations services can lead to better architecture

Outline of Services for Operations Programming and Planning of Industrial Buildings:

I Research

By means of study and exploration with clients, equipment manufacturers and others, determination of data such as:

A Total production goals

B Quantities of raw materials required

C Methods of receiving, storage and handling of these materials

D Equipment and methods for processing or assembly of products

E Methods of packaging products

F Materials required for packaging products

G Production quantities to be stored

H Methods of storage

I Mode of shipments

J Frequency of shipments

II Analysis

A Analysis of present operating methods and space utilization

B Analysis of data gathered through research in order to determine, for each phase of the operations, the optimum rack or storage spacing of materials, arrangements and spacing of equipment, aisle widths, clearance heights and other important factors from which computations may be made of floor areas and other building and site requirements

C For additions to existing facilities, analysis of important factors such as existing utilities

III Programs and Plans

Preparation of operations program and plans, describing present and future needs, in written form and in the form of equipment layouts and flow diagrams

IV Cost Analysis

A Estimates of costs of equipment for manufacturing, materials handling and storage

B Comparisons of labor-cost savings possible with new equipment as related to costs of recommended new equipment

C Estimates of the costs of complete new facilities or alterations to existing facilities (together with the costs for mechanical alterations and moving or replacement of equipment).

34

Building Programming

BY LOUIS ROSSETTI, FAIA

In the past often performed sketchily, if at all—or left for clients to perform for themselves—building programming has now become an essential phase of comprehensive architectural practice, a phase that can point the way toward improved professional services in the design and construction phases

Need for building programming

Building programming, in actuality a primary phase of an architect's service, is often romantically discussed, but in practice almost invariably leaves much to be desired.

Today, when crash projects are so prevalent in many endeavors of architectural development, building programming obviously has become even more significant. Accelerated design schedules need not have a detrimental effect on programming. In fact, architects can often perform crash design efforts without impairment of the quality of their efforts, by judicious assignment of staff. Programming can be staffed in a similar way if it is given the same high priority. Of course, this will only be possible when the necessity for programming and its importance as a phase of project development have been conveyed to the owner. A glorified definition will hardly suffice.

Perhaps an illustration or two will serve to demonstrate the widespread need for programming and how it is performed. Within the past two years, the author's firm was retained by two clients whose end goals were varied, but for whom programming was essential. One example that will illustrate such an assignment was a commission for the programming and master planning of a new campus for a college in New York State. The starting place for the study was the academic requirement for a twelve-building complex to accommodate an increase in the student body to 1200 from a present enrollment of 600 students. The report on the study was broken down into three major divisions:

Program and master plan for a college

1) Objectives of master plan
2) The proposed master plan
3) Development of master plan

The report on the studies of all of these divisions were to be supported with scale models, delineations, area plans and recommended floor plans. The objectives of the studies were:

1) Facility requirements and occupancy
2) Space requirements

Campus master plan based on complete programming   *Campus at time of programming and planning studies*

3) Site characteristics and potential
4) Traffic and parking
5) Review of previous recommendations
6) Space requirements for various phases of construction
7) Master plan studies for the whole campus, based on various projected phases of construction
8) Engineering studies for master plan site work and main utilities distribution for various construction phases
9) Engineering evaluations of heating plant arrangements
10) Schematic concept studies of all buildings in plan.

Finally, each of the buildings had to be assigned to one of three construction phases. Selection of the construction phase for each building was based on the urgency of the need for it and the capital budget outlay it required. Soil investigations were made. Traffic patterns and parking areas were established, to avoid a "sea of cars." The topography of the site was to our advantage in this regard, since the campus is rolling, bounded by golf courses and fine residences.

Importance of costs

In the programming for this college, more than just a cursory look was given to costs. A complete budget was determined for each stage of construction. These budgets included the costs of structures, site work, utilities, fees, furnishings and other contingent requirements. The cost data was then transcribed to construction schedules and area breakdowns.

Program and master plan for a foundry

In a second instance, a leading foundry operator asked for a program and master plan for production consolidation along with more extensive administrative and employee facilities than those generally found in the foundry field. The first step was an analysis of the owner's basic requirements. The results of the analysis were put in a report covering such phases as:

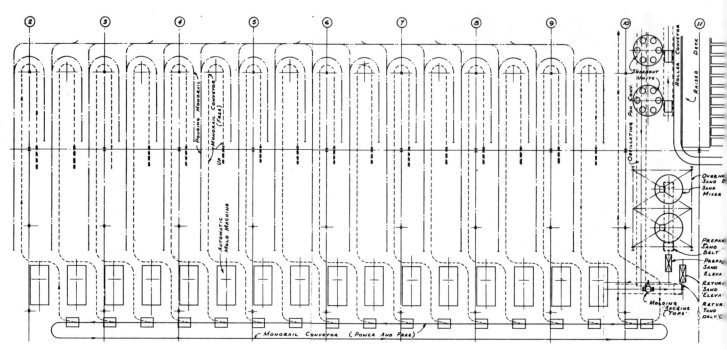

Layout of foundry production lines based on programming studies

1) Production requirements
2) Production methods
3) Economics of the facility
4) Conceptual design and estimates of construction and equipment
5) Site factors
6) Equipment specifications.

Preparation of definitive specifications

Definitive specifications were then prepared for much of the major equipment for the foundry and subsequently submitted by the owner to manufacturers for bidding purposes. These clear specifications made it possible for each of the bidders to save considerable money in the preparation of his bid. Of even more importance was the fact that the owner received objective and realistic quotations. This phase of architectural services provided a second benefit; it eliminated what is referred to by so many in the equipment field as "free engineering."

Programming may be performed by personnel in architectural offices

To reiterate a point made earlier, in both of these projects, the programming was conducted by key personnel of the architectural firm, with the management of the firm taking an active role in all phases of the work, including field visits and personal supervision. The same procedures are followed on design assignments. Programming, because of its nature, deserves and requires the same sort of concern as design; indeed, perhaps even greater concern is needed in programming. Design may be performed by specialists who have had training and experience in certain areas. Programming, if it is to be tailored to the best interests of clients, is an area in which there are few fully qualified practitioners.

How then can the talent for programming be nurtured in architectural offices? Selected staff members should be given the opportunity to participate in programming assignments, not in the delineation or schematic phases alone, but in all of the areas of costing, scheduling and field investigations. Some knowledge of programming can be acquired by extracurricular training; and this should be encouraged in architectural offices. The time so expended, even though it may not be reimbursed for in all instances, will inevitably add to the scope of architectural services and help insure a continuation of successful practice. Also time spent in this way can provide an uplift in the morale of those who hope to make their marks in the profession.

Plant layout services

Plant layout is the "veteran" of all services adjunct to programming, if a significant portion of a firm's volume consists of industrial assignments. Qualified personnel in this area of project development are quite scarce. No degrees are conferred in plant layout; it is a talent that must be nourished. In the author's firm, approximately twenty-five per cent of the industrial projects call for plant layout. However, the availability of this service is made known to each plant owner.

Even though the plant layout may be prepared by his own staff, the owner feels more secure when he knows that the building design is being developed with a full understanding of the operational aspects. On such projects, our plant layout engineers are often called upon to provide staff consulting services to the design group. The fact that only twenty-five per cent of our projects require plant layout services in no way makes such efforts simply an appendage to other services. In recent years, in our firm, projects requiring plant layout services have kept a staff up to twenty persons busy over periods of long duration. Such a department is as important as any other in any architectural and engineering practice in which industrial work is important.

Scheduling services

Scheduling—particularly the critical path method (CPM) —has been much discussed of late. General contractors, the Federal government and many industrialists are putting the method to effective use. More architects should do so.

One of our design concepts that was recently accepted by an automobile manufacturer included a suggested construction time schedule based on a typical CPM diagram. The project involves the complete modernization of an existing headquarters building. The study of project scheduling will make possible the continuation of administrative work with a minimum of shutdown. In this instance, the owner spent as much time on the schedule as he did on the design concept. This owner was concerned with work output in the building during construction; he had no apprehensions about the ability of our firm to maintain his corporate image in the design of the refurbished building. Our concern about the work output in the structure may have been the key for his giving us the go-ahead signal on the project.

Training for CPM services

Care should be taken in the selection of a person in the firm to be trained in CPM or in a similar scheduling method. Knowledge in design should be coupled with a practical understanding of field conditions. Once a person has been trained, he can then provide in-house schooling for others of the staff.

What then is building programming? What does it encompass? How is it practiced? Obviously it is a needed growth service for the smaller or newer architectural firm and an expanded service for the larger, longer established organization.

35

Project Analysis Services For Community Colleges

BY EBERLE M. SMITH, FAIA

How comprehensive architectural services in the area of project analysis for community colleges are performed, and how these services may be augmented by promotional activities which support the building programs of clients

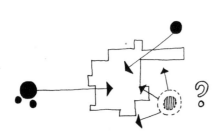

The community college is a relative newcomer to the American scene. In the simplest terms, a community college is an institution of higher learning offering programs beyond the high school level, but less than four years in length. Such colleges offer unusual opportunities for the architect to be of service in the areas of project analysis and promotional services because they grow out of the unique needs of the localities they serve, draw financial support from a number of different sources and usually must be planned in a series of steps according to the most immediate needs and the availability of funds.

For many youngsters, the community college bridges a difficult gap between high school and employment. Because it is a

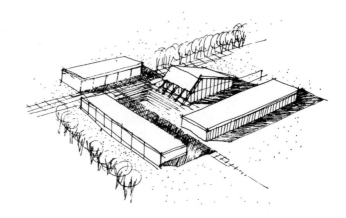

local institution, easily accessible and inexpensive to attend, the community college enables and encourages youngsters to continue their education. The modern community college offers preparatory programs for high school graduates planning to transfer later to four-year colleges, terminal programs for those who do not plan to go further in college and continuing adult education.

The community college is responsive to local needs in that it furnishes terminal education in skills needed by local business and industry. It offers a very good bargain in education to the individual since operating expenses are largely met by various governmental agencies and tuition fees are generally low. It is within commuting range of the area it serves so that, in general, students incur no expense for board and room.

These are the usual steps to be taken in the development of a community college:

1 Determine the need for a community college
2 Determine the area to be served
3 Determine methods of financing initial, operational costs
4 Determine what is to be taught
5 Determine location and size of site
6 Develop the physical plant
7 Provide the staff and personnel to operate

As these steps are taken, the governing body of the community college will have to make decisions at each stage. Information must be presented so that these decisions can be made promptly and in an orderly manner; in this, the architect can be of inestimable aid to the governing boards of the colleges.

Ordinarily, the first step in establishing a community college is to determine the existence and degree of the need for it, based on projected school enrollments, the area to be served, local and state employment trends, courses of education not provided by existing schools in the area, and intellectual and cultural goals of the community. Determining the need is often the function of a study group, drawn from business and educational leaders of the locality, and brought into being by a realization that lack of technical training and education is denying opportunity to many individuals within the community and is creating a public burden of unemployment. Many high schools maintain records on their graduates; statistics of this type and school district enrollment projections based on the anticipated growth of the community furnish a sound basis for assessing the magnitude of the problem to be solved in a community college building program.

The study group may draw on a number of sources in order to develop a background and an improved understanding of community college experience in other localities. These sources may include state and Federal departments of education, schools of education in large universities, educational consultants and administrators at other community colleges.

Local and state employment trends may be established in consultation with local chambers of commerce, representatives of local industry, labor unions, employment agencies and governmental units concerned with welfare, social security and employment. In addition, community leaders and planners may be able to suggest

new goals which the community may wish to set in order to reach a better balance between industry, commerce, culture and the professions. As an example, the community might plan a hospital as part of its future growth and include nursing and pre-medicine in the curriculum of the college.

The size of the college community may be established according to three major considerations. First, of course, there must exist a socially and geographically integrated group which needs and wants a community college. Second, the area to be served must conform to the requirements of the enabling act of the state. Third, the area must have an adequate tax base in order to carry its share of the support of the community college. Such considerations are of material value in the selection of the site and in promoting the community college program.

Frequently, the architect first enters the picture at this stage. He may begin his services by assembling data from planning and statistical sources and incorporating these data into visual displays for presentation to various groups and to the general public. Such displays might well include graphic presentations of the locality, of the expected stages of growth, of the needs for a community college and of the benefits to be derived from it.

Before the college issue can be presented to the vote of the community, it is essential that the financing of the project be planned. The vote may come before final selection of the site. It may precede determination of the area to be served, since a negative vote in a given district may take that district out of the project. Nevertheless, the proposal presented to the voters must be realistic and adequate, in most cases, to finance the entire project. It is not easy to go back to the community for additional funds, particularly if the need arises from poor planning or lack of foresight in the initial request.

Among the possible sources of support are individual donors, local tax revenue, fees for tuition, state aid to education and Federal funds. Part of the architect's service is the development of a master plan and a construction schedule that will best take advantage of each of these sources. Usually, construction must take place in several stages, as funds become available year by year. Periodically, some units may be added and others may be expanded or converted to new uses as required by increases in enrollment and enlargement of the curriculum.

As an example, consider a proposed community college planned initially for 3000 students on a 150-acre site. Cost of the land is estimated at $600,000, and of the buildings, $9 million. An additional $400,000 is to be allowed for fees and preliminary work and for assembling the beginnings of a staff.

Assume the community has an assessed valuation of about $2 billion. If the property tax is increased by one mill, the annual tax revenue available to the college will amount to $2 million.

In addition, the state contributes, let us say, $200 per student toward operating expenses. Many states also contribute to capital expenditure, usually on some sort of a matching fund basis. The formulas for these funds vary widely from state to state. In this case, let us assume a formula that will provide from $40,000 to $150,000 in matching funds according to enrollment.

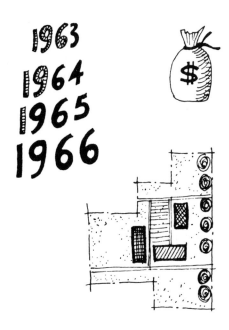

A Federal long-term, self-liquidating loan at low interest is presently available for construction of the student center, which is estimated to cost $500,000.

Operating costs are expected to be $600 per student. If $200 of this is covered by tuition and $200 is contributed by the state, there remains $200 per student which must be paid out of tax revenue.

The accompanying table shows how the cash position varies over the first few years. It will be noted that a bond issue of $7 million is adequate, and that of this amount over $5 million is available for reinvestment during the first year of construction. Conceivably, a smaller bond issue would serve the purpose, but a margin of safety is desirable to cover construction expenses accruing in 1965-66 prior to collection of taxes. As a result a reserve fund of slightly over $2 million is available in 1965 and this fund increases approximately $700,000 each year. At the same time the college will undertake $300,000 of new construction each year, so as to take full advantage of state aid.

In this particular case no individual gifts or bequests have been included in the financing. These may have a profound effect on the financing, the design and construction sequence of the project, etc; a gift may include a site for the college or funds for a specific building.

In order to qualify for state and Federal aid to construction, and often as a necessary preliminary to receiving a gift, the portions

Capitalization and Expenditures of a Hypothetical Community College

YEAR	1963–64	1964–65	1965–66	1966–67
No of Students	0	0	1500	3000
Operating Costs	$ 400,000 (1)	$ 150,000	$ 900,000	$1,800,000
Construction Costs	600,000 (2)	4,500,000	4,500,000	300,000
Debt Amortization	—	550,000	550,000	550,000
Total Outlay	$1,000,000	$5,200,000	$5,950,000	$2,650,000
Tax Revenue	$2,000,000	$2,000,000	$2,000,000	$2,000,000
Tuition	—	—	300,000	600,000
State Aid for Operation	—	—	300,000	600,000
State Aid for Capital Expeditures	40,000	40,000	90,000	150,000
Federal Loan	500,000	—	—	—
Bond Issue	7,000,000	—	—	—
Total Funds Received	$9,540,000	$2,040,000	$2,690,000	$3,350,000
Total Unexpended Funds (3)	$8,540,000	$5,380,000	$2,120,000	$2,820,000

1) Fees and Preliminary Expense
2) Site Cost
3) Does not include earned interest

of the project for which the funds are intended must be studied and presented in detail with realistic cost estimates. To the architect these are still analysis and promotional services, but in completeness and refinement they go several steps beyond the analysis and general promotion of the program to the community that was previously described.

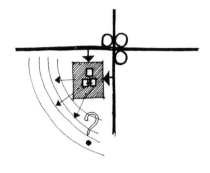

Some community colleges begin with the gift of a site; others must select one. Ideally, the site should be located close to the center of population of the area it serves, now and in the future. Nearly all of the students and faculty will probably use automobiles to reach the college; consequently access roads must be planned to meet the needs of this traffic without creating serious hazards or disturbances in the neighborhood.

Also a survey should be made of the site and the neighborhood to uncover any problems of sewers, storm drainage or essential utilities.

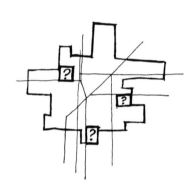

It is not always possible to find a sufficiently large piece of suitable land under single ownership. When land of various sizes, shapes and costs must be assembled into a workable site, it becomes the architect's problem to recommend the combination which represents the best compromise between price and suitability. In arriving at his conclusions, he must take into account not only the cost of purchasing the land but also those of grading, filling and developing the site. Nor should he omit to verify the present or proposed uses of adjacent land; for example, an airport is not a good neighbor for a community college.

Even though he is well qualified by education and experience to consider the interdependent factors of finance, real estate, community growth and planning, the architect will be well advised to make use of consultants and other resources within the community in order to insure that he has given proper consideration to all of the specific problems of the locality. Ignorance is no excuse for a bad recommendation.

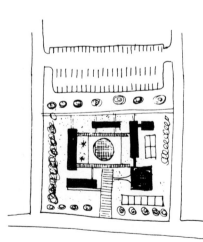

There is one further aspect of the architect's service with respect to the planning of community colleges which deserves special mention; that is, his relationship with administration and staff. The current concept of the public elementary school has had more than a century to evolve. Community colleges are infants by comparison and their pattern is not set; each is a challenge and an opportunity to be met jointly by the educator and the architect. Much of the approach may be frankly experimental, and the architect may find it necessary to range far and wide to fit himself to perform an effective role in areas in which he has had no previous experience. The details must all be worked out in conferences with administration and staff. These conferences cannot be limited to the preliminary stages, since the staff will still be in the process of formation at this time. In fact, some conferences or seminars may be necessary when the first stages of construction are essentially complete in order to acquaint key personnel with the arrangement of the physical plant and the maintenance and operation of equipment.

By comparison with more traditional practice, the community college requires a much more active and continuing exchange of ideas between the architect and client.

Part Six:

Related and Supporting Services

36

Comprehensive Architectural Services: Related and Supporting

BY DUDLEY HUNT JR, AIA

Engineering and the newer specialties that support complete architecture and the activities such as research that relate to complete architecture are expanding as rapidly as architecture itself and can be expected to become more and more important in comprehensive architectural services as the years go by

As architecture has become more complex, a great variety of specialists in phases of architectural services or services that closely support—or relate to—architecture have come into being. In recent times, the lighting specialist and the acoustics specialist have come into relative importance and have taken their places beside the consulting engineers and others who have worked closely with the architect for many years. In addition, numbers of architects now go into fields related to architectural practice such as consulting work with industry. In the future, it can be expected that these trends will continue. Surely, there will be more and more specialists engaged in smaller and smaller portions of the total area of architecture as time and progress expand the demands on the architect and his consultants or collaborators.

One thing all of these pursuits have in common is that they all contribute to the over-all value of architects to society.

In the pages following, only a token look at the role of the architect in such services has been possible. Perhaps the limited attention given here to such services in the construction industry will serve to indicate the vast needs and opportunities in related and supporting services.

37

Architecture and Industrialization

BY CARL KOCH, FAIA

How comprehensive services, used with intelligence and imagination, can lead to future accomplishments in the largely unexplored area of mass-produced, standardized and interchangeable components that can be combined into varied, successful and satisfying designs for buildings and the entire environment

"What matters to a society is less what it owns than what it is and how it uses its possessions. It is civilized insofar as its conduct is guided by a just appreciation of spiritual ends, insofar as it uses its material resources to promote the dignity and refinement of the individual beings who compose it."
(R. H. Tawney, "Equality," New York: The Macmillan Co., 1961)

In Classic Greece, architects designed and built beautiful buildings using almost identical elements over and over again, refining them over long periods of time. In the Middle Ages, the cathedrals, which expressed man's hopes and aspirations better than ever before or since, derived their breathtaking beauty from the necessity to use a single material—stone—in an imaginative way. Involved in a process of very slow evolution, architects of these eras accepted the rigorous discipline necessary to build in the media available to them.

Today, we can do an almost limitless number of things with our new processes and new materials. We can simulate natural materials. We can support buildings with air. We can do almost any job with a bewildering choice of methods and materials. We can, as one engineer has said, ". . . correct almost any design mistake with technology." Yet we somehow seem to lack the imagination necessary to harness the industrialized process by accepting the disciplines it imposes on us.

Buildings part of larger environment

Almost no building today is sufficient unto itself. Rather it is a part of a much larger environment; and industrialized components, designed with imagination and discipline, can be instrumental in making this a better environment. By the kind of discipline required to achieve efficient, economical and beautiful in-

Sketches by Gardner Ertman

dustrialized components, we can harness industry to achieve an

221

In industrialization, basic word is repetition

attractive, civilized environment we can afford in our communities.

Before attempting to relate industrial components and community design, it will be well to look briefly at the relation of repetition, the basic word in industrialization, to the other design aspects required in a civilized society. First of all, industrialization is only a means, not an end. Secondly, the main features of industrialization are mass production and distribution. Today it is volume which reduces costs. The key features of any factory-produced item are repetition and interchangeability. The *assembly* of components may vary considerably, provided that the components themselves are repetitive. In other words, to achieve both beauty and economy, flexibility must be achieved within a standardized repetitive system.

The word "repetition" conjures up, for many people, a nightmare of monotony and ugliness, but it shouldn't because repetition is actually a key element in every esthetically satisfying composition. The standard component is found universally in nature—and in art. For example, most organic cells appear to reproduce repetitively. With only the 26 interchangeable parts of the alphabet as the elemental components of literature, and with words as sub-assemblies, we are able to build sentences, express ideas and construct an essay, a novel or a poem.

The number of letters in our alphabet is quite arbitrary; the Chinese, for instance, have thousands of "letters." The form of their literature is necessarily different from ours and therefore presents tremendous complications of mechanics. For the Chinese, written communication requires, for complete understanding, considerably more scholarship than it does for us. Other examples of the use of components could be cited: our nine digits and the cipher, zero, permit extreme variety and, in music, our 13-note scale allows us to create almost inexhaustible variations that are meaningful and beautiful.

Industrialization can lead to esthetic quality

Neither architecture nor any other art is a process of evasion or concealment of the discipline of repetition. Rather all of the arts must react to, and treat of, this discipline with creative intelligence and imagination. Indeed, the industrialization of buildings, in imaginative hands, can lead to esthetic quality in architecture through intelligent discipline and repetition.

It is quite possible to apply the repetitive principles of mass production very effectively and still permit the outward appearance of the building to be treated individually. In fact, it can be demonstrated that in a three-story building the exterior walls represent only about 20 per cent of the surface area of the building shell. If the balance of the building surface were built from standardized parts, the facades could be varied considerably without a large increase in costs. At the same time, if the standardized components have been carefully proportioned, the total building can be made intrinsically sound in proportion; and it will form a strong framework in which variety of the surfaces can add interest without deteriorating into chaos. The discipline afforded by standardization can go a long way toward the elimination of the most immediately obvious failure of modern buildings in cities and suburbs—the lack of coherence which stems from partly accidental and partly deliberate, if abortive, attempts to achieve individuality. True individual expression is not only possible, but is enhanced, by incorporation into an over-all pattern, rather into the current artificial multiplicity of materials, heights and roof slopes. Historically, this principle may be seen in the basically repetitive nature of the patterns of the 18th and 19th century architecture of Bath, England, in that of Beacon Hill in Boston or of the Greek island towns, all composed of basic patterns and similar materials, colors and textures, but with rich variation in detail.

Cannot house construction be as intelligent as that of automobile engines?

Granting that a house and an automobile engine have different sets of functional and esthetic factors, cannot the house be built in as intelligent a way as the engine? A house certainly presents no more difficult a problem and, on the whole, the materials used in a house, because of the static nature of their use, are subject to fewer restrictions. An automobile engine built the way an average house is built might well cost $10,000. That engine built in Detroit costs $200; yet it is an incredibly complex assembly of precisioned machined parts—parts that by functional necessity are far more complex and far more precise than in a house; and the engine is made of special alloys that are far more expensive than any of the materials in the average house. The simple fact is that the components of this potentially expensive assembly have been standardized in order to allow production to be large enough to justify the use of tools, dies, machines and processes—at every stage—which drastically reduce the time required to convert raw materials to machined parts.

Limitations of present-day industrialized building components

A great many of the components of buildings are available as standard items, it is true. Three observations, however, may be made on this point. First, most standard items are developed largely in isolation from all other standard items. Thus, plywood and plasterboard are 4 ft wide, bathtubs 5 ft long and floor tiles 9 x 9 in, illustrating only the simplest form of our irrationality in this respect. Secondly, even within the existing framework of standardization, the common tendency is to fail to take maximum advantage of what exists. Thus, dimension lumber comes in standard lengths, but usually, on visits to constructions jobs, we find lumber being sawed to odd lengths. In the third place, the available components, on the whole, are in smaller increments than they should be. For example, when plywood and plasterboard precut studs and machine cut shingles are being used, assembly is ordinarily performed at the site. Clearly this whole wall could be factory produced in large sizes.

Indeed, a whole house can be factory-built with potentially substantial savings. For some housing problems this is often the best answer. But people vary; so do weather, topography, soil and density requirements. A more flexible approach for our larger needs would entail, therefore, a system of standard parts which themselves are designed for mass production. The optimum size of such components would obviously be a compromise between the complete factory-produced house and the bits and pieces that are commonly used for most housing today. The key word in this is "system" since only through interrelated systematized standardization of all of the necessary elements can the volume necessary today be established.

Another aspect of the mass production of standardized, systematic building components is that more intelligent use can be made of human resources through intelligent use of manufacturing processes. We are approaching a stage in most areas of our socio-economic organization in which routine mechanical and heavy work can be performed by machines, so that, for those with the capacity and interest, work can become more skilled and creative. One can visualize an industrial process designed to permit statistically correct proportioning of work so that all phases of it are geared to the varied capacities of the workers. The ideal component system is so perfectly interchangeable that assembly can be done by totally unskilled personnel. This goal is normally thought of as related primarily to cost savings, but the human values involved may be equally as valid a goal. Waste in many forms is inherent in the so-called building industry today. This industry, if it can be called such, in fact, is not unlike a giant centipede whose legs are quite uncoordinated.

Today, almost every single building is treated as a unique creation in every respect. Two hundred pages of specifications (full of time-worn phrases, paragraphs and sections) are necessary to describe it. In contrast, a standard mass-produced product can be described in a page, since the quality and attributes of all the parts are controllable and predictable. A large proportion of the motions involved in the design and construction of a building are, in fact, repeated over and over again. In almost every field except building, we have placed the production of the constants in our factories.

Improvement of construction industry is feasible now

Every facility is now at hand for vast improvement of the construction industry, for improvement of the livability of our buildings and our cities and for the enhancement of our esthetic environment. Why have we resisted it so long? Many reasons could be cited, but it seems self-evident that in his traditional role as professional leader of the whole field, it is the architect, above all, who must meet the challenge. In the next few years the architect must face up to this problem, or face being written off as an interesting example of surviving customs from the past, like the Beefeaters at the Tower of London.

Opportunities industrialization offers in urban design

Urban renewal and the construction of new city housing and related physical facilities make up, perhaps, the largest building construction market any society ever had. This great market represents, particularly to architects, opportunities for improvement in the environment that are limited only by our capacities. Perhaps the largest part of this market—and the hardest to crack—is in mass housing for middle- to low-income groups.

There would seem to be no better target than this at which to aim the skills and concerns of architects today. On the pages following, is described a study of the genesis of a series of urban building components designed by architects for other architects to use and improve upon. One of the main aims of the study was to provide better, bigger "bricks" to build with so that the architect may be freed by the machine from some of the endless and ever-changing minutiae of building design and construction—that he may turn his thoughts and imagination to better building groups and, finally, to a better complete living environment.

Excerpt from Edward Logue memo to BRA:

"A key element in the rehabilitation of residential neighborhoods is the construction of moderate-rental housing to provide not only for the relocation of displaced families but for the stabilization of such neighborhoods through new residential investment and construction. The opportunity to develop new private housing both for relocation and for low- and moderate-income families is better now than ever before because of the adoption by Congress of Section 221 (d) (3) of the Housing Act of 1961.

"The terms . . . provide for mortgage loans at an interest rate of 3⅛%, substantially under the market rate. Preliminary studies by the Authority staff indicate that this 'under market' interest rate will make it possible to provide two- to four-bedroom family dwellings at rentals ranging from $85 to $105 per month, including heat. In order to obtain such rentals, however, developers . . . must be prepared to take advantage of every possible economy in design, construction, administration and management while developing structurally sound, easily maintainable, livable dwellings of maximum architectural quality. . . ."

With an experienced young builder, Mark Waltch, our firm was hired by Edward J. Logue, Development Administrator, Boston Redevelopment Authority (BRA), to develop prototype plans for housing of maximum architectural quality, consistent with the use of optimum low-cost construction materials and methods so that the units could be leased at the lowest possible rentals. The studies will also develop construction cost data, financing and operating cost information for this high-quality low-cost housing.

The essence of the project, then, is the initiation of an approach to the residential portion of Boston's renewal program which will answer the following needs:

1 Provision of a rich living environment, urban in character, and purpose; not a weak imitation of suburban attractions, but a new statement of the vitality of city life;

2 Establishment of a visual pattern expressive of urban vitality, without resort to chaos, in order to find again the proportion between anonymity and the richness of individual expression of the Beacon Hills and Georgetowns of yesterday;

3 Provision of these values, together with the more obvious aspects of good housing, at a monthly cost range low enough to meet the requirements of the relocated and/or poorly-housed families for whose needs the program is primarily intended;

4 To find these answers, or their beginnings, in a program for which construction can begin immediately.

As suggested previously, all of these goals may be met in a program, founded on a system of standard parts, which will:

1 Reduce construction costs by taking advantage of volume production of standard components;

2 Reduce construction time;

3 Create an inherent discipline within which individual

expression of architects, owners and tenants will enhance the patterned proportion of the whole;

4 Establish a framework for better cost, quality control;

5 Through reduction, for architect, developer and builder, of some of the time-consuming mechanics of working drawings, estimating and other processes now necessary, increase the time available for important studies of planning and design;

6 Insure a repeatable—not a unique—demonstration of the values cited previously.

Basic premise of study:
500 dwelling units under construction
in first year of program

The studies, planning and ideas of the present project were founded on the premise that the construction of at least 500 dwelling units could begin during the first year of the program. Not all mass-producible elements can be made ready for use within such a short time schedule; but enough elements can be made ready to make a significant initial demonstration. Five hundred units is the minimum quantity of standard components which will amount to a volume large enough to obtain significant cost advantages. This minimum quantity for the first year is, therefore, the basis on which this study was made. Undoubtedly, additional cost reductions might accrue if the production volume were increased.

In addition to the establishment of a single family of parts that would be interchangeable in whole or in part, and that could be combined into a system of components, the following factors were also considered important:

1 Efficiency one-, two-, three- and four-bedroom family units at moderate rentals;

2 Two-, three- or four-story, and eventually high-rise, buildings adaptable to varied site, soil and density conditions;

3 Ideally, both frame or skeleton construction (in wood, steel or concrete) and bearing wall-slab construction. Of these, the basic shell of concrete appears to offer the most advantages, not the least of which is its promise of significant lowering of costs within the next few years;

4 Adaptability to varied exterior treatments that would permit sympathetic placement in the existing environment and also permit individual expression and creativity on the part of architects and owners.

Need for flexible modules

In other words, a search was made for a basic module, flexible enough for the desired variations, that would permit moderate-sized basic unit sizes yet allow for increased sizes if cost factors permitted. Dimensions were to be suitable to a variety of structural elements and readily divisible into sizes for component parts that could be produced from materials on the market. Each system of components had to be composed of interchangeable parts.

With these aspects of the problem in mind, as well as the criteria set forth by BRA, a number of progress studies were made of the elements of the over-all problem.

In order to ensure maximum standardization of floor and roof components, the number of breaks through these elements had to be minimized. While the need for this is most obvious in a concrete system, whether precast or preformed, in terms of mass-production, this is equally valid for framed floors of wood or steel.

Importance of standardized stairs
and mechanical systems

Since special floor panels or slabs are necessary where stacks, vents or stairs penetrate the structure, these elements should be standardized within their special functions. Approaches to a solution of this problem include: establishment of specialized structural panels for such things as plumbing, heating and stairs; grouping all of these elements and locating them between, and along, party walls; and, as in the example shown here, grouping the elements in a central location. The separation of stairs from mechanical is practical in a frame system but precast concrete slabs require an in-line arrangement of these elements. A number of systems of this type were studied.

On this page is shown one basic in-line grouping, from those possible, for a mechanical core and, on the following page, one such system for stairs. All of the elements shown may be standard regardless of unit size, building type or structural system.

The mechanical elements have been divided into: 1) chase, which contains the stack, water supply, flues, vents, ducts and electrical service and 2) prebuilt baths, kitchens, heating units and electrical panels for individual apartments. This standard chase would serve the requirements of up to four apartments, each with an individual heating unit, where conditions call for this. Central heating, and/or central domestic hot water would permit simplification, but the chases have been sized for the more stringent condition. Baths are standard and should, eventually, be preplumbed, with field connections required only at the main stacks and supplies. The kitchen will also have a standard pre-wired preplumbed base unit (sink, range and washer) with cabinets that can be added for different plan situations.

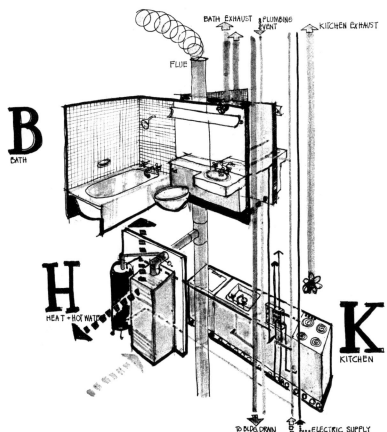

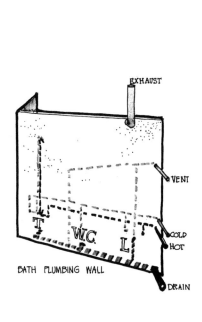

Mechanical System

The basic component of the stair is the half-run, which may be assembled to form a variety of stair types as shown. Public access stairs may be fabricated on the same basis, and the principles may be applied in either wood or precast concrete.

As shown across-page, the first structural system studied combines structure, enclosure and finish in a precast concrete system. Present indications are that such concrete structures are economically feasible—they may, in fact, be nearly competitive in initial cost with conventional frame structures—and that they provide definite savings in operating costs. While box-frame construction may eventually prove to be less expensive, at the present time available plant equipment and know-how seems more adaptable to a system employing precast, prestressed floor slabs (the extruded-core types seem to be the most competitive in price) and solid or extruded bearing walls.

It may be seen that the grouped core of vertical elements permits the maximum use of identical slabs, the special elements being limited to the central area; in this way, even the special elements can be made standard. With this approach, a 500-unit project can generate a volume of rigidly standardized production sufficient to make competitive prices possible. Walls may be built-up of the same cored units, running the full height, or precast in flat beds full width and one story in height. At the present stage of development, unfinished concrete block still runs slightly below precast concrete in cost; but to bring concrete block to the performance level of precast concrete in fire rating, acoustic value and

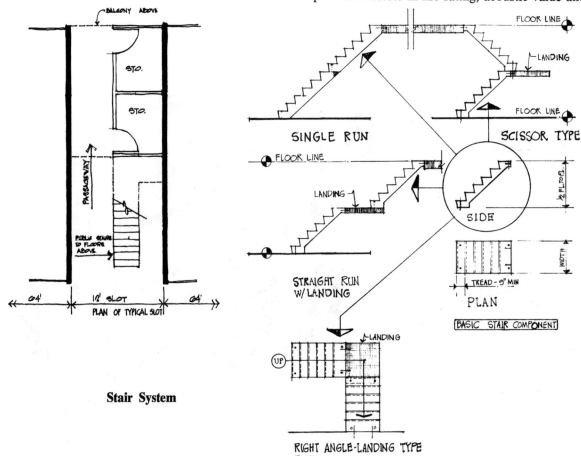

Stair System

finishes would probably make it cost more than precast, particularly if the minimum is 500 units.

In the future, there is every reason to believe that large precast elements will not only cost less (and perform better) than concrete block, but will also cost less than conventional frame materials. On the other hand, there seems to be very little room for significant cost reductions in wood framing.

Development of structure 2:
Skeletal systems

A second basic concept studied is a skeletal structure with infill for shelter and finish. The grouped core may also be used with such a system. The frame may be light steel or precast concrete; floor and roof and walls may be steel, wood or concrete, or a mixture of these. We are also working on a system of prestressed wood floor panels set into a light steel frame. In the immediate future, this system is the one most likely to meet the cost requirements. To support a light frame, more foundation work is required than for the precast slab, and more steps are required in construction. However, where fire and acoustic protection are of lesser importance, and where buildings are generally limited to two stories, a system which continues traditional wood frame residential construction remains useful.

Development of plan systems

The stair and mechanical core plus the structural elements form a block within which all of the requisite plan types are obtainable. In the case of concrete, any number of stories can be built, subject to design criteria and site conditions. The basic units may be enlarged by adding structural components, without changing the core elements. Thus a family of plan types and sizes can

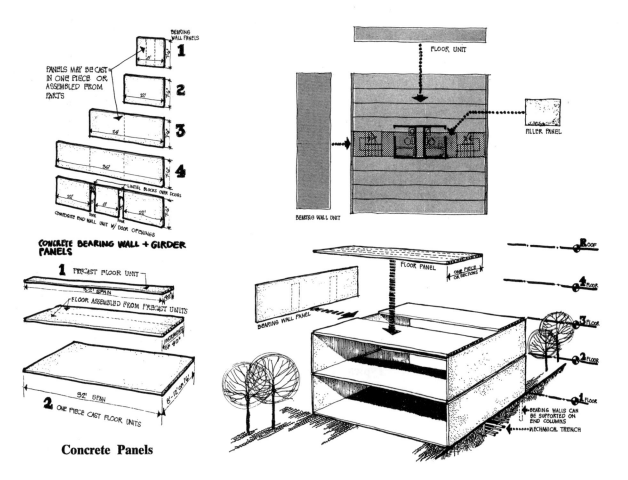

Concrete Panels

be established. The larger units can be built in such a way that extra space is considerably lower in square foot cost than space in the smaller base unit.

The key dimension (32 ft, divisible by two for frame systems) was arrived at as a result of considerable study of planning flexibility in conjunction with structural requirements; and 20-, 24- and 28-ft planning bases were also tried. All presented drawbacks when several unit sizes were involved. The 20-ft block is too small to take full advantage of the characteristics of prestressed concrete and too large for practical frame components. Neither 24 nor 28 ft can be divided into two good living room widths. Also, the 32-ft size gives three bedrooms with more workable widths than the two possible in 24 ft or three in 28 ft.

At this time, it should be in order to point out again that what is being developed here is a series of standard parts which can be repeated regardless of structural methods or materials; the modular discipline of the system can be similarly repeated. Such orderly repetition results in cost savings through standardization and in an orderly urban environment through the application of esthetic disciplines.

Within the party walls, and around the cores, interior partition placement is entirely flexible, since none are fixed structural walls. Also a modular system of standard partition and closet components can be established.

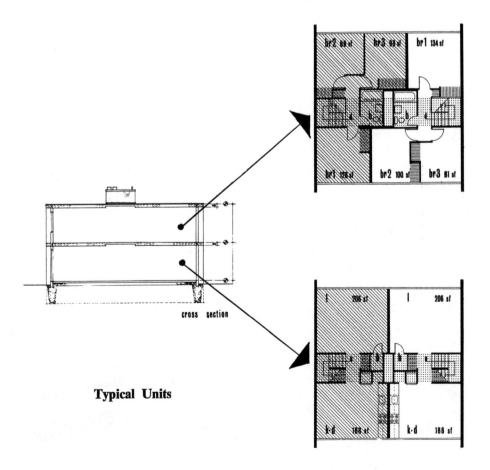

cross section

Typical Units

Standard exterior walls will be proposed when specific projects are developed under this program. However, the over-all intent of the program is to provide a framework for considerable variety within the bounds of the structural module. The complete shell of these buildings represents about 30 per cent of their total cost. In a typical example, about one-fourth of this is in the exterior non-bearing walls. Thus with only some six to nine per cent of the total cost involved, the non-bearing walls may be varied considerably without significant increases in the total costs; in this way, allowances have been made for preferences in material, color, texture, fenestration and even variation in planes.

The disciplines established in the studies allow considerable latitude in adapting the buildings to varied topographic conditions. In addition, the structural systems proposed—in particular, the precast concrete system—are suitable for poor soil areas.

Considerable variation possible for varied topography

The Way Ahead

In order to avoid any misinterpretation of the foregoing, it should be pointed out here that what we have accomplished so far is little enough indeed. Even though my own main interest, as an architect, has been in research and development in housing and its immediate surroundings, we have found no client, public or private, who is able—or willing—to employ us on other than a very tentative, short-term basis. The approach of our private industrial clients has been limited to the short-term utilization of their materials and products in housing, with little reference to the

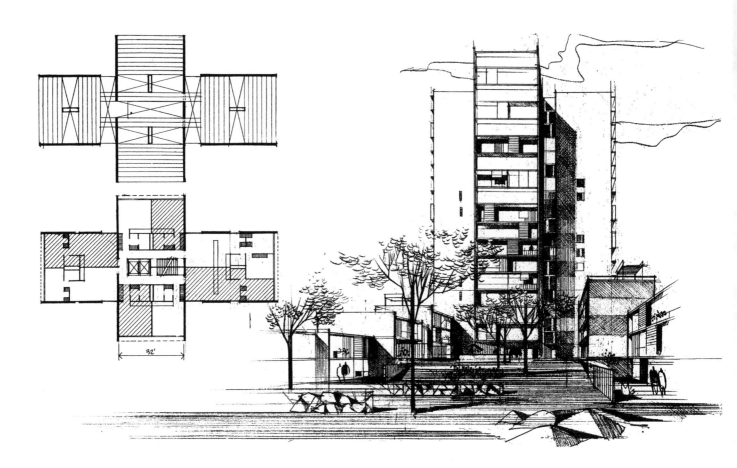

32'

rest of the house or the environment. The approach of public clients has also been short term, for political or budgetary reasons. Our experience is not unusual in this respect; on the contrary, our office seems to be one of the very few that is able to eke out even a part of its income from this marginal business of research and development in housing, if what we do can be called research at all in the real sense of the word.

In "Better Housing for the Future," a report prepared at the request of the Office of Science and Technology of the Executive Office of the President, the conclusion was reached that, because of the present state of the housing industry, government sponsorship of research in this area is, in the public interest, necessary in order to unlock the flood of new technology in other fields so that it may provide the much-needed flow of life blood in this segment of our economy. The same report suggests that the experimental program of FHA and the demonstration program of HHFA are pointing the way. This is, I am afraid, only a hope, not a fact. After several years, the FHA appropriation of $1 million for this purpose is almost entirely intact, except for the money spent for three or four small projects, each costing $25,000 or so. Ironically, none of these may be experimental enough to entirely pay for itself without using any of this fund. Yet, as anyone who has worked with low-income housing of any sort is well aware, the FHA, in a very real sense, is more definitely in control of design than the architect, builder or client. And because of the staff and budget control limitations of the FHA, there are almost irresistible pressures to take no step that does not have 20 years of experience behind it and whose shortcomings have, through long usage, been accepted as inevitable.

The report mentioned also states that most growth industries spend an average of about 1½ per cent of their sales income on research and development, that at this rate the amount spent for these purposes in the housing industry should total $360 million a year, but that only one-sixth to one-tenth of this amount is actually spent. Though the report does not make the point clear, it is my assumption that the amount actually spent includes—and in fact, is almost entirely made up of—*product* research, which leads to almost nothing that is applicable to the dwelling as a whole, much less the environment of which the dwelling is only one part.

In order to meet our needs in this area, I believe we must do at least three things: 1) We must learn from the neighborhoods we have already built, 2) We must build neighborhoods from which we can learn even more, and 3) We must encourage young architects, and related professionals such as sociologists and economists, to educate themselves for work in this area.

How little we have learned from the billions of dollars of housing we have already built is illustrated very well by a search made recently by our office for information on the mundane, and very practical, subject of refuse and garbage disposal in multi-family housing units—a problem of increasing dimensions in our planned-obsolescence society. The end of this search was well summed up, in a thoughtful letter received from Thomas E.

How can housing research be encouraged and performed?

Basic current needs

Thompson, Assistant Commissioner for Development of PHA, approximately as follows: "We have found no satisfactory means of handling this problem, but are hoping to engage a foundation to make a study. . . ." (Any other suggestions will be much appreciated.)

Essentially, in housing today, we are faced with the problem of building new neighborhoods. Any further delay in solving this problem can only multiply our difficulties in the future. A word or two about how we can go about solving the problem—and about the great opportunities open to us, if only we take advantage of them—is surely in order at this time.

We have learned, from such varied sources as St Augustine, Plato and the Bagavadghita, that there are four essentials in making anything—including an urban neighborhood—well. The first of these is over-all *purpose*—or *motivation*. The American constitution lays down such a set of purposes, all providing for the ultimate good of man. The second essential is *concept* or *idea*. Here again, in the America of the past, we have provided a solid foundation in our New England towns and in certain residential areas in older cities such as Boston, Philadelphia, Washington and San Francisco. Even as late as the 1930's, the greenbelt towns provided a real answer to the first two essentials. The third and fourth essentials are the *materials* from which things may be well made and the *techniques* for accomplishing our purpose and concept with the materials. There are few who have any doubts about the American ability to accomplish, with awesome effectiveness, in the material and technique areas, whatever we set our minds to. In this lies our dilemma.

In developing our materials and techniques, we have, to a frightening degree, forgotten our purposes and concepts—the first two essentials for making things well. In our concentration on materials and techniques, we have developed a degree of power and wealth that is unprecedented in history but, as Senator William Fulbright has said, "Neither power nor wealth is, in itself, the condition of the good life." And power and wealth cannot be substituted for the first two essentials—purpose and concept.

A few years ago, after searching for several years for effective methods of building good mass housing at low cost, I came upon a plant producing a precast, prestressed concerete material that obviously was better for my purpose than any I had seen in Europe or Russia and of already proven quality. At that time, the product had already been installed in supermarkets and warehouses at prices as low as 80 cents per square foot. Today, the product is being used in a number of states; but not for housing for Boston specifically designed to permit the use of this product on a completely standardized basis and in quantity. Here, after receipt of a written quotation at an acceptable figure from the president of a supply company, at the last minute he was overruled by his management; now we are faced with a floor system 40 per cent more expensive. The reasons for this are not all clear, but enough are clear to make a good essay on futility.

As one way of escaping from our dilemma, I have dreamed up a project based on the four essentials—purpose, concept, ma-

Basic problem is building new—and better—neighborhoods

Four essentials of new and better neighborhoods

Purpose and concept can be lost sight of in development of materials and techniques

A proposal for future housing development

terials and technique—and founded on my own recent experience in housing. First, it would be necessary to pick a number and a time-span, say 5000 housing units to be built within three years. These figures are based on the experience of Bill Levitt, for whom we are trying to develop a new group of house designs. Using the current Levitt materials and techniques as basing points (and nowhere is better housing space and equipment provided per building dollar), any changes made in materials or techniques would have to be proven by their producers to be equal or better than those currently in use, at the same or a better price.

Fitting of concept, materials and techniques to purpose

Non-profit financing and tax formulas, similar to those of Boston under which we are now building our project in Roxbury, would be necessary for the success of this project. In addition, the project should be a cooperative. In American multi-family housing, the cooperative is the nearest present equivalent to individually owned homes that is practical. Also, monthly costs can be lowered considerably in a co-op since a considerable amount of the management and maintenance responsibility is placed on the individual families. To these ingredients must be added the principles of the design philosophy heretofore expounded. Thus armed with concept, materials and techniques, three of the essentials, it would be necessary to present the program to the trustees of the first essential—purpose—personified in Boston by Mayor Collins and Edward J. Logue. Optimistically assuming that these trustees of the public purpose will remain in office for the full three years necessary for the project, it should then become possible to carry out the provisions of the 1949 National Housing Act, "A decent home and a suitable living environment for every American," or at least for our 5000 families. In doing this, we would accomplish our first essential—purpose.

Good design plus cooperative equals lowered rents and better environment

In a project we designed in New Haven, a two-bedroom apartment rents for $88 a month with heat. The rents for the Roxbury homes in Boston are expected to be at a similar level, but are of better construction and have more amenities than the New Haven example. At the estimated construction cost of Roxbury, about $8.50 a square foot, the rental of a two-bedroom apartment in a cooperative should run as much as $25 a month less than the $88 cited above. This may be accomplished because FHA procedures for co-ops allow a reduction in vacancy allowances from seven to two per cent and all interior decorating, repairs and maintenance to be performed by tenants, thus eliminating reserves for replacement of equipment, reducing annual fixed charges for curtailment and including the allowable income tax offset. If we can also reduce the construction cost with sacrificing quality, rentals can be reduced even further. There would seem to be no insurmountable reason why this cannot be done.

In our studies for Boston, I think we have made a small start toward solutions to our problems, in spite of the obstacles we have encountered. However, as in other cities, more, and better, professional and business help is needed, along with far greater public understanding, and backing, for the efforts that are being made. Our children, and those in the rest of the world, are at least as dependent on what we accomplish in this as on the question of whether we reach the moon before—or after—the Russians.

38

Architectural Consultation with Industry

BY WAYNE F. KOPPES, AIA

Working with those associated with the building industry, architectural consultants perform a number of services that are necessary if comprehensive architectural practice is to result in the greatest benefit to clients and society

Architectural consultation offers increasing opportunities for architects

The term "architectural consultant" has at least two different connotations. The term may refer to one who offers consulting services to architects, as an expert in some aspect of building design, or it may apply to a person with architectural training and experience who offers advice regarding architectural problems to manufacturers or others who require such information. In my own case the latter definition applies; my work has been chiefly with manufacturers of building products and with industry associations. On occasion, I've assisted architects with specific technical problems, but in the main I've been concerned with interpreting the architect's requirements to manufacturers.

Importance of product manufacturers

Like it or not, the work of architects is becoming more and more dependent upon the manufacturers of building products. For proof of this, it is only necessary to compare the size of Sweet's today with its size in 1950. As Phil Will has said, ". . . producers are now members of our design team, and must be regarded as a creative force in the building industry. This must be so, for the architect can only use that which someone is willing to produce." Manual craftsmanship in building has given way to the erection of preformed components. A growing proportion of the labor of building the typical commercial structure is performed off-site by the manufacturers of materials and components; and in the interests of greater economy efforts are being made to increase the ratio. Before World War II the prefabricated house was a rarity; now prefabrication accounts for about one-fifth of all of our single family dwelling units.

The expanding role of the producer, then, as well as the expanding role of the architect, requires attention. An ever-increasing number of established and experienced producers of building products are cognizant of their growing responsibilities as "members of the design team," and are increasing their efforts to cooperate more effectively. The new and less experienced producers *want* to cooperate, too, but sometimes don't quite know how to go about it. These producers often recognize that their survival in this competitive field depends largely on their qualifying for the team, and this may require a bit of coaching. In a sense, it is this kind of coaching that the architectural consultant can provide.

Role of the product manufacturer

Many of the older and larger companies producing for the building industry have long been familiar with the architect's *modus operandi,* his idiosyncracies and his requirements. Some have their own competent architecturally trained personnel. However, a great many other producers, who lack such experience, recognize that they need professional guidance, both in the development of products and in making their products known to the architect. Some of these are small companies just going into business; others are among the largest and best-known companies, whose diversification programs are bringing them into contact for the first time with the building industry. Those in the latter category, recognizing that the ways of the building industry are unique as compared with, for instance, the automotive or the aircraft industries, often feel the need of a guide in exploring this unfamiliar territory. Some even sense a language barrier, and consequently have a need for the assistance of an "interpreter," who can "speak the architect's language."

It is regrettable, but nevertheless true, that the architect—and his capabilities—are not always highly esteemed by the average producer, probably as the result of some unfortunate experience. The producer's impression of the architect sometimes seems to range from the sublime to the ridiculous—from that of an unapproachable and omnipotent authority to that of one who is fussy and unreasonable. Probably the average architect's concept of the producer is no more complimentary, and just as inaccurate. He may think the producer is most unreasonable, too—with no feeling at all for esthetic values, who puts salesmanship first and responsibility second.

Need for communication

This lack of understanding between producer and architect is unfortunate; it exists chiefly because of the lack of adequate intercommunication. The producer too often doesn't look beyond the salesman's order, to see how his work relates to the architect's overall concept; the architect, on the other hand, frequently fails to state his requirements clearly, having at best a very hazy concept of the manufacturer's work and problems. If the architectural consultant, acting as a liaison between the two parties, can effect a better understanding by explaining to each the functions and limitations of the other, he then performs a service of value to both.

The work of the architectural consultant is likely to be quite

Nature of architectural consulting work

varied in nature; it may be concerned with evaluation of a concept, or assistance with the design of a product or with the promotion of a material or product. When a new product or system of construction is under consideration, feasibility studies may be required for investigation of the pros and cons—or the potential merits—of the proposal. Such studies usually require research work, including surveys and interviews with sources of information, and often result in technical reports. Design assistance may involve advice on appropriate testing procedures, as well as guidance in preparing useful technical data for architects. Questions of conformity with building code requirements or of comparative costs, may require investigation. Frequently architectural consulting service entails assistance with the preparation of technical literature, architectural advertising, and perhaps, Sweet's catalog inserts.

Companies which are suppliers of base materials, rather than manufacturers of specific products, often need suggestions for architectural uses of their materials or ideas for product applications. If the previous experience of a company has been in fields other than building construction, it will need advice, first of all, concerning the general operation of the building business and the architect's role in this business. Salesmen or distributors may require instruction on how the architect thinks and works, and how he should be approached. If the company has no architect on its regular staff, the consultant may be called upon for liaison work with architectural offices, to provide first-hand technical advice in the uses of the company's products, or to assist in the detailing of specific applications.

Examples of consulting work

Some representative examples drawn from the author's own experience may serve to illustrate the nature of architectural consulting services: a) for a plastics manufacturer—study of potential uses of plastics in building, and review of pertinent restrictions in state building code; b) for another plastics manufacturer—evaluation of potential of a plastic-faced building block; c) for architectural metalwork manufacturer—assistance with design, testing and promotion of one of the first successful commercial metal curtain walls; d) for architectural metals manufacturer—assistance with preparation of product catalogs for architects; e) for stainless steel supplier—liaison work with architects, preparation of technical and promotional literature, educational work with sales force, assistance in product development; f) for insulation supplier—study of comparative costs of school wall and roof constructions; g) for elastomeric sealants manufacturer—guidance in testing and promotion for architectural uses; h) for branch of armed forces—study of feasibility of prefabricated overseas bases; i) for lumber manufacturer—study of possible uses of wood in fallout shelters and evaluation of potential uses of fire-retardant treated lumber; j) for basic aluminum supplier—evaluation of new method for production of building panels, and; k) for rigid insulation manufacturer—study of possible uses in residential work.

Working with industry associations

The architectural consultant may also be of service to industry associations allied to the construction industry. Organizations of this sort serve the common interests of groups of manufacturers.

Usually these associations are more concerned with general standards and technical service than with specific product applications. With the support of their member companies, some of these groups undertake research projects related to architectural problems; others make efforts to formulate technical data to assist architects in the proper use of their products. In much of this work architectural experience and an understanding of the architect's viewpoint are essential. Unless an association has architecturally trained personnel on its own staff, a need usually exists for outside architectural consultation in connection with such work. If chiefly research and investigation, the work often is turned over entirely to an architectural consultant on a contract basis.

Manufacturer's literature and advertising

Competent guidance is particularly needed in the field of manufacturer's literature and advertising. Much of the advertising directed to architects is ineffectual. However, neither the publishers of the magazines nor the companies whose products are represented are generally at fault. Both use what the advertising agencies provide; thus the agencies must be held largely responsible for any waste. Of course there are fortunate exceptions to the general rule. Some advertising is both tasteful and helpful. But on the whole, the manufacturer's advertising to architects could be greatly improved. The Producers' Council has demonstrated that advertising *can* be improved, and in a few cases at least, agencies have produced excellent work. Most agencies handling this sort of work might be well advised to consider using the services of competent architectural consultants in order to better serve agency clients and their audience—the architect.

Qualifications for consultants

What qualifications are needed in this business of architectural consulting? The architectural consultant should be research-minded. He should have a background of well-rounded experience in the architectural profession, and probably in research work and teaching. He should be knowledgeable enough to be able to interpret the actual problems and needs architects are finding in the field and to assist manufacturers in producing products to meet these needs and solve these problems. A knowledge of materials and construction, and a continuing interest in the broadening of this knowledge, are necessities. Architectural design ability is a valuable asset; and a certain amount of technical writing ability is essential because the preparation of reports, specifications and brochures is an important part of the work. In order to work with manufacturers, a reasonable knowledge of production processes is also helpful.

How consultants work

Some architectural consultants work independently, others as members of consulting firms. Some consultants work full time, while others combine consulting work with teaching or practice. On occasion, architectural firms are commissioned to do research or investigatory work that is not related to specific architectural projects. A few architectural firms, in addition to their architectural practice, regularly perform such consulting work for manufacturers and industry groups. However, the number of people who are now actively engaged in this branch of the architectural profession is quite small —far too small to adequately meet the increasing needs of industry and the future potentials the architectural consulting field offers.

Consultants needed

Index

A

Advertising, 24, 238
Agency, 5, 23–24, 29, 32–36, 177
Agreements, owner-architect, vii, ix, 29, 32, 150–151
owner-contractor, 32
AIA JOURNAL, iv–v, 6
Alerts to architectural profession, x–xii
Alexander, Robert E., vi, 5, 72
American Telephone & Telegraph Co., 108–120
Analysis, vector, in human engineering, 197–200
Analysis services, 7, 11, 170–171, 214–218
feasibility, 7, 61–63, 73, 76–77, 152–158, 178–186, 214–218
financial, 7, 49, 69–71, 76–77, 178–186, 187–193, 216–217
human factors, 194–200
location, 7, 49, 156–157, 164–165, 172–177, 216–218
market, 69–70, 153–154, 156
programming, building, 7, 50, 56, 65–66, 210–213
operational, 7, 56, 65, 73–74, 77–78, 171, 201–210
site, 7, 49, 172–177
Appraisal forms, 69–70
Arbiter, architect as, 32–33
Architectural Practice, AIA Handbook of, 32
Architectural Record, 6
Architectural services, basic, vii, 4, 14, 45
comprehensive, 44–47
alerts, x–xii
bank buildings, 76–80
books on, 6
colleges and universities, 72–75
future developments, vi, xii, 5–6
industrial buildings, 53–59
multifamily housing, 68–71
outline of, 7–9
principles, 44–47
research & development buildings, 81–90
shopping centers, 60–67
techniques, 48–52
Architecture, definition of, 3–4, 127–129
and industrialization, 221–234
Art in buildings, 51, 80
Associations, consultation with, 237–238
Authority of architects, 115–116

B

Bacon, Sir Francis, 26
Balance sheets, 19–20
Bank buildings, services for, 76–80
Bell system, 108–120

Belluschi, Pietro, 47
Better Housing of the Future, 232
Blumberg, Frederick, 140
BRA (Boston Redevelopment Authority), 225–226
Budgets, construction, 187–193
Burgin, Robert A., 87
Burke, Dr. Cletus J., 197
Business of architecture, 16–22, 94–99
Business development, architectural, 102–107
budget for, 104
criteria for, 106–107
measurement of 105–107
program for, 105
sales tools, 104
Business district studies, central Albany, Ore., *illus.,* 50–51
Bylaws, AIA, 23–25

C

Catalogs, product, 238
Chicago, location and site analysis for office building, 172–177
Civic activities of architects, 97
Clients, architectural, 92–94
concern with business, 94
controllers instead of owners, 94
corporate, 63–64, 108–120
decision-makers, 103–104
entrepreneurial, 29–30, 53, 61, 94, 136–139
governmental, 121–124
home builder, 93
industrial lessee, 140–151
large and complex, 94
organizational, 93, 108–120
presentation to, 125–132
promotional, 29–30, 94, 136–139
as providers of space, 94
Colleges, services for, 72–75
analyses, 214–218
building programming, 210–211
Collins, Mayor John F., 234
Commissions, architectural, 103–107
commission agents prohibited, 25, 30
Communications, 86, 97–98, 120, 131, 236–237
as design and planning element, 196–197
standard for, 24
within architectural offices, 19
Communications buildings, services for, 108–120
Community, fitting architecture into, 110
Compensation, architectural, 24, 29, 51–52, 117, 123, 136–139, 151, 173–174, 208
of employees, 20, 25
Competence, professional, 24, 26–28

Competition, 4
architects with others, 4, 52, 140
between architects, 24–25, 30
Components, building, 221–234
Concurrency system of design and construction, 84–85, 90
Configuration, building, 84, 88–89, 188
Connor, Neil A., 68
Construction services, 8, 12
bank buildings, 80
building contracting, standard, for architects, 24, 28–29
colleges, 75
improvement of, pointers for, 120
industrial buildings, 59
relationships with contractors, 32
research & development buildings, 83–85, 90
shopping centers, 67
Consultants, 25
architectural, 235–238
real estate, 159–168
Consultation, architectural, with industry, 235–238
Contracts, 32
owner-architect, vii, ix, 29, 32, 150–151
owner-contractor, 32, 67
Controls, cost, for construction, 24, 28, 85–86, 114–115, 154–156, 187–193
Coordination of building projects, 117–118
Coplan, Norman, 31
Corporate clients, 108–120
communications buildings, 108–120
shopping centers, 63–64
Costs, of construction, 179, 187–193
control, 24, 28, 85–86, 114–115, 154,–156, 187–193
costs vs. rent, 62–63, 142
estimating, 24, 28, 180, 187–193
of finishes, 192–193
of mechanical systems, 190–192
of structural systems, 189–190
of vertical transportation, 190
CPM (Critical Path Method), 213

D

Daly, Leo A., 95
Data sheets, FHA, 69–70
De Moll, Louis, 201
Depreciation of buildings, 64
Design, 19
freeze, 17–18
Design and construction, concurrent, 84–85, 90
Design and planning services, 8, 12
bank buildings, 77–79
building, 8, 58–59
colleges, 74–75